HARCOURT SCIENCE
WORKBOOK
TEACHER'S EDITION

Harcourt School Publishers

Orlando • Boston • Dallas • Chicago • San Diego

www.harcourtschool.com

Printed in the United States of America

ISBN 0-15-323721-X

6 7 8 9 10 022 10 09 08 07 06 05 04

Contents

Safety in Science

Doing investigations in science can be fun, but you need to be sure you do them safely. Here are some rules to follow.

1 **Think ahead.** Study the steps of the investigation so you know what to expect. If you have any questions, ask your teacher. Be sure you understand any safety symbols that are shown.

2 **Be neat.** Keep your work area clean. If you have long hair, pull it back so it doesn't get in the way. Roll or push up long sleeves to keep them away from your experiment.

3 **Oops!** If you should spill or break something, or get cut, tell your teacher right away.

4 **Watch your eyes.** Wear safety goggles anytime you are directed to do so. If you get anything in your eyes, tell your teacher right away.

5 **Yuck!** Never eat or drink anything during a science activity.

6 **Don't get shocked.** Be especially careful if an electric appliance is used. Be sure that electric cords are in a safe place where you can't trip over them. Don't ever pull a plug out of an outlet by pulling on the cord.

7 **Keep it clean.** Always clean up when you have finished. Put everything away and wipe your work area. Wash your hands.

In some activities you will see these symbols. They are signs for what you need to be safe.

Be especially careful.

Wear safety goggles.

Be careful with sharp objects.

Don't get burned.

Protect your clothes.

Protect your hands with mitts.

Be careful with electricity.

Science Safety

_____ I will study the steps of the investigation before I begin.

_____ I will ask my teacher if I do not understand something.

_____ I will keep my work area clean.

_____ I will pull my hair back and roll up long sleeves before I begin.

_____ I will tell my teacher if I spill or break something or get cut.

_____ I will wear safety goggles when I am told to do so.

_____ I will tell my teacher if I get something in my eye.

_____ I will not eat or drink anything during an investigation unless told to do so by my teacher.

_____ I will be extra careful when using electrical appliances.

_____ I will keep electric cords out of the way and only unplug them by pulling on the protected plug.

_____ I will clean up when I am finished.

_____ I will return unused materials to my teacher.

_____ I will wipe my area and then wash my hands.

Chapter 1 • Graphic Organizer for Chapter Concepts

From Single Cells to Body Systems

LESSON 1
CELLS

All living things are made up of one or more

_____ cells

Cell Structures

Plant	Animal
1. nucleus	1. nucleus
2. chromosomes	
3. cell membrane	
4. cell wall	
5. cytoplasm	
6. chloroplasts	
7. vacuole	
8. mitochondria	

LESSON 2
BODY TRANSPORT SYSTEMS

Circulatory System Parts

1. heart
2. blood vessels
3. blood

Respiratory System Organs

1. trachea
2. bronchi
3. lungs

Excretory System Organs

1. kidneys
2. ureters
3. bladder

LESSON 3
BODY MOVEMENT SYSTEMS

Skeletal System Organs

1. bones
2. tendons
3. ligaments

Muscular System
Types of Muscles

1. voluntary muscles
2. smooth muscles
3. cardiac muscle

Nervous System Parts

1. brain
2. spinal cord
3. neurons

Name _____

Date _____

Observing Cells

Materials

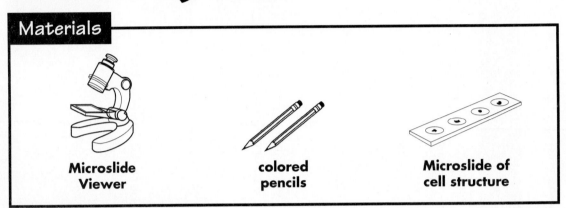

Microslide Viewer **colored pencils** **Microslide of cell structure**

Alternate Materials

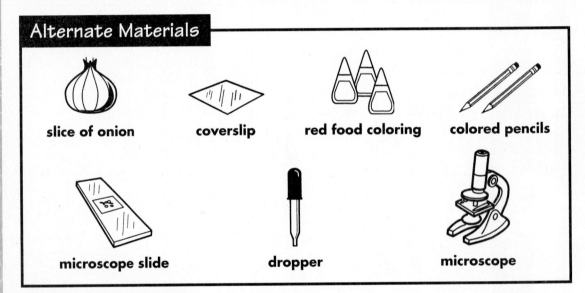

slice of onion **coverslip** **red food coloring** **colored pencils**

microscope slide **dropper** **microscope**

Activity Procedure

❶ Insert the Cell Structure Microslide in the slot on the Microslide Viewer. Turn the focus knob until you can see the cells clearly.

❷ **Observe** the onion skin cells and the human cheek cells. **Record** your observations by using the colored pencils to make drawings.

❸ Now **observe** the green leaf cells and the nerve cells. Again, **record** your observations by making drawings.

❹ Now **compare** your drawings. Make a Venn diagram with two large, overlapping circles. Label the circles *Plant Cells* and *Animal Cells*. Label the area where the circles overlap *Both Cells*. Draw the cell parts that you **observed** in the proper circles. Leave enough room to label the parts as you read about them in this lesson.

Name _____

Draw Conclusions

1. **Compare** the outer layers of plant and animal cells. The plant cells have a
   thick outer "wall," while the outer layer of the animal cells is much thinner.

   _____

2. In the centers of most cells are structures that control the cells' activities.
   How many of these structures are there in each of the cells you **observed**?
   one

3. **Scientists at Work** Scientists often **infer** characteristics of a group of objects
   by **observing** just a few of the objects. From your observations, what do you

   infer about the number of controlling structures in a cell? Every cell has a
   single controlling structure.

   _____

Investigate Further Now that you have **observed** photomicrographs of cells,
what questions do you have about living cells? Use the materials in the *Alternate
Materials* list to **plan and conduct a simple experiment** based on **this
hypothesis**: All cells have certain parts in common. See page R3 for tips on using

a microscope. Experiments should support the hypotheses. Students should
note the similar structures, such as a nucleus and cytoplasm, present in all
plant and animal cells.

_____

_____

Name _____

Date _____

Observe and Infer

Observing is the most basic science skill. Making good observations will allow you to develop other important science skills, like inferring, comparing, classifying, and measuring. Inferring involves the use of logical reasoning to make conclusions based on observations. Inferences are explanations for events, are based on judgments, and are not always correct.

Think About Observing and Inferring

You looked at cells during the investigation for this lesson. Imagine you come to class and find that all the microscope slides have been removed from their holders and had their labels removed. Use your observations and your knowledge of cells to answer the following questions and make inferences.

1. Your teacher asks you and other students to help relabel the slides by separating the cell slides from the other slides. What do you need to look

   for to decide whether or not you are looking at a cell slide? cell wall or
   membrane and a "controlling structure" (nucleus)

   _____

2. Next your teacher asks you to separate the plant cell slides from the animal cell slides. What do you need to look for to decide whether or not you are looking

   at a plant cell slide or an animal cell slide? If the cell has an outer cell wall,
   it's a plant cell.

   _____

3. What would you look for to decide whether you were seeing that structure?
   a rigid layer supporting the plant cell

   _____

4. What inference could you make about why such a difference is found in plant

   and animal cells? Possible answer: cells in plants and cells in animals
   perform different functions, so they require different cell parts.

   _____

    Use with page A5.

Use Context to Determine/Confirm Word Meaning

Read the selection. Use context clues to decide the meaning of each italicized term. Then check each meaning in a dictionary.

Sickle-Cell Disease

Sickle-cell disease, often known as sickle-cell *anemia*, is an illness affecting the red blood cells. It is a genetic disorder that a person inherits from his or her parents. People with sickle-cell anemia have an abnormal form of hemoglobin in their red blood cells, making the cells sickle-shaped (curved). This *abnormality* causes the blood to flow more slowly and the blood cells to carry less oxygen than normal cells. Sickle-cell disease eventually causes infection and damages internal organs. It is painful and is treated with pain relievers and antibiotics. People with this disease sometimes require blood *transfusions* to replenish red blood cells. A bone-marrow transplant can help treat the disease, but it is a risky procedure.

Term	Possible Meaning	Dictionary Meaning
anemia	an illness affecting the red blood cells	a condition in which blood is deficient in red blood cells, in hemoglobin, or in total volume
abnormality	a condition that is not normal	the quality or state of being not normal
transfusions (See *transfuse.*)	to give blood to someone	to transfer (as blood) into a vein of a person or animal

Name _____

Date _____

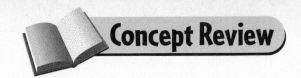

What Are Cells, and What Do They Do?

Lesson Concept

Living things are made of one or more cells, each able to support the functions of life. Plant cells differ from animal cells in that they have cell walls and chloroplasts.

Vocabulary

cell (A6)	**cell membrane** (A8)	**nucleus** (A8)
cytoplasm (A9)	**diffusion** (A10)	**osmosis** (A10)
tissue (A12)	**organ** (A12)	**system** (A12)

Match the name of each structure or process with its function.

_____ **1.** muscle tissue

_____ **2.** chromosomes

_____ **3.** diffusion

_____ **4.** nervous tissue

_____ **5.** chloroplasts

_____ **6.** cell membrane

_____ **7.** nucleus

_____ **8.** vacuoles

A make food in plant cells

B store food, water, and waste materials for the cell

C can move an animal's skeleton by contracting and relaxing

D holds parts of the cell together and separates the cell from its surroundings

E the way most materials move in and out of cells

F threadlike structures that contain information about the characteristics of the organism

G carries electrical signals that affect muscle tissue

H controls the cell's activities

Cells and Tissues

Materials

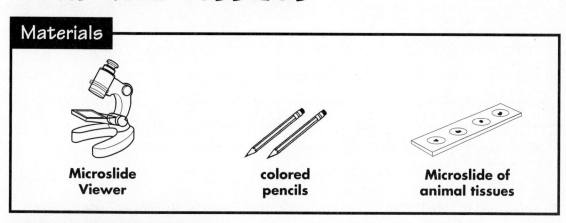

Microslide Viewer

colored pencils

Microslide of animal tissues

Alternate Materials

prepared slides of epithelial, connective, and nervous tissues

microscope

Activity Procedure

1 Insert the Animal Tissues Microslide in the slot of the Microslide Viewer. Turn the focus knob until you can see the cells and tissues clearly.

2 **Observe** the voluntary muscle cells. **Record** your observations by using the colored pencils to make a drawing. Label your drawing with the name of the tissue. Then describe the tissue. You may use the Microslide text folder to help you write your description.

3 Repeat Step 2 for the smooth muscle cells and the heart muscle.

4 **Compare** the three kinds of muscle tissue.

Draw Conclusions

1. How are the three kinds of muscle tissue alike? How are they different?

    The voluntary muscle tissue has long, thin cells. The cells of the smooth
    muscle tissue are shorter and more tightly packed. Cells of the heart
    muscle seem to be interconnected.

2. The dark-stained organelles you **observed** in the muscle tissues are
    mitochondria. Which kind of muscle tissue has the most mitochondria?

    heart muscle

3. **Scientists at Work** When scientists **compare** objects, they often **infer** reasons
    for any differences. What do you infer about why one kind of muscle tissue has
    more mitochondria than the others? Since the heart is always beating, heart
    tissue needs more energy than other muscle tissue.

Investigate Further Now that you have **observed** several kinds of tissues, develop
a testable question about differences among tissues. Use the materials in the
Alternate Materials list to study other kinds of tissue. Observe the tissues under
the microscope, and draw and label any differences you see. **Form a hypothesis**
about how these tissues are different from the muscle tissues you observed. See page
R3 for tips on using a microscope. Students might hypothesize that the cells
making up each of the other tissues look different from the cells of the muscle
tissue but still have the same basic cell parts.

Name _____

Date _____

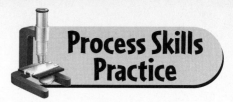

Compare and Infer

When you compare data, you arrange your information so that you
can see similarities and differences. Inferring involves the use of logical
reasoning to make conclusions based on observations.

Think About Comparing and Inferring

Rajean was doing a comparative study to test a new preservative. She made a
nutrient solution for microorganisms from beef broth. Then she put 100 mL
of the broth in three different beakers. She put 0.1 mL of the preservative in
Beaker A, 0.01 mL in *Beaker B*, and 0.001 mL in *Beaker C*. The next day Rajean
checked the beakers and found the broth discolored and cloudy in two of them.
So, she used a microscope to check a sample from each of the three beakers. She
recorded what she observed.

	Beaker A	**Beaker B**	**Beaker C**
Amount of preservative added to beaker	0.1 mL	0.01 mL	0.001 mL
Appearance of broth	Clear	Somewhat cloudy	Very cloudy
Microorganisms seen under microscope	None	Yeast cells	Yeast and bacteria

1. Compare the mixtures in each beaker. How are they different?
   by the amount of preservative added to each one
   _____

2. How are they alike? They each contain the same amount of the same nutrient
   solution. All other conditions except the preservative added were the same.

3. After 24 hours, how do the beakers compare? Two of them are cloudy.
   _____

4. What can you infer about how effective the preservative is in keeping yeast
   from growing in the solution? It is not as good at keeping yeast from growing
   as it is at keeping bacteria from growing.

Arrange Events in Sequence

Read the selection on page A18 about the respiratory system. Then number the steps below according to the order in which they occur.

___5___ Carbon dioxide diffuses out of the blood through the thin walls of the capillaries, into the alveoli.

___8___ From the heart, oxygen-rich blood is pumped to other parts of the body.

___1___ When you inhale, air is pulled into your body.

___4___ Air travels through bronchial tubes into your lungs.

___2___ The air is filtered by tiny hairs in your nose and warmed by capillaries.

___6___ At the same time, oxygen from inhaled air diffuses through the thin walls of the alveoli and into the capillaries.

___3___ Warm, clean air travels down your trachea.

___7___ The oxygen-rich blood then flows from the capillaries into the pulmonary veins and back to the heart.

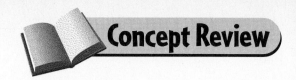

How Do Body Systems Transport Materials?

Lesson Concept

Body cells are organized into tissues, organs, and systems that work together to keep the body alive. Four of the major systems are the circulatory, the respiratory, the digestive, and the excretory.

Vocabulary

capillaries (A17)   **alveoli** (A18)   **villi** (A19)   **nephrons** (A20)

Match the name of each structure or process with its function.

_C_ **1.** circulatory system

_H_ **2.** platelets

_K_ **3.** alveoli

_B_ **4.** esophagus

_A_ **5.** capillaries

_D_ **6.** ureters

_J_ **7.** trachea

_E_ **8.** arteries

_G_ **9.** heart

_F_ **10.** saliva

_L_ **11.** pancreas

_I_ **12.** sweating

A blood vessels so small that blood cells have to move through them in single file

B a long tube that leads to the stomach

C transports oxygen, nutrients, and wastes through the body in the blood

D tubes that empty wastes into the bladder from the kidneys

E vessels through which blood leaves the heart

F moistens food and begins to break down starchy foods

G pumps blood through blood vessels

H cause blood to clot when a blood vessel is cut

I eliminates excess body heat

J sometimes called the windpipe

K tiny air sacs in the lungs

L produces a fluid that neutralizes stomach acid

How Muscles Cause Movement

Materials

tape measure

Activity Procedure

1 Place your left hand on top of your right arm, between the shoulder and elbow. Bend and straighten your right arm at the elbow. **Observe** the movement by feeling the muscles in your right arm.

2 The muscle on the front of the upper arm is called the *biceps*. The muscle on the back of the upper arm is called the *triceps*. **Compare** the biceps and the triceps as you bend and straighten your arm. **Infer** which muscle controls the bending movement and which controls the straightening movement.

3 Have a partner use the tape measure to **measure** the distance around your upper arm when it is straight and when it is bent. **Record** the measurements.

4 Repeat Steps 2 and 3, using your right hand and your left arm.

5 **Compare** the sets of measurements.

Name _____

Draw Conclusions

1. What did you **infer** about the muscles controlling the bending and the straightening of your upper arm? The biceps bends the arm, and the triceps straightens it.

_____

2. Why are two muscles needed to bend and straighten your arm? Why can't one muscle do it? A muscle only works one way; it can only contract to move a bone in one direction.

_____

3. Scientists at Work Scientists often hypothesize about things they **observe**. **Hypothesize** about any differences between the measurements of your right arm and the measurements of your left arm. Students might hypothesize that the arm that does more work has larger muscles.

_____

Investigate Further **Plan and conduct an experiment** with different pairs of muscles. For example, try bending your leg at the knee while **observing** the muscles in your thigh. See if these measurements also support your hypothesis. Draw conclusions about differences in muscle sizes from the data you collected.

Decide whether more data is needed to support your conclusions. In the experiments, students should find that data using leg muscles will parallel that using arm muscles. Individual responses will vary.

_____

_____

Name _____

Date _____

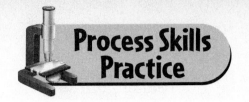

Hypothesize

When you hypothesize, you make an educated guess about the results of an experiment you plan to do. A hypothesis is based upon observation, prior knowledge, and prior experimental outcomes. A hypothesis is often altered based on the outcome of experiments that test it.

Think About Hypothesizing

A group of students decided to test the effect of sleep on reaction time. Their hypothesis was that reaction time would improve with more sleep. Each student in the test was asked to push a button as soon as he or she heard the sound of a bell. The amount of time between the sound of the bell and the pushing of the button was recorded as the reaction time.

The table below lists reaction times for three students on different days after receiving different amounts of sleep the night before. Each student underwent two trials on each day of testing.

| Amount of Sleep | Reaction Time in Seconds | | | | | |
| | Student A | | Student B | | Student C | |
	Trial 1	Trial 2	Trial 1	Trial 2	Trial 1	Trial 2
8 hours	0.20	0.16	0.15	0.12	0.25	0.19
6 hours	0.17	0.17	0.19	0.24	0.25	0.32
4 hours	0.30	0.45	0.35	0.47	0.40	0.45
2 hours	0.82	1.10	0.75	1.08	0.80	1.02

1. Was the hypothesis correct? _Yes, reaction time improved with more sleep._

2. Use the data to form a hypothesis about the effect of sleeping less than eight hours a night on reaction time. _Possible answer: Sleeping less than six hours will increase reaction time considerably._

_____

3. How would you test this hypothesis? _Possible answer: by repeating the experiment with more and different students._

Name _____

Date _____

Compare and Contrast

Read the selection. Then complete the chart by comparing and contrasting the three kinds of muscles.

There are three types of muscles in the human body—voluntary, smooth, and cardiac. All of the body's more than 600 muscles are made of cells called muscle fibers. All the muscles contract, depending on the body's movements and functions. Voluntary muscles move bones and support the skeleton. They range in size from those in the eye to those in the thigh. Smooth muscles are in the body's organs and move slowly, controlling bodily functions. The cardiac muscles make up the walls of the heart and pump blood to the rest of the body. Some cardiac muscles work together to set the pace of the heartbeat.

Type of Muscle	Compare	Contrast
voluntary	ability to contract; made of cells called muscle fibers	many different sizes; move bones; support the skeleton
smooth	ability to contract; made of cells called muscle fibers	contract slowly and control bodily functions
cardiac	ability to contract; made of cells called muscle fibers	make up the walls of the heart; pump blood; some cardiac muscles set the pace of the heartbeat

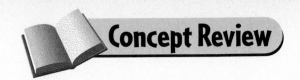

How Do Bones, Muscles, and Nerves Work Together?

Lesson Concept

Skeletal bones move because of the action of pairs of voluntary muscles. Smooth muscles line digestive organs and blood vessels. The walls of the heart are made of cardiac muscle. Nerves carry signals from sensory organs to the brain and from the brain to the muscles.

Vocabulary

bone marrow (A24)	**joints** (A24)	**tendons** (A25)
ligaments (A25)	**neuron** (A26)	**receptors** (A26)

Match the term in the left column with its description in the right column.

___E___ **1.** bone marrow

___H___ **2.** ligaments

___D___ **3.** tendons

___A___ **4.** smooth muscles

___F___ **5.** cardiac muscles

___J___ **6.** joints

___B___ **7.** central nervous system

___C___ **8.** receptors

___I___ **9.** neurons

___G___ **10.** synapse

A line digestive organs and blood vessels

B is made up of the brain and the spinal cord

C are nerve cells that detect conditions in the body's environment

D attach bones to muscles

E produces red and white blood cells

F make up the walls of the heart

G is a gap between the axon of one neuron and the dendrite of the next neuron

H attach bones to each other

I are the cells that nerves are made of

J are where the bones meet to attach to each other and to muscles

Name _____

Date _____

Recognize Vocabulary

Listed below are scrambled vocabulary terms from Chapter 1. Use the clues to unscramble the terms. Write the unscrambled terms on the lines provided.

1. S M O O S S I _____
the movement of water and dissolved materials through cell membranes

2. L L R C A S E I A P I _____
blood vessels so small that blood cells move through them in single file

3. R U N N E O _____
a specialized cell that can receive and transmit signals to other cells like it

4. L Y M O C P S T A _____
a jellylike substance containing chemicals that keep the cell functioning

5. G R O A N _____
tissues that work together form this

6. L C L E _____
the basic unit of structure and function of all living things

7. J S T O N I _____
where bones meet and are attached to each other and to muscles

8. P R E E T O C R S _____
nerve cells that detect conditions in the body's environment

9. I I L V L _____
tiny tubes sticking out from the walls of the small intestine

10. O M N O E A W B R R (2 words) _____
connective tissue that produces red and white blood cells

11. F D N I U F I O S _____
the way most materials move in and out of cells

12. M C L N E E M E R L B A (2 words) _____
a thin covering that encloses a cell

13. I G L E S A N T M _____
bands of connective tissue that hold the skeleton together

14. V I O A L E L _____
tiny air sacs at the end of the smallest tubes in the lungs

Name _____

Date _____

Write a Sensory Poem

Expressive Writing–Poem

Think of one of your favorite places to be. Write a poem about how you experience that place through your sensory organs. Use vivid, descriptive words. Complete the concept web below to help you generate ideas for your poem.

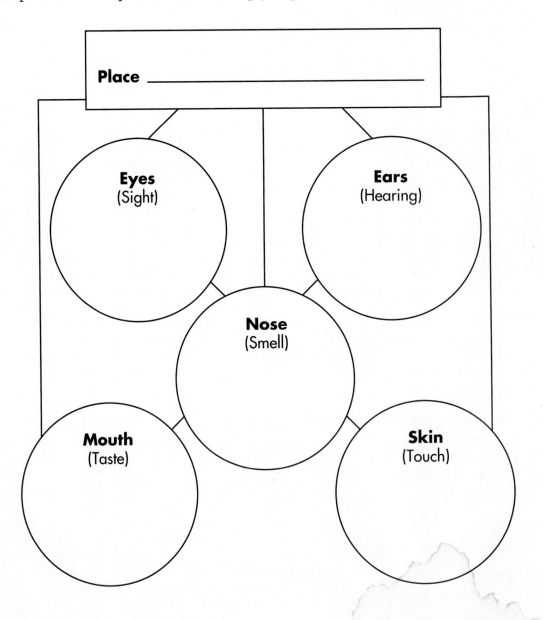

Chapter 2 • Graphic Organizer for Chapter Concepts

Classifying Living Things

LESSON 1
CLASSIFYING

Why Classify?

To organize living things so they

can be more easily studied

and discussed.

The Five Kingdoms

1. monerans

2. protists

3. fungi

4. plants

5. animals

LESSON 2
CLASSIFYING ANIMALS

Animals with Backbones Are

Called vertebrates

Examples

1. mammals

2. reptiles

3. amphibians

4. fish

5. birds

Animals Without Backbones

Are Called invertebrates

Examples

1. anthropods

2. mollusks

LESSON 3
CLASSIFYING PLANTS

Two Groups of Plants

1. vascular plants (have tubes)

2. nonvascular plants (no tubes)

Classifying Shoes

Materials

shoes

newspaper or paper towels

Activity Procedure

1 Take off one shoe and put it with your classmates' shoes. If you put the shoes on a desk or table, cover it first with newspaper or paper towels.

2 Find a way to **classify** the shoes. Begin by finding two or three large groups of shoes that are alike. Write a description of each group.

3 **Classify** the large groups of shoes into smaller and smaller groups. Each smaller group should be alike in some way.

My classification: _____

_____

_____

4 Write a description of each smaller group.

My descriptions: _____

_____

_____

_____

_____

5 Stop classifying when you have sorted all the shoes into groups with two or fewer members.

Name _____

Draw Conclusions

1. What features did you use to **classify** the shoes? _Possible answer: use of_ _shoes, material, color, length, height, slip-on or lace up, and so on._ _____

2. **Compare** your classification system with a classmate's system. How are your systems alike? _Answers will vary. Students should include specific examples of_ _how systems are alike._ _____

How are they different? _Answers will vary. Students should include specific_ _examples of how systems are different._ _____

3. **Scientists at Work** Scientists **classify** living things to show how living things are alike. Why might it be important for scientists to agree on a set of rules for classifying living things? _Possible answers: to make it easy to find or to talk_ _about specific living things; to find out why living things are alike in some ways._ _____

Investigate Further **Classify** other groups of things such as toys, cars, or pictures of plants and animals. Write a brief explanation of your classification system.
You may wish to have students share their classifications and explanations.
How were students' explanations of their groupings alike? How were they
different? _____

Name _____

Date _____

Classify

When you classify living things, you group them based on similarities.
Things with many similarities may be classified in more than one way.

Think About Classifying

Observe these pictures of shells. Classify the
shells into two or more groups. Fill in the
chart to describe your classification
system. Then answer the questions.

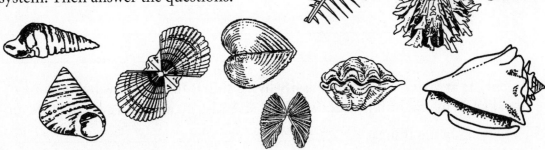

Characteristic Used for Classifying	Name of Group	Shells in Group

1. Look at the shells in each of your groups. How could you classify the shells in
each group into smaller groups? _Answers will depend upon how students
classified shells on the chart. For example, if students classified shells as
spiked or not spiked, they could break them down into whether they had one
or two parts._

2. Compare your classification with that of a classmate. How were your
classifications similar? How were they different? _Accept reasonable answers.
Comparisons should focus on characteristics used for classification, such as
those described in the answer to question 1._

Use with page A37.

Arrange Events in Sequence

Read the selection. Then fill in the organizer with the five basic plant groups and the divisions of one of the groups mentioned in the selection.

Plants are categorized into five groups: seed plants, ferns, lycophytes, horsetails, and bryophytes. Most plants are seed plants, which are further divided into angiosperms and gymnosperms. The word *angiosperm* comes from two Greek words that mean *case* and *seed*. This type of plant produces flowers and fruits, and it varies greatly in size. Monocots are a type of angiosperm that have a seed leaf called a cotyledon. Dicots are another type of angiosperm with two cotyledons in their seeds.

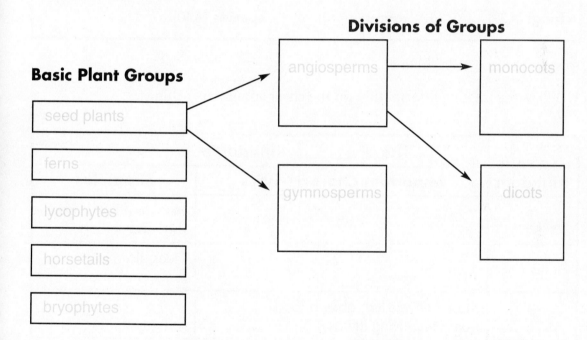

Divisions of Groups

Basic Plant Groups

seed plants

ferns

lycophytes

horsetails

bryophytes

angiosperms

gymnosperms

monocots

dicots

Name _____

Date _____

How Do Scientists Classify Living Things?

Lesson Concept

Scientists organize living things so they can be easily studied and discussed.

Vocabulary

classification (A38)   **kingdom** (A39)   **moneran** (A39)   **protist** (A39)

fungi (A39)   **genus** (A40)   **species** (A40)

Answer the questions below.

1. Fill in the missing information on the chart about living things.

The ___Five___ Kingdoms		
Kingdom	**Important Characteristics**	**Examples**
Animals	Many-celled, feed on other living things	Monkeys, birds, frogs, fish, and spiders
Plants	Many-celled, make their own food	Trees, flowers, ferns, and mosses
Fungi	Most many-celled, absorb food from other living things	Mushrooms, yeast, and mold
Protists	Most one-celled with nuclei; some make their own food, others do not	Algae, amoebas, and diatoms
Monerans	One-celled, no cell nuclei; some make their own food, some feed on living things	Bacteria

2. The white oak tree has the scientific name *Quercus alba*. This is also the name

of the _____species_____. What genus does the white oak belong

to? _____Quercus_____ What kingdom does the white oak tree

belong to? _____plants_____

Building a Model Backbone

Materials

chenille stem

wagon wheel pasta, uncooked

candy gelatin rings

Activity Procedure

CAUTION **Never eat anything you use in an Investigate.**

1 Bend one end of the chenille stem. Thread six pieces of wagon-wheel pasta onto the stem. Push the pasta down to the bend in the stem. Bend the stem above the pasta to hold the pasta in place.

2 Bend and twist the stem. What do you see and hear? _____

_____

3 Take all the pasta off the chenille stem except one. Thread a candy gelatin ring onto the stem, and push it down.

4 Add pasta and rings until the stem is almost full. Bend the stem above the pasta and rings to hold them in place.

5 Bend and twist the stem. What do you see and hear? _____

_____

6 Draw pictures of the model backbones you made. **Compare** your models with that shown in the picture on page A57.

Draw Conclusions

1. A real backbone is made of bones called vertebrae (VER•tuh•bray) and soft discs that surround the spinal cord. What does each part of your final model stand for? The chenille stem is the spinal cord, the pasta pieces are the vertebrae, and the candy rings are the soft discs. _____

_____

_____

2. How is your final model like a real backbone? It can bend or twist. It is also stiff enough to give the body support. _____

_____

_____

3. Study your final model again. What do the soft discs do? The discs cushion the bones—they keep the bones from rubbing against one another. _____

_____

_____

4. **Scientists at Work** Scientists use models to study how things work. **Make a model** to test this **hypothesis**: A piece of dry, uncooked spaghetti or some other material would work better than a chenille stem to stand for the spinal cord in a model. **Investigate** to see. Then write a report of your investigation. Be sure to include the results of any tests you conducted with other materials, and any conclusions you drew about using those materials in a model

backbone. The chenille stem is a better model because it can bend like the spinal column does. Uncooked spaghetti would break if bent too far. _____

_____

_____

_____

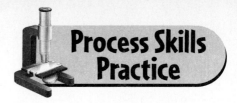

Make a Model

You don't always need to see the whole thing to understand how part of it works. Models can be built to help you see just one part of a thing.

Think About Making a Model

Todd wanted to show his younger sister Rebecca how a frog leaps. He decided to make a poster to show the leaping movements of a frog. He found a book with pictures of a frog leaping. The book showed that when a frog leaps, it makes six basic movements.

First the frog crouches down, bending all its legs. Then its feet and legs move straight out away from its body, pushing the frog away from the crouched position. While in midair, it pulls its front legs back to its sides and leaves its hind legs straight. Right before the frog lands, it puts its front legs in front of itself. The frog lands on its front feet first. Then it pulls its back legs toward its body and puts them on the ground.

1. Why would it be hard to understand the movements by just watching a frog leap? It would be hard to see the individual motions of the frog's body, because they would happen faster than anyone could see.

2. Why do you think Todd made a poster instead of a working model of a frog? Accept reasonable answers. Students may say that it is easier to see the movements in a series of pictures than in one working model.

3. Do you think Todd's poster was a model? Explain. Accept reasonable answers. Some students may consider the poster a model because it shows individual movements. Some students may not consider pictures to be models because they're not three-dimensional, but in fact a picture is a kind of model.

4. Besides Todd's poster, what other ways could Rebecca use to learn about how a frog leaps? Accept reasonable answers. Students may suggest watching a slow-motion video of a frog leaping.

Name _____

Date _____

Compare and Contrast

Read the selection about vertebrates and invertebrates. Then use the Venn diagram to compare and contrast these two kinds of animals.

Animals are either vertebrates or invertebrates. A vertebrate has a spinal column, or backbone, and a cranium, or skull. An invertebrate does not have a spinal column. There are more than 1 million known species of invertebrates but only about 55,000 species of vertebrates. Vertebrates are bilaterally symmetrical, meaning that the right and left sides mirror each other. Vertebrates also have no more than two pairs of limbs.

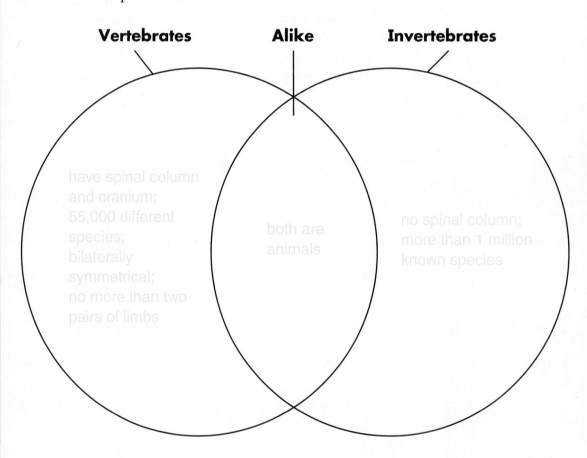

Vertebrates   **Alike**   **Invertebrates**

have spinal column and cranium; 55,000 different species; bilaterally symmetrical; no more than two pairs of limbs

both are animals

no spinal column; more than 1 million known species

How Are Vertebrates Classified?

Lesson Concept

Animals with backbones are classified into five groups.

Vocabulary

vertebrate (A44)   **mammal** (A44)   **reptile** (A44)   **amphibian** (A44)

invertebrate (A45)   **bird** (A45)   **fish** (A45)

Fill in the missing information on the chart.

Vertebrates		
Group	**Important Characteristics**	**Examples**
Amphibians	Have moist skin; begin life in water	Frogs, newts, toads, and salamanders
Birds	Have wings and feathers; lay eggs	Eagles, owls, accept any other bird
Fish	Have scales; spend their entire lives in water	Salmon, trout, and accept any other fish
Mammals	Have hair; make milk for their young	Cats, dogs, and accept any other mammal
Reptiles	Have dry, scaly skin; lay eggs	Lizards, snakes, alligators, dinosaurs, and turtles

Plant Stems

Materials

fresh celery stalk with leaves	plastic knife	two containers	water
red food coloring	blue food coloring	hand lens	paper towels

Activity Procedure

1. Use the plastic knife to trim the end off the celery stalk. Split the celery from the middle of the stalk to the bottom. Do not cut the stalk completely in half.

2. Use the chart below.

3. Half-fill each container with water. Add 15 drops of red food coloring to one container. Add 15 drops of blue food coloring to the other container.

4. With the containers side by side, place one part of the celery stalk in each container of colored water. You may need to prop the stalk up so the containers don't tip over.

5. **Observe** the celery every 15 minutes for an hour. **Record** your observations on your chart.

6. After you have completed your chart, put a paper towel on your desk. Take the celery out of the water. Cut about 2 cm off the bottom of the stalk. Use the hand lens to **observe** the pieces of stalk and freshly cut end of the stalk.

Time	Observations

Draw Conclusions

1. Where did the water travel? The water traveled up the stalk to the leaf blades.

_____

How do you know? The leaf blades had red and blue color in them.

_____

2. How fast did the water travel? The water traveled up the tubes in the stalks.
The speed of the water transport depended on the freshness of the stalk.

How do you know? The tubes were colored, and the material around the
tubes was not.

_____

3. Scientists at Work Scientists **infer** what happens in nature by making careful
observations. Based on this investigation, what can you infer about the

importance of stems? Stems transport water from the roots to the leaves.

_____

_____

Investigate Further Hypothesize about how you could change a white carnation
into a flower with two colors. **Plan and conduct an experiment** to test your
hypothesis.

In their experiments, students should split the carnation's stalk and put the

two stalk parts in two containers, each with a different color of water.

_____

_____

_____

Name _____

Date _____

Infer

Inferring is using what you observe to explain what has happened. An inference may be correct or incorrect. Once you have made an inference, you may need to make more observations to confirm your inference.

Think About Inferring

Hope was helping decorate her house with flowers she cut from her garden. She made two similar bouquets in different vases with water. The pictures show what happened to Hope's bouquets after a few days. After the third day, Hope wondered why the flowers in the black vase stayed fresh, but those in the smaller white vase wilted. She looked inside the black vase. There was water in it. She looked inside the white vase. It was completely dry.

Day 1 **Day 2** **Day 3**

1. What observations did Hope make? Hope observed that the flowers in the white vase wilted after three days while the flowers in the black vase did not. She also observed the black vase had water and after three days the white vase did not.

2. Infer why the flowers in the white vase wilted, but those in the black vase did not. Students may say that the flowers wilted because they had no water. They may also say the flowers wilted because the vase was a different color or different size.

3. What do you infer happened to the water in the white vase?
The flower stems drew up all the water in the white vase. It was all gone because there was less water in the vase to start with than in the black vase.

4. How could you test your inference? Cut some more flowers, and put them in the vases. Mark the water levels, and observe what happens over a few days.

Summarize and Paraphrase a Selection

Read the selection. Then complete the organizer below by writing the main idea, three supporting facts and details, and a two- or three-sentence summary.

An Unusual Vascular Plant

If you live in a dry climate, you may be familiar with the cactus. Cacti are flowering plants that belong to the plant kingdom, but they are different from other flowering plants. One important difference is the ability of the cactus to store water in its leaves or stems, which makes it a succulent. Another difference is the cactus's areola, or crossways bud or shoot, which grows on the base of a leaf. The spines, leaves, hairs, and flowers grow from the areola. Cactus flowers are distinctive because they are usually large and single, and have many stamens.

Main Idea	**Supporting Fact/Detail**
The cactus is an unusual member of the plant kingdom.	Cacti can store water in their leaves or stems.
	Supporting Fact/Detail
	The spines, leaves, hairs, and flowers grow from an areola.
	Supporting Fact/Detail
	The flowers are large and single and have many stamens.

Summary

Cacti are unique vascular plants with large, single flowers. They store water in their leaves or stems and have areolas from which the spines, leaves, hairs, and flowers grow.

Name _____

Date _____

Concept Review

How Are Plants Classified?

Lesson Concept

Plants are classified by whether or not they have tubes.

Vocabulary

vascular plant (A50)   **nonvascular plant** (A52)

Fill in the blank with the letter of the correct answer.

1. The main difference between plants and animals is that ____B____.
   A animals make their own food   **B** plants make their own food

2. In plants with tubes, the tubes ____B____.
   A take in air from around the plant
   B carry water, food, and nutrients to different plant parts

3. Where would you look for tubes in a plant? ____D____
   A in the stem   **B** in the leaves   **C** in the trunk   **D** all of these

4. In plants that do not have tubes, food travels in water ____B____.
   A around the outside of the plant   **B** from cell to cell

5. Nonvascular plants are always ____A____.
   A very small   **B** found in dry places

6. The ____B____ is the part of a tree trunk that has the living tubes.
   A heartwood   **B** sapwood

7. This tree was ____B____ when the trunk was cut down.
   A eight years old   **B** ten years old

8. Label the parts of the tree trunk.

   bark _____   sapwood _____

   heartwood _____   growth ring _____

Recognize Vocabulary

Match the definition in column A with the term in column B.

Column A

_____G_____ **1.** name of the second-smallest group

_C,H,P, or J_ **2.** animal with a backbone

_____M_____ **3.** plants with tubes

_____D_____ **4.** grouping things by a set of rules

_____I_____ **5.** name of the largest group

_____B_____ **6.** have many cells and absorb food from other living things

_____L_____ **7.** name of the smallest group

_____O_____ **8.** invertebrates with legs and several joints

_____F_____ **9.** plants without tubes

_____N_____ **10.** some one-celled with nuclei

_____J_____ **11.** vertebrate that has fur and makes milk

_____A_____ **12.** invertebrates that may or may not have a hard shell

_____E_____ **13.** animal without a backbone

_____C_____ **14.** vertebrate that begins life in water

_____K_____ **15.** one-celled, no nuclei

_____H_____ **16.** vertebrate with dry, scaly skin

Column B

A mollusks

B fungi

C amphibian

D classification

E invertebrate

F nonvascular plants

G genus

H reptile

I kingdom

J mammal

K monerans

L species

M vascular plants

N protists

O arthropods

P vertebrate

Writing Practice

Compare and Contrast Arthropods

Informative Writing–Compare and Contrast

Imagine that you have been asked to help scientists from another planet classify arthropods found on Earth. Write a set of directions for distinguishing insects from other arthropods. Give examples of each group of arthropods. Use the Venn diagram below to help you brainstorm points of comparison and contrast.

Insects   **All arthropods**   **Non-insect arthropods**

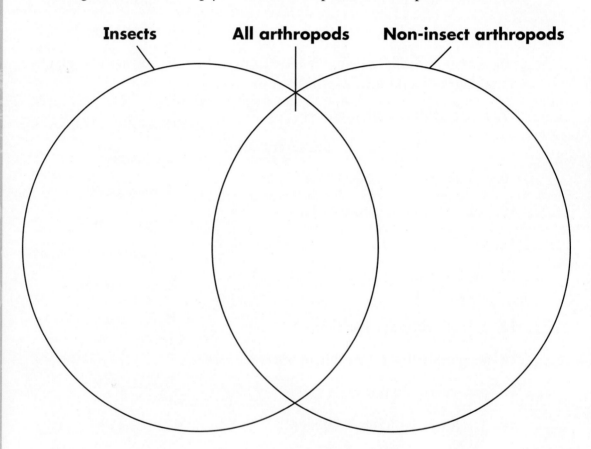

Chapter 3 • Graphic Organizer for Chapter Concepts

Animal Growth and Heredity

LESSON 1
CELL REPRODUCTION

1. mitosis

   produces 2 identical cells

2. meiosis

   produces gametes

LESSON 2
TYPES OF LIFE CYCLES

1. direct development

2. incomplete metamorphosis

3. complete metamorphosis

LESSON 3
INHERITED TRAITS

1. dominant trait

   purebred

   hybrid

2. recessive trait

   purebred

Name _____

Date _____

Cell Reproduction

Materials

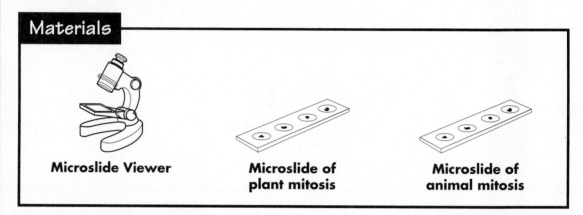

Microslide Viewer

Microslide of plant mitosis

Microslide of animal mitosis

Alternate Materials

microscope

prepared slides of plant cells dividing

prepared slides of animal cells dividing

Activity Procedure

1. Insert the Plant Mitosis Microslide into the slot in the Microslide Viewer. Turn the focus knob until you can see the cells clearly.

2. **Observe** the plant cells dividing. **Record** what you observe in each stage of cell division. The descriptions on the Microslide card may help you. Then draw pictures of what you see at each stage.

3. Now insert the Animal Mitosis Microslide into the slot of the Microslide Viewer. Again turn the focus knob until you can see the cells clearly.

4. **Observe** the animal cells dividing. **Record** what you observe in each stage of cell division. Again you may use the descriptions on the Microslide card to help you. Then draw pictures of what you see at each stage.

5. Now **compare** the stages of plant cell division with the stages of animal cell division. How are the stages alike? How are they different? **Record** your observations.

Name _____

Draw Conclusions

1. What part of the cell changes as cell division occurs? What changes take place?

The nucleus; in some cells the nucleus disappears, cross-shaped structures

line up in the center of some cells, and some cells look as if they are splitting

into two cells.

2. How many new cells does each dividing cell produce? two

3. What similarities and differences did you **observe** between the dividing plant

cells and the dividing animal cells? Possible answers: Both plant and

animal cells had a visible nucleus, materials inside the nucleus divided in

both, and the stages of cell division were the same in both. The plant cells

had cell walls and the animal cells did not.

4. Scientists at Work Scientists **observe** cells and ask questions based on their

observations. What questions do you have about cell division, based on what

you observed? Questions will vary.

_____

_____

Investigate Further Now that you have **observed** photomicrographs of plant and
animal cells dividing, use the materials on the *Alternate Materials* list to observe
other cells dividing. See page R3 for tips on using a microscope.

Name _____

Date _____

Observe

Observing is the most basic science skill. Making good observations will allow you to develop other important skills, such as comparing and classifying.

Think About Observing

Do all plant cells look alike? Do all animal cells look alike? Observe the drawings below, and compare them to what you know about cells. Then classify them by writing *plant* or *animal* beneath the drawing.

1. What observation can you make to determine which cells are plant cells?
Plant cells have a cell wall. Therefore, cells 3 and 6 are plant cells.
_____

2. Do you observe anything unusual about one of the plant cells and one of the animal cells? One of the plant cells has no chloroplasts (it is a root cell).
One of the animal cells has no nucleus (it is a red blood cell).
_____

4. _____ animal (white blood cell) _____

3. _____ plant (plant cell) _____

5. _____ animal (red blood cell) _____

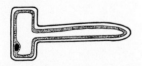

6. _____ plant (root hair cell) _____

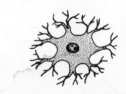

7. _____ animal (nerve cell) _____

Use with page A63.

Arrange Events in Sequence

Read the steps below about planarian regeneration. When you have finished, number the steps in the correct order. Circle the word clues that help you know the order of events.

Planarian Regeneration

___2___ | Next, the flatworm splits in half.

___3___ | After this, the flatworm halves regenerate body parts.

___1___ | First, most common planarian reproduce asexually, beginning with a rupture that starts behind the mouth.

___4___ | Finally, if any parts are missing, the planarian will grow them back.

Name _____

Date _____

 **Concept Review**

Growth and Reproduction

Lesson Concept

Organisms grow when their cells divide. Body cells divide through mitosis. Reproductive cells divide through meiosis.

Vocabulary

chromosome (A65)	**mitosis** (A65)	**asexual reproduction** (A67)
sexual reproduction (A68)	**meiosis** (A68)	

Use the terms from the box to fill in the blanks in the paragraph that follows. Watch out! One term is used twice.

sexual reproduction	**regenerate**	**planaria**
mitosis	**meiosis**	**zygote**
asexual reproduction	**chromosomes**	**planarian**

Organisms grow when their cells divide in a process called _____mitosis_____.

To prepare for this process, a cell makes copies of its _____chromosomes_____. After this process, each of the new cells has an exact copy of the original cell's

_____chromosomes_____. When a cut or scrape on your skin heals, it is because this

process of cell division has allowed the damaged tissue to _____regenerate_____.

The freshwater flatworm, called a _____planarian_____, can regenerate most of its body through mitosis. Many simple one-celled organisms, like yeast or bacteria, can use this process of cell division to produce new organisms through

_____asexual reproduction_____, in which a single parent produces offspring through mitosis. Most organisms, however, are reproduced from two parents in a process

called _____sexual reproduction_____. In this process cells from two parents combine

to form a _____zygote_____, which contains genetic material from each parent. Organisms produce reproductive cells through a process called

_____meiosis_____, which reduces the number of chromosomes in the reproductive cells, so they don't end up with twice as many as they need.

The Stages of a Mealworm's Life

Materials

mealworm culture   paper plate   hand lens

Activity Procedure

1. Your teacher will give you a mealworm from the mealworm culture.

2. Put the mealworm on the paper plate. Using the hand lens, **observe** the mealworm closely. Draw what you see.

3. Label these parts on your drawing: head, segment, antenna, outer shell, claw, mouth, and leg.

4. **Observe** the mealworm's movements. Does it move straight forward or from side to side? Does it move quickly or slowly? **Record** your observations.

5. Now your teacher will give you a beetle from the mealworm culture. Repeat Steps 2–4 with the beetle.

6. Finally, **observe** the mealworm culture. Try to find evidence of other stages of a mealworm's life, such as eggs and pupa cases. Draw pictures of what you find.

7. **Compare** your drawings of the eggs and pupa cases with your drawings of the mealworm and the beetle. Form a **hypothesis** about the order of these life stages. Then list the ways in which a mealworm changes as it grows.

Draw Conclusions

1. How are the mealworm and the beetle similar? _Possible answers: Both have_ ___
heads and antennae, both have segmented bodies, and both have legs. ___

_____

2. How is the beetle different from the mealworm? _Possible answers: The_ ___
beetle has a hard shell and wings, and the mealworm doesn't; the beetle has ___
more legs. ___

3. Scientists at Work Scientists often **observe** an organism and then **hypothesize** about their observations. What observations enabled you to form your hypothesis about the order of the life stages? _Accept all reasonable answers._ ___

_____

_____

Investigate Further Plan and conduct an experiment to test your hypothesis about the life stages of a mealworm. Decide what equipment or technology you will need to use to test your hypothesis. Then use the equipment or technology in your experiment. _One possible experiment is to separate an egg from the_ ___
culture and then observe its development on a regular basis as it changes ___
over time. ___

_____

_____

_____

Name _____

Date _____

Hypothesize

To explain your observations you may form a hypothesis. A hypothesis is an explanation that you can test. Tests cannot prove a hypothesis. They can only support it. If test results don't support your hypothesis, then you need to form a new one.

Think About Hypothesizing

People used to believe that certain forms of life developed directly from nonliving things, such as dead animals or mud. This was known as spontaneous generation. The belief was a hypothesis based on observation. Eventually the hypothesis was subjected to scientific testing and found to be incorrect. See if you can think of ways to test the following hypotheses.

1. Many years ago maggots were believed to come from decaying meat. Suppose you are living in those days and you propose a new hypothesis that maggots hatch from fly eggs laid on the meat. How can you test your hypothesis?

Have two samples of meat. Let one be exposed to flies. Keep flies away from
the other, perhaps by keeping it in a jar covered with mesh. See if the
maggots appear only in the exposed meat. Any reasonable variation of this
should be accepted.

2. Microorganisms were believed to arise spontaneously in water under certain conditions. For example, if you add hay to water and wait a few days, you will be able to use a microscope and find microorganisms in the water. What hypothesis could you form about this observation? How could you test it?

Answers should include that the microorganisms came from the hay.
Tests may include sterilizing the hay and boiling the water. Accept all
reasonable answers.

3. In 1745 an Englishman named John Needham wanted to show that microorganisms spring spontaneously from meat broth. It was known that boiling would kill any microorganisms in the broth. His hypothesis was that if microorganisms appeared in broth that had been boiled, then spontaneous generation would be proved. Do you agree with his hypothesis? Why or why not?

Disagree; organisms can enter the broth from the air after the broth has
been boiled.

Compare and Contrast

Read the selection about grasshoppers and butterflies. Then complete the diagram by comparing, contrasting, and finding likenesses between these two insects.

    Metamorphosis of grasshoppers is different from that of butterflies. Grasshoppers go through incomplete metamorphosis, meaning that there are only three stages of this process. The process for butterflies is complete—there are four stages. Both grasshoppers and butterflies first form in eggs, but each emerges in a different form. Although butterflies emerge as caterpillars, grasshoppers hatch into nymphs that resemble the adult but lack wings. As the adult grasshopper grows, it molts, or sheds, its outer skeleton. After emerging from the egg, the butterfly larva metamorphoses into a pupa in which it then develops into a butterfly.

Compare and Contrast

Grasshopper	Alike	Butterfly
incomplete metamorphosis; emerges from egg as nymph; molts skeleton when adult	both go through metamorphosis; first form in eggs	complete metamorphosis; emerges from egg as caterpillar; metamorphoses into pupa, then butterfly

Use with page A74.

What Is a Life Cycle?

Lesson Concept

A life cycle is made of the stages that make up an organism's life. Some organisms grow through direct development, in which the only change is size. Others go through metamorphosis, which means they change shape and characteristics as they grow.

Vocabulary

life cycle (A72)   **direct development** (A72)   **metamorphosis** (A73)

Match the term on the left with the sentence on the right that describes it by writing the letter of the description in the blank next to the term.

Column A

___E___ **1.** molting

___F___ **2.** metamorphosis

___G___ **3.** larva

___H___ **4.** life cycle

___D___ **5.** complete metamorphosis

___C___ **6.** pupa

___B___ **7.** adult

___A___ **8.** cocoon

Column B

A A pupa may bury itself in the ground or it may make a protective covering around itself.

B When an organism reaches its final stage of development, it is able to reproduce.

C During the third stage of complete metamorphosis, insects neither eat nor move.

D Some insects have a life cycle that includes four distinct stages.

E Some insects that go through incomplete metamorphosis must shed their outer skeletons as they grow.

F Some organisms go through drastic changes in the shape or characteristics of their bodies.

G In complete metamorphosis, when an insect hatches from its egg, it enters the second stage of its development.

H Most organisms grow and mature through several distinct stages of life.

Inherited Characteristics

Materials

mirror

Activity Procedure

1 Use the chart below for this activity.

2 **Tongue Rolling** Use the mirror to **observe** what you are doing. Stick out your tongue, and try to roll its edges up toward the center. **Record** your results in the chart.

3 **Ear Lobes** Use the mirror to **observe** the shape of your ear lobes. Are they attached to your cheek, or do they hang free? **Record** your results in the chart.

Characteristic	Results (Circle one)		Class Totals
Tongue rolling	Yes	No	
Ear lobes	Attached	Free	
Folded hands	Left	Right	

4 **Folded Hands** Clasp your hands in front of you. **Observe** which of your thumbs falls naturally on top. **Record** your results in the chart.

5 Your teacher will now ask students to report the results of their observations. Tally the results in the chart as students report them. Total the number of students for each characteristic. Then **calculate** what fraction of the class has each characteristic.

Investigate Log

Draw Conclusions

1. Infer whether a person could learn tongue rolling. Explain. _If tongue rolling is inherited, a person could not learn to roll his or her tongue._

_____

2. What other inherited characteristics could you have **observed?**

Possible answers include eye color, hair color, left- or right-handedness, and freckles.

_____

3. Scientists at Work Scientists often **use numbers** to summarize the data they collect. Which trait in each pair occurred most often in your class?

Answers will vary.

_____

Investigate Further Do your class results suggest how often these traits occur in other people? Choose one or two of these characteristics. **Hypothesize** whether the results will be the same for another group. Then ask some of your friends, neighbors, and family members to participate in this activity, and **collect data**. **Draw conclusions**, and share them with your class.

_____

_____

_____

_____

Process Skills Practice

Use Numbers

When you use numbers, you summarize the data you collect. You can also use numbers to estimate, to count, and to figure out ratios or percentages.

Think About Using Numbers

Greg was experimenting with cross-breeding pea plants. He started with 100 plants. One of the things he wanted to study was seed color. When Greg crossed 50 plants having yellow seeds with 50 plants having green seeds, all the offspring had yellow seeds.

1. What percentage of this first generation had yellow seeds? _100 percent_

2. Greg knew there would be two factors for seed color in each plant and that the factors would pair up. He represented this first generation with the following chart, using Y for what he began calling the yellow seed factor and G for the green seed factor.

	G	G
Y	YG	YG
Y	YG	YG

The parents with green seeds were GG and the parents with yellow seeds were YY. Looking at his chart, he realized that even though every offspring's seed was yellow, each offspring's seed also carried a factor for green.

3. Next Greg planted all the yellow seeds from the offspring. When the plants grew up, he checked their seeds and found that 75 percent of them were yellow. The rest were green seeds. What percentage of this second generation of

pea plants had green seeds? _25 percent_

4. Greg represented this second generation with another chart. This time he knew that each parent plant had factors of both Y and G. Each square in the chart represents one-fourth the total number of seeds. What percent is represented by GG?

	Y	G
Y	YY	YG
G	YG	GG

25 percent

5. What percent of the total number of seeds carried at least one Y factor?

75 percent

Summarize and Paraphrase a Selection

Read the selection about gene mapping. Then write important details that support the main idea, and write a brief summary of the paragraph.

Gene mapping today is much different from Gregor Mendel's mapping of pea-plant genes in the nineteenth century. Modern gene mapping has enabled scientists to complete a map of the human genome by researching DNA. A *genome* is a set of chromosomes that make up the genetic material of an organism. Scientists make maps of chromosomes by adding special enzymes that cut DNA into specific pieces about the size of genes. When they cut DNA, they separate the pieces, each of which may contain a gene. Then scientists map the position of the gene, based on where the DNA was cut. There are up to 100,000 genes in every genome, which makes this a difficult task.

Main Idea: Modern gene mapping has enabled scientists to complete a map of the human genome by researching DNA.

Support: Scientists make maps of chromosomes by adding enzymes that cut DNA into specific pieces about the size of genes.

Support: When scientists cut DNA, they separate pieces, each of which may contain a gene.

Support: Scientists map the position of the gene based on where the DNA was cut.

Summary: Because of modern gene mapping techniques, scientists have made a complete map of the human genome. They use enzymes to cut DNA into individual genes. They then note the genes' locations and construct a map.

Concept Review

Why Are Offspring Like Their Parents?

Lesson Concept

Many traits are inherited by offspring from their parents. These traits are determined by genes. Gene combinations determine if traits are seen (dominant traits) or hidden (recessive traits).

Vocabulary

inherited trait (A78)   **dominant trait** (A79)

recessive trait (A79)   **gene** (A80)

Look at the traits shown for two generations in this family. Label the traits *D* for "dominant," *R* for "recessive," or *N* for "not inherited."

First Generation

Dad
Free earlobes
Short eyelashes
Plays tennis
Speaks English and French

Mom
Attached earlobes
Long eyelashes
Grows tomatoes
Speaks Spanish and English

Second Generation

Son
Free earlobes _____ D
Plays basketball _____ N
Speaks Spanish and English _____ N
Short eyelashes _____ R

Daughter
Free earlobes _____ D
Grows tomatoes _____ N
Speaks Spanish, French, and English _____ N
Long eyelashes _____ D

Daughter
Attached earlobes _____ R
Plays basketball _____ N
Speaks only English _____ N
Long eyelashes _____ D

Son
Free earlobes _____ D
Plays tennis and basketball _____ N
Speaks Spanish and English _____ N
Long eyelashes _____ D

Name _____

Date _____

Recognize Vocabulary

Underline the vocabulary term that best completes each sentence.

1. Gametes, or reproductive cells, are formed during ____.
   A meiosis   **B** mitosis   **C** metamorphosis   **D** asexual reproduction

2. The DNA codes for a certain trait are found on a ____.
   A inherited trait   **B** dominant trait   **C** recessive trait   **D** gene

3. The code that tells each cell when to divide is contained in a threadlike ____.
   A gene   **B** life cycle   **C** mitosis   **D** chromosome

4. Worms change only in size as they grow to be adults, because they go through ____.
   A direct development   **B** mitosis   **C** metamorphosis   **D** asexual reproduction

5. When two parents each contribute a cell to form one cell, that's ____.
   A asexual reproduction   **B** sexual reproduction   **C** meiosis   **D** gene

6. Development and growth in an egg is the first stage of a bird's ____.
   A metamorphosis   **B** direct development   **C** life cycle   **D** asexual reproduction

7. Hair color is an example of a(n) ____.
   A inherited trait   **B** dominant trait   **C** recessive trait   **D** gene

8. The transformation of a caterpillar to a butterfly is an example of ____.
   A direct development   **B** mitosis   **C** metamorphosis   **D** asexual reproduction

9. If you scrape your skin, your body creates new skin cells through ____.
   A meiosis   **B** mitosis   **C** metamorphosis   **D** sexual reproduction

10. Yeast, a one-celled organism, reproduces by budding, a type of ____.
   A asexual reproduction   **B** sexual reproduction   **C** meiosis   **D** gene

11. Gregor Mendel found that in peas, tallness was a strong, or____,trait.
   A inherited   **B** dominant   **C** recessive   **D** gene

Name _____

Date _____

Writing Practice

Tell an Animal's Story

Narrative Writing–Story

Choose an animal that undergoes metamorphosis. Write a story for a
young child about the animal's life cycle. Tell the story from the
animal's point of view, using colorful language and interesting details.
Use the story map below to help you plan your narrative.

Character (Animal):	**Setting (Habitat):**
First stage:	
Second stage:	
Third stage:	
Last stage:	

TIP Add or subtract stages as necessary for the animal you have chosen.

Chapter 4 • Graphic Organizer for Chapter Concepts

Plants and Their Adaptations

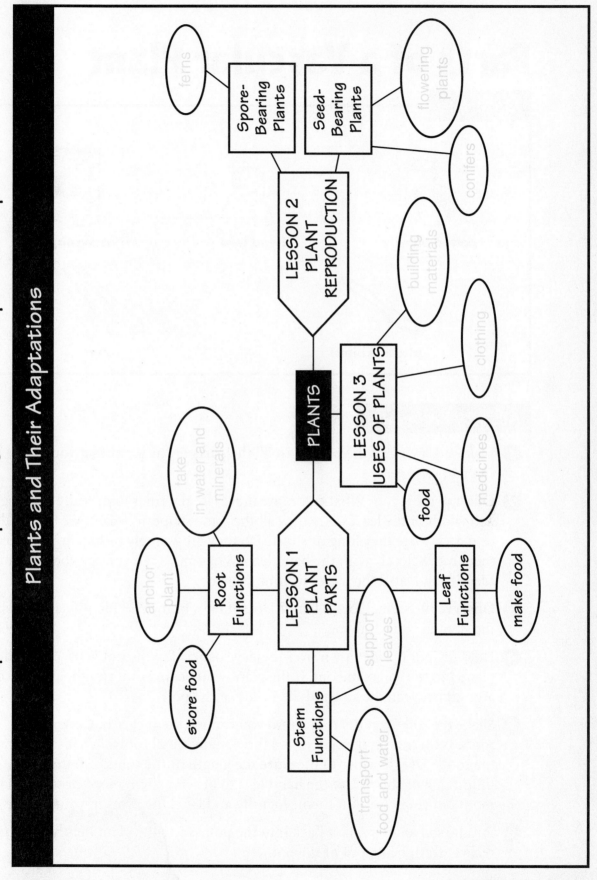

Parts of a Vascular Plant

Materials

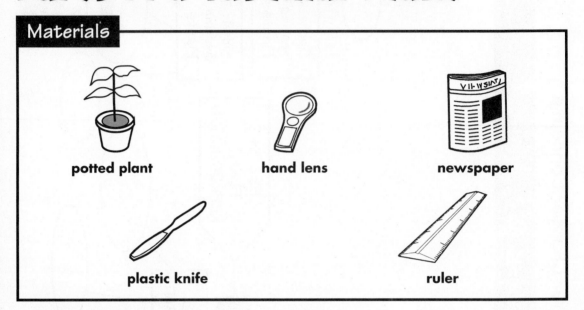

potted plant   hand lens   newspaper

plastic knife   ruler

Activity Procedure

1 Make a drawing of the plant. List all the parts of the plant that you can name.

2 **Observe** the leaves. What colors are they? Use the ruler to measure the length and width of the leaves. Are they all the same shape and size? Are they wide or narrow? Are they long or short? Do they grow singly or in pairs? Observe them more closely with the hand lens. What more can you say about them? Identify and label the leaves in your drawing.

3 **Observe** the stem. Does it bend? Does it have branches? Identify and label the stem in your drawing.

4 Hold the pot upside down over the newspaper. Tap the pot gently until the plant and the soil come out. If the plant won't come out, run the plastic knife around between the soil and the inside of the pot.

5 Shake the soil from the roots until you can see them clearly. **Observe** the roots. Is there a single root, or are there many small roots? What shape are the roots? Use the ruler to **measure** the length of the roots. Are they thick or thin? Long or short? Use the hand lens to observe them more closely. What more can you say about them? Identify and label the roots in your drawing.

6 Put the soil and the plant back into the pot. Water the plant lightly to help it recover from being out of the pot.

Name _____

Draw Conclusions

1. What are the parts of the plant you **observed**? leaves, stem, roots
_____

2. **Compare** the plant parts you identified with the parts of a large tree. How are they the same? How are they different? Possible answers: A tree's stem, or trunk, is harder, taller, and larger than a potted plant's stem; the tree leaves are larger; the roots of a tree are larger and hard like the trunk.

_____

_____

3. **Scientists at Work** Scientists learn by making observations. What did you **observe** about each part of the plant? Answers could include: veins or tiny hairs on the leaves, different leaf shapes, branched stems, flexible stems, branched roots, root hairs, and different colors and shapes of leaves.

_____

Investigate Further What questions about plant parts could you answer if you had other measuring tools? Form a **hypothesis** about the function of plant parts. Then **plan and conduct an experiment** to test your hypothesis.

Make sure that you have a wide selection of measuring tools, such as rulers, metersticks, balances, and spring scales for students to use.

_____

_____

_____

Observe

Observing involves using one or more of the senses to perceive properties of objects or events. Sometimes you need to use an instrument, such as a microscope, to extend your senses.

Think About Observing

Suppose you are walking beside a river on a summer afternoon. You observe several large slabs of concrete on the riverbank. When you look across the river, you observe more concrete slabs on the opposite bank. You are curious about them, but you decide to move on. After a short while, you come to a pipe that empties into the river. The water is foamy and cloudy near the pipe. It has no smell. You observe a lot of plants growing in the cloudy water and on the riverbank near the pipe.

1. What objects have you observed on your walk? Answers include concrete slabs, a pipe, foam, and plants. Some students may suggest more.

2. What senses have you used? sight and smell

3. You observed something coming from the pipe. From your observations, do you think it was harmful to the plants? It was causing no immediate harm. Students should realize that it would be difficult to tell by this brief observation about long-term effects.

4. How could you make a better observation about what was coming from the pipe? by getting a sample and observing it with a microscope

5. If you decided to observe the foam more closely, what do you think you should be looking for? Possible answers include microorganisms and chemicals. Accept all reasonable answers.

6. If you decided to observe the concrete slabs more closely, would you need instruments to extend your senses? Probably not, but some students may suggest otherwise. Accept all reasonable answers.

Use with page A91.

Summarize and Paraphrase a Selection

Read the section on Stems on pages A94 and A95. Next, complete the chart with a few of the facts about stems. Finally, write a paragraph that tells in your own words what you have learned about stems.

Important Facts About Stems
Stems hold plants up.
Stems support the leaves so that they can receive sunlight.
Stems carry water and food to other parts of plants.
Stems have the ability to turn toward the light.
Some stems can store food and water.

Summary:

_____

_____

_____

_____

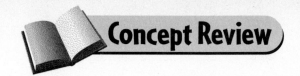
What Are the Functions of Roots, Stems, and Leaves?

Lesson Concept

Each part of a plant has a different function. Roots anchor the plant and take in minerals and water. A stem supports the plant and moves materials between its parts. Leaves make food.

Vocabulary

xylem (A95) **phloem** (A95) **chlorophyll** (A96)

photosynthesis (A96)

Match each term on the left with its description on the right.

Column A

_____ **1.** fibrous roots

_____ **2.** phloem

_____ **3.** stomata

_____ **4.** chlorophyll

_____ **5.** xylem

_____ **6.** taproot

_____ **7.** stem

_____ **8.** leaf

_____ **9.** root hairs

_____ **10.** chloroplasts

_____ **11.** photosynthesis

Column B

A tiny holes in a leaf where carbon dioxide enters and oxygen exits

B a pigment that helps plants use light energy to make sugars

C a plant part that holds the plant up and carries food and water to other plant parts

D tiny parts of roots that take in water and minerals from the soil

E a root that goes straight down so it can reach water deep underground

F a plant part that is the "food factory" of the plant

G roots that form a thick and tangled mat just under the surface of the soil

H the parts of leaf cells where the food-making process takes place

I tubes in plant stems that carry water and minerals

J tubes in plant stems that carry food made in the leaves to other parts of the plant

K the process in which a plant makes food from water, carbon dioxide, and sunlight

Nonvascular Plants

Materials

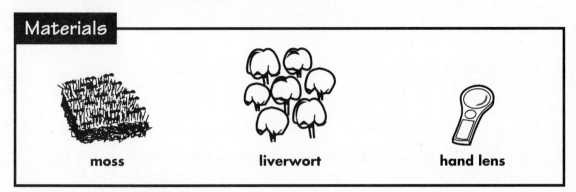

moss   liverwort   hand lens

Activity Procedure

1 **Observe** the moss and the liverwort. **Record** what you see.

2 Now **observe** the plants with a hand lens. Can you see different parts? Do any of the parts you see look like the parts of the potted plant you observed in Lesson 1?

3 **Observe** the plants by touching them with your fingers. Are they soft or firm? Are they dry or moist? What else can you tell by feeling them? Describe what they feel like.

4 Touch the plants with a pencil or other object while you **observe** them through the hand lens. Do the parts bend, or are they stiff? Do you see anything new if you push a part of the plant to one side? Describe what you see.

5 **Observe** the plants by smelling them. Do they have any kind of odor? Try to identify the odors. Describe what you smell.

6 Make drawings of the moss and liverwort, identify the parts you observed, and **infer** what each part does.

Name _____

Draw Conclusions

1. What plant parts did you **observe** on the moss? What parts did you observe on the liverwort? Students should observe stemlike, leaflike, and rootlike structures on both plants.

2. What do you **infer** each part of the plant does? Students may infer that the leaflike structures make food, the stemlike structures hold the leaves, and the rootlike structures anchor the plants and absorb water.

3. **Scientists at Work** Scientists use observations to **compare** things. Use the observations you made in this investigation to compare the moss and liverwort with the plant you observed in Lesson 1. The parts of the moss and liverwort seem similar to the parts of the potted plant.

Investigate Further Observe a fern. Based on your observations, would you classify a fern as a nonvascular plant, like the moss and the liverwort, or as a vascular plant, like the potted plant in Lesson 1? The fern's parts look more like the roots, the stems, and the leaves of the vascular plant than do the parts of the moss and the liverwort.

Compare

When you compare, you observe objects or events and try to find out how they are alike or different. You ask yourself questions while you are observing. Which plant is the smallest? Which plant has the most leaves? What does this plant have that the other does not have?

Think About Comparing

When you shop for fruits and vegetables, you see all different shapes and colors. You know from your experience that each of the items also has its own special taste and smell. All the shapes, the colors, the tastes, and the smells come from plants. Answer the questions about the following items: watermelon, cantaloupe, strawberries, carrots, apples, mushrooms, and lettuce.

1. Compare the mushrooms to the strawberries. Do they share any characteristics? How are they different? Shared characteristics: They are of similar size and they are both living things. Students may also recognize that they share a similar function: scattering reproductive cells (seeds and spores). Differences: color, taste, texture, and many other attributes students may recognize.

2. How is the carrot different from all the other items? It is a root.

3. Compare the lettuce to all the other items. Can you think of an important difference? Students should be able to see that all the items except the lettuce could be used to make new plants. That is, the melons, the apples, and the strawberries have seeds, the mushrooms have spores, and the carrot is a root that might grow a new top under the right conditions. Students may find other differences that are also acceptable.

4. Choose the two items you think are most similar to one another. Explain your choice. Answers will vary, but students should be able to support their choices with reasonable explanations.

5. Choose the two items you think are most different from one another. Explain your choice. Answers will vary, but students should be able to support their choices with reasonable explanations.

Name _____

Date _____

Reading Skills Practice

Compare and Contrast

Read the selection. Then complete the graphic organizer with characteristics of the tomato and potato and how they are alike.

Tomatoes and Potatoes

Tomatoes are often called vegetables, but they are fruits. The tomato plant is an angiosperm that protects its seeds by surrounding them with fruit, much like apples, oranges, acorns, and peanuts. The tomato plant grows aboveground and spreads outward while growing, producing clusters of yellow flowers.

Potatoes are vegetables, and more specifically *tubers*, which grow underground on the stems. The aboveground part of the plant has dark green leaves and white, purple, or pink flowers, and it grows three to four feet tall. Also an angiosperm, the potato plant has flowers that grow seedballs containing seeds that can be used by scientists to grow new varieties of potatoes.

Both the tomato and potato are thought to have originated in Central America. Both tomatoes and potatoes are grown in nearly every part of the United States.

Tomato　　　　**Alike**　　　　**Potato**

fruit; grows aboveground; grows outward; yellow flower clusters

angiosperm; grows flowers; thought to have originated in Central America; grown almost everywhere in the United States

vegetable; grows underground; grows upward 3–4 ft. tall; plant has dark green leaves; white, purple, or pink flowers

Name _____

Date _____

How Do Plants Reproduce?

Lesson Concept

Vascular plants have xylem and phloem. Nonvascular plants do not have these tubes. Nonvascular plants and simple vascular plants reproduce with spores. Gymnosperms and angiosperms are seed-producing vascular plants. Plants go through several stages in their life cycles.

Vocabulary

spore (A101)   **gymnosperm** (A102)   **pollen** (A102)

angiosperm (A103)   **germinate** (A105)

Put each term on the following list into the Venn diagram below. Remember, in a Venn diagram, the areas that overlap are areas that include both categories shown in the areas. If a term belongs in or applies to both categories, put it in the area where the ovals overlap. If it belongs in or applies to only one category, put it only in the correct oval.

spore	**conifer**	**pollen**	**flower**
fruit	**mosses**	**ferns**	**apples**
xylem	**phloem**	**chloroplasts**	**life cycle**

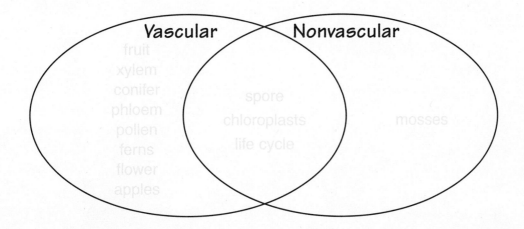

Popcorn

Materials

large plastic measuring cup   balance   unpopped popcorn

Activity Procedure

1. Cover the bottom of the measuring cup with unpopped popcorn seeds.

2. **Estimate** the volume of the unpopped seeds. Put the cup on the balance, and **measure** the mass of the unpopped seeds.

3. **Predict** what will happen to the mass and the volume when the seeds are popped.

4. Your teacher will help you pop the popcorn. Return the popped seeds to the measuring cup.

5. **Measure** the volume and mass of the cup of popped popcorn. Were your **predictions** correct?

Draw Conclusions

1. How did the volume of the popcorn change? The volume increased.

_____

2. How did the mass change? Explain. The mass of the popped popcorn should

be slightly less, because the water escaped as steam during popping.

_____

3. Scientists at Work One reason why scientists **experiment** is to test predictions. If an experiment doesn't turn out the way they predicted, it may mean that their predictions were wrong. Or it may mean that they did not consider everything that could affect the experiment. Did you predict the volume and mass of the popped popcorn correctly? Explain.

Possible answer: No; failure to predict the mass correctly was probably due

to forgetting about the water that was lost from the seeds as steam.

_____

Investigate Further What other questions do you have about popcorn? Plan and conduct **an experiment** to answer your question. Have students state a clear

question for their investigation.

_____

_____

_____

_____

_____

Name _____

Date _____

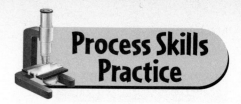
Experiment

When you experiment, you gather data to test a hypothesis. A well-designed experiment will allow you to test for certain variables while controlling others so you will know which factors affect the outcome.

Think About Experimenting

Juan and Ahmal were planning an experiment to see which of four different fertilizers would grow the biggest and healthiest plants. Juan gathered four pots from the garage, labeled them *Pot A* through *Pot D*, and filled them with dirt from his backyard. He put various seeds into each pot. He labeled the fertilizers *A* through *D* and put a teaspoon of *Fertilizer A* into *Pot A*, *Fertilizer B* in *Pot B*, and so on until each pot had a spoonful of different fertilizer. Ahmal watched him do this. Then he reminded Juan that he had not controlled his experiment. Juan agreed. They started over again.

1. What are some variables Juan should control? Answers should include type and species of seed, origin of seed, type of soil, size of container, schedule of watering, and exposure to sunlight. Students may suggest others.

2. Juan and Ahmal also need a control sample. How do they make one? Use five pots and don't put fertilizer in one of the pots, but keep all the other conditions the same.

3. As he was filling the pots with potting soil he had bought at the hardware store, Juan thought of another problem. What if, without meaning to, they paid more attention to one of the plants, because they had already formed a hypothesis that *Fertilizer A* worked better than the others? How could they avoid this? They could set up the experiment so that only one boy would know which fertilizer was added to which pot. The other boy would then take care of the plants without knowing which fertilizer was used.

4. What do you think would be the best way to gather data from this experiment? Answers will vary but may include using a table to keep track of conditions and how tall each plant is growing.

Name _____

Date _____

Use Graphic Sources for Information

Read the information about grains. Then summarize the information
in one or two sentences.

What is grain?
Grain is the seed or
fruit of cereal grasses.
The main grains are
wheat, corn, rice,
barley, oats, rye,
sorghum, and millet.

Where is grain grown? Grains grow
almost everywhere on Earth. The countries
that produce the most grains are China, the
United States, India, and the Russian
Federation. France, Indonesia, Canada,
Brazil, Ukraine, and Germany also produce
large supplies of grains.

Grain

**What are the
nutritional
benefits of grain?**
Grain is a nutritious
food. Grains supply
most of the
carbohydrates in the
human diet throughout
the world. They
provide energy as well
as protein, vitamins,
and minerals.

How is grain used? Grains are used
mostly as food for humans and as feed for
livestock. Grains also are used in industry to
make starch, malt, oils, and plastic products.
Starch is used in paper production, and
gluten is separated from wheat for baking
products.

Summary:

Grain is a nutritious food for humans and livestock that is grown in many

countries. It also is used to make plastics, oils, and starch for paper products.

Grain comes from cereal grasses such as wheat, corn, and rice.

How Do People Use Plants?

Lesson Concept

People eat the leaves, the stems, the roots, the seeds, the fruits, and the flowers of various plants. When they are sick, people often use medicines made from plants. In fact, many things people use every day come from plants.

Vocabulary

grain (A110)   **fiber** (A112)

Read the statements below. Put a *T* in front of the true statements and an *F* in front of the false statements. If the statement is false, write a correction in the space provided after it.

_____ **1.** People use plants more for food than for any other purpose.

_____

_____

_____ **2.** Fruits form the largest part of the Food Guide Pyramid.

Grains form the largest part of the Food Guide Pyramid.

_____

_____ **3.** Quinine, which is made from the bark of a tree, is used to treat

measles. Quinine is used to treat malaria.

_____

_____ **4.** Grains are the seeds of certain types of grasses. _____

_____

_____ **5.** Digitalis, which is made from the leaves of the maple tree, is a heart

medicine. Digitalis is made from the leaves of the foxglove plant.

_____

_____ **6.** A fiber is any material that can be separated into thread.

_____

_____

Recognize Vocabulary

Read the clues to decide which vocabulary term to use to fill in the word puzzle.

Across

1. tubes that carry food in plants

2. a reproductive cell that grows into a new plant

3. a plant with seeds covered by fruit

4. plant structures that contain male reproductive cells

5. tubes that carry water and minerals in plants

Down

6. a plant whose seeds are not protected by fruit

7. a pigment that helps plants produce sugar from light energy

8. another word for the process of a seed sprouting

9. the process by which plants turn water and carbon dioxide into food

Report on a Plant

Informative Writing–Description

Imagine that you are a nature educator at a public garden or state park. Write a report that you will give to visitors about a plant that grows in your garden or park. The report should describe the plant's parts and its life cycle. In the box below, draw the plant you have chosen, and label its parts. Then use the organizer to make notes on the plant's life cycle for your report.

Plant _____

Drawing of Plant with Parts Labeled	Outline of Plant's Life Cycle
	Kind of plant
	How plant begins life
	How plant grows to maturity
	How plant reproduces

Chapter 1 • Graphic Organizer for Chapter Concepts

Cycles in Nature

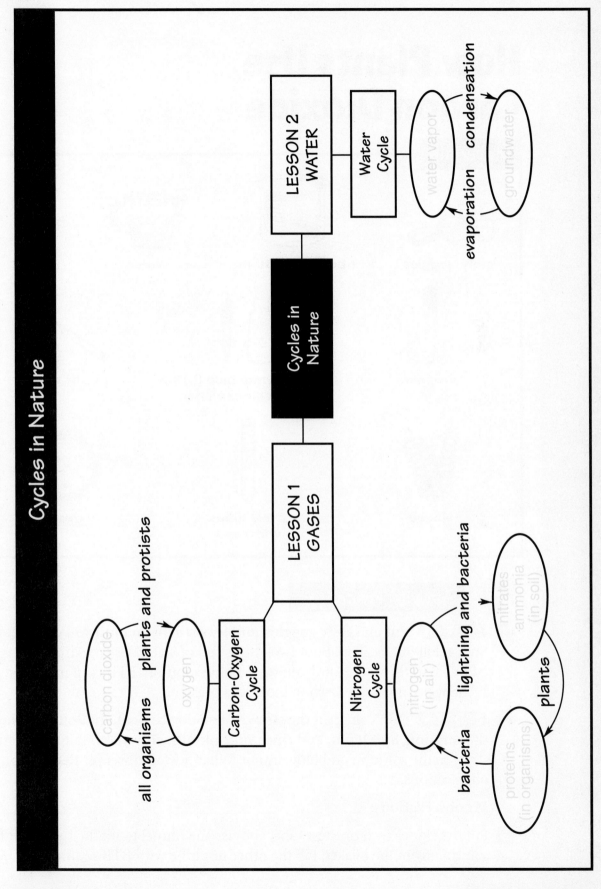

LESSON 2 WATER

Water Cycle

water vapor — condensation → groundwater

evaporation

Cycles in Nature

LESSON 1 GASES

Carbon-Oxygen Cycle

carbon dioxide ← all organisms — plants and protists → oxygen

Nitrogen Cycle

nitrogen (in air) — lightning and bacteria → nitrates ammonia (in soil)

bacteria

proteins (in organisms) ← plants

How Plants Use Carbon Dioxide

Materials

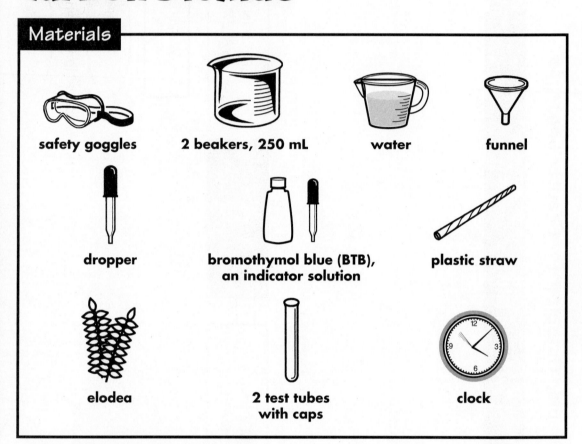

safety goggles   2 beakers, 250 mL   water   funnel

dropper   bromothymol blue (BTB), an indicator solution   plastic straw

elodea   2 test tubes with caps   clock

Activity Procedure

1 **CAUTION** **Put on safety goggles, and leave them on until you complete Step 4.** Fill one beaker about two-thirds full of water. Use the dropper to add BTB to the water until you have a blue solution. BTB is an indicator. It changes color when carbon dioxide is present.

2 **CAUTION** **Don't suck on the straw. If you do accidentally, don't swallow the solution. Spit it out, and rinse your mouth with water.** Put the plastic straw in the solution and blow into it. What do you **observe**? **Record** your observations.

My observations: _____

3 Put the elodea into one test tube, and use the funnel to fill the tube with BTB solution from the beaker. Fill the other test tube with BTB solution only.

4 Seal the test tubes with caps. Carefully turn the test tubes upside down, and place them in the empty beaker.

5 Put the beaker containing the two test tubes in a sunny window for 1 hour. **Predict** what changes will occur in the test tubes. After 1 hour, **observe** both test tubes and **record** your observations.

My prediction: _____

_____

My observations: _____

_____

Draw Conclusions

1. What changes did you **observe** in the BTB solution when you blew into it through the straw? Explain. It turned yellow because of the carbon dioxide blown into it.

2. What changes did you **observe** in the test tube of BTB after the elodea plant had been in it for 1 hour? It turned blue again.

3. **Compare** the color of the BTB solution in the test tube that had the elodea with the color of the BTB in the test tube that did not have the elodea. Describe any differences. The tube of BTB without the plant stayed yellow.

4. **Scientists at Work** Scientists **observe** changes that happen during experiments. Then they **infer** what caused the changes. What can you infer about any changes that took place in the test tubes? Students may infer that the elodea used up the carbon dioxide.

Investigate Further What is the importance of sunlight in this investigation? **Hypothesize** about the importance of sunlight. Then **plan and conduct a simple experiment** to test your hypothesis.

_____

_____

_____

_____

_____

Observe

Observing is a basic science skill. Making good observations will allow you to develop other important science skills, like inferring, comparing, classifying, and measuring.

Think About Observing

Cecelia likes to grow tomatoes. She wanted to see if adding certain things to the soil would improve her tomato harvest. She treated different parts of her garden with kitchen-scrap compost, leaf-litter compost, and nitrogen fertilizer. Some parts of the garden were not treated. For five years she treated the soil and recorded the number of tomatoes produced by the plants in each area of her garden.

	Untreated Soil	Kitchen-Scrap Compost	Leaf-Litter Compost	Nitrogen Fertilizer
Year 1	130	145	140	165
Year 2	125	155	155	155
Year 3	110	160	165	155
Year 4	95	155	170	145
Year 5	70	165	180	150

1. Which treatment produced the best results over time? _leaf-litter compost_

2. Cecelia thought she should make a bar graph of her results. Do you think it would be easier to read her data this way? _Accept reasonable answers._
   Most people read a bar graph more easily than a table.

3. What inference could you make about how Cecelia could improve the yield of plants grown in the untreated area of her garden? _Accept reasonable_
   answers. Students may suggest adding compost or fertilizer.

Predict Probable Future Actions and Outcomes

Natural Gas

One of Earth's naturally occurring sources of energy is *natural gas*. Natural gas is a fuel that has taken hundreds of thousands of years to form in the earth. As plants and animals die, their remains are covered by layers of sand, mud, and rock. As these remains decay, tiny bubbles of natural gas are trapped under this heavy layer of earth. Eventually some of this gas escapes to the surface and mixes with the oxygen in the air, igniting small flames.

Natural gas is a valuable source of energy. Efficient ways have been developed to get the gas out of the ground and pipe it into homes and businesses. Today natural gas is used for heating, cooking, and many other uses in the home. It is used in industries to help manufacture automobiles, steel, and other products. Scientists continue to discover new ways to conserve the use of natural gas while expanding the benefits it can provide to people throughout the world.

Predict the Outcome

It takes hundreds of thousands of years to replenish the natural gas that humans use. If it is not conserved, what might happen to this natural resource?

The supply of natural gas might be depleted. Humans then

would have fewer sources of energy available to them.

_____

Predict the Outcome

Natural gas has no color or odor. A strong-smelling chemical called mercaptan is added to natural gas before it is piped to homes and businesses. If this additive weren't used, what might happen if gas escaped from the earth or pipeline?

People would have no warning. Natural gas might be too

dangerous to use, causing sudden explosions and fires, and

sickening or even killing people.

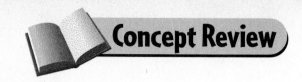
How Does Nature Reuse Materials?

Lesson Concept

Many of the materials organisms need are cycled through nature.

Vocabulary

nitrogen cycle (B7)   **respiration** (B8)   **carbon-oxygen cycle** (B8)

Choose the correct caption from the table below each diagram, and write the appropriate letter below each picture.

A

C

B

A	Animal wastes and decaying organisms return nitrates and ammonia to the soil.
B	Animals get nitrogen by eating plants and other animals.
C	Plants make proteins from nitrogen in the soil.

C

A

B

A	Plants use carbon dioxide and release oxygen during photosynthesis.
B	Plants and animals use oxygen and release carbon dioxide during respiration.
C	Bacteria and fungi use as food some carbon from the tissues of dead animals. The rest is released as carbon dioxide.

Water, Water Everywhere

Materials

graduate   water   small plastic cup   zip-top plastic bag

Activity Procedure

1 Using the graduate, **measure** and pour 100 mL of water into the cup.

2 Open the plastic bag, and carefully put the cup inside. Then seal the bag. Be careful not to spill any water from the cup.

3 Place the sealed bag near a sunny window. **Predict** what will happen to the water in the cup.

My prediction: _____

4 Leave the bag near a window for 3–4 days. **Observe** the cup and the bag each day. **Record** what you see.

My observation: _____

_____

5 Remove the cup from the bag. **Measure** the amount of water in the cup by pouring it back into the graduate. **Calculate** any difference in the amount of water you poured into the cup and the amount of water you removed from the cup.

My measurement: _____

My calculation: _____

Draw Conclusions

1. What did you **observe** during the time the cup was inside the bag?
Water drops appeared on the inside of the bag.

2. Where do you infer the water in the bag came from? Explain.
From the cup; the amount of water poured out of the cup was less than the
amount poured into the cup.

3. Scientists at Work Scientists often **infer** the cause of something they **observe**.
What can you infer about the amount of water in the bag? The amount of
water in the bag is the same as the amount of water missing from the cup.

Investigate Further How could you test the following **hypothesis**? The amount
of water in the bag is the same as the amount of water missing from the cup.
Decide what equipment you would need to use. Then **plan and conduct a simple
experiment** that would test the hypothesis.
Students may choose to test their hypotheses by weighing the cups and the
plastic bags before and after the experiment.

_____

_____

_____

_____

_____

Infer

When you infer, you draw conclusions to explain events.
Your inferences may not always be correct.

Think About Inferring

1. Dion lives in a town with a lake nearby. People use the lake to swim, fish, and go boating. Dion reads in the newspaper that the rainfall in the area has been less than normal for the summer. When he went to the lake, he noticed that the water level in the lake was lower than usual for the time of year. What could Dion infer caused the water level in the lake to be below normal?

Accept reasonable answers. Students may say there was less rain than normal.

2. Since there had been little rain in Dion's town, people were told not to water their lawns. Many plants in Dion's yard and garden turned brown and died. But the big trees were still green and leafy. What could Dion infer caused some plants to die and the trees to survive? Accept reasonable answers. Students may say that without water, plants die. The trees didn't die because their roots were deep enough to get water or they had water stored in their tissues.

3. Last year Dion's uncle Jeb had a house built outside Dion's town. Jeb built a deep well to pull water up into his house. This year Jeb was not able to get any water from his well. What could Jeb infer caused him to not get water from his well this year? Accept reasonable answers. Students may infer that the lack of rain was directly related to the lack of groundwater.

4. Jeb found out that he needs to dig his well deeper to get water. The county engineer explained to Jeb that many people built houses and drilled wells near Jeb. This caused the groundwater level to drop several feet when everyone started using their wells. The county engineer also told Jeb that his groundwater comes from an underground river. The lack of rain during the summer would not affect the groundwater level. Knowing this, tell whether your inference was correct in Question 3. This depends on the answer above.

5. What does Question 4 show you about making inferences? Accept reasonable answers. Students may say that correct inferences can be made only when you know everything about an event.

Arrange Events in Sequence

Water as a Source of Energy

Use the transition words below to arrange the events of hydroelectric power in correct sequence.

You already know how important the water cycle is for humans, animals, and the environment. Did you know that water also is used as a source of energy?

When water is used as energy, it is called *hydroelectric power*. First, stored water from a lake, river, or other source flows through a pipe and pushes against turbine blades. Then, the turbine blades turn, spinning a generator that produces electricity. After that, the electricity travels along wires to a transformer. The function of the transformer is to change the electric power from low voltage to high voltage. Once the electricity is at a high voltage, it can be moved along more efficiently to a substation. Next, the electricity is changed back into low voltage so that it can be used in homes and businesses. Finally, once the electricity is back at low voltage, it passes out of the substation through distribution lines and into homes, offices, and factories.

Hydroelectric Power

First, stored water from a lake, river, or other source flows through a pipe and pushes against turbine blades.

Then, the turbine blades turn, spinning a generator that produces electricity.

After that, the electricity travels along wires to a transformer. _____

Next, the electricity is changed back into low voltage so that it can be used in homes and businesses.

Finally, once the electricity is back at low voltage, it passes out of the substation through distribution lines and into homes, offices, and factories.

Name _____

Date _____

Why Is the Water Cycle Important?

Lesson Concept

Earth's water moves through the environment in the water cycle. All the water on Earth today is the same water that was here billions of years ago.

Vocabulary

water cycle (B14) **evaporation** (B14) **condensation** (B14)

precipitation (B15) **transpiration** (B15)

Complete each sentence with a term from the list above.

1. The sun's heat changes water at the surface of a lake to water vapor. This is called _____evaporation_____.

2. Water can move through the environment as liquid, vapor, or ice in the _____water cycle_____.

3. Water falls as _____precipitation_____ when clouds rise over a mountain.

4. Plants give off water through their stomata during _____transpiration_____.

5. High in the air, water changes into tiny droplets to form clouds. This process is called _____condensation_____.

Write the numbers of the above sentences that would make the best captions for this picture.

Recognize Vocabulary

nitrogen cycle	**water cycle**	**precipitation**
transpiration	**evaporation**	**condensation**
carbon-oxygen cycle		

Underline the vocabulary term that best completes each sentence.

1. Heat changes liquid water into vapor during ____.

   A evaporation   **B** transpiration   **C** precipitation

2. The process in which plants give off water through their stomata is ____.

   A evaporation   **B** condensation   **C** transpiration

3. Gases needed for respiration are exchanged between organisms in

   the ____ cycle.

   A nitrogen   **B** water   **C** carbon-oxygen

4. In the ____ cycle, bacteria fix a gas that plants and animals need for producing protein. Sometimes this gas comes from the air, and sometimes this gas comes from decaying organisms.

   A nitrogen   **B** water   **C** carbon dioxide-oxygen

5. Molecules in the ____ cycle can move through the environment as a solid, liquid, or gas.

   A nitrogen   **B** water   **C** carbon–oxygen

6. Water vapor changes to liquid during ____.

   A transpiration   **B** condensation   **C** precipitation

7. Water is moved from the atmosphere to Earth's surface during ____.

   A transpiration   **B** condensation   **C** precipitation

Name _____

Date _____

Explain the Nitrogen Cycle

Informative Writing–Explanation

Write an explanation of the nitrogen cycle in the form of a video script. Use the storyboard—a script outline—below to sketch or write about the visual images you will show and to make notes for the narration that will accompany the visuals.

Visual	Narration
	How plants and animals use nitrogen
	Where nitrogen is found
	One way nitrogen is fixed
	Another way nitrogen is fixed
	One way nitrogen is returned to the soil
	Another way nitrogen is returned to the soil

Chapter 2 • Graphic Organizer for Chapter Concepts

Living Things Interact

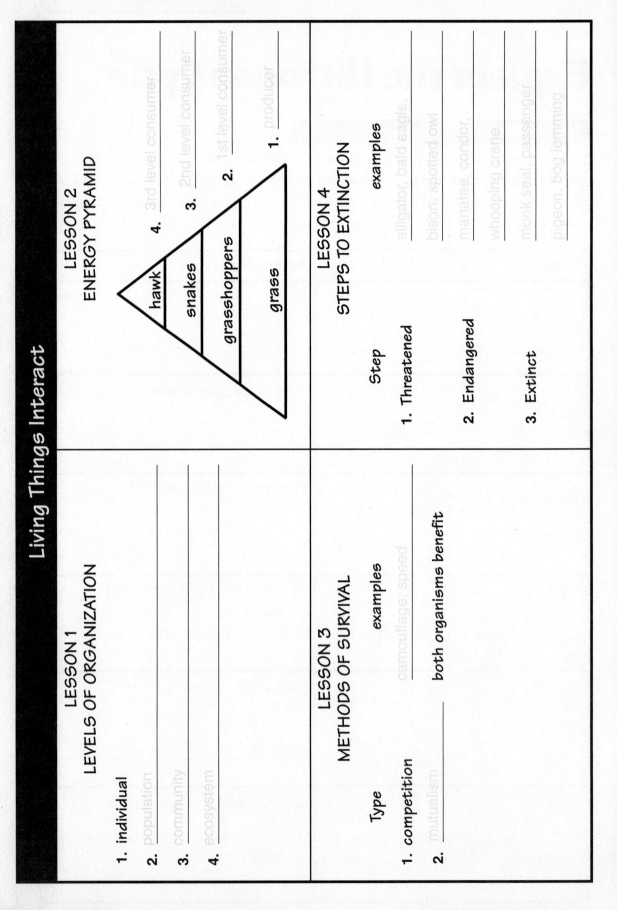

LESSON 1
LEVELS OF ORGANIZATION

1. individual
2. population
3. community
4. ecosystem

LESSON 2
ENERGY PYRAMID

4. 3rd level consumer
3. 2nd level consumer
2. 1st level consumer
1. producer

hawk
snakes
grasshoppers
grass

LESSON 3
METHODS OF SURVIVAL

Type   examples

1. competition   camouflage; speed
2. mutualism   both organisms benefit

LESSON 4
STEPS TO EXTINCTION

Step   examples

1. Threatened   alligator, bald eagle,
                    bison, spotted owl
2. Endangered   manatee, condor,
                    whooping crane
3. Extinct   monk seal, passenger
                    pigeon, bog lemming

Name _____

Date _____

The Local Environment

Materials

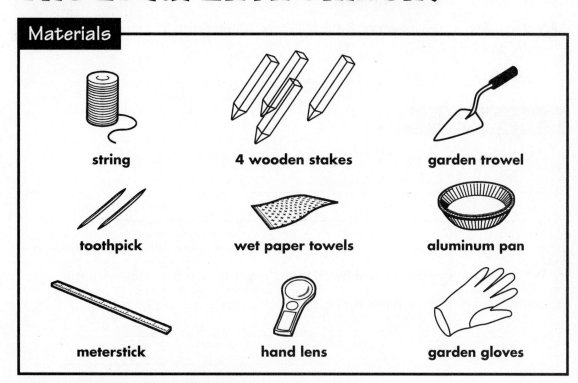

string

4 wooden stakes

garden trowel

toothpick

wet paper towels

aluminum pan

meterstick

hand lens

garden gloves

CAUTION ## Activity Procedure

1 **CAUTION** **Wear garden gloves to protect your hands.** Your teacher will send you to a grassy or lightly wooded area near your school. Once you are there, use the meterstick to **measure** an area of ground that is 1 m² (1 m × 1 m). Push a stake into each corner of the plot. Tie the string around the stakes.

2 Before observing the plot, **predict** what living organisms and nonliving things you might find in this environment. **Record** your prediction.

My prediction: _____

3 **Observe** the plot carefully. Use the hand lens to look for small things in the plot. **Record** your observations by making lists of the living organisms and the nonliving things in this environment.

My observations: _____

4 Sit back and continue to **observe** the plot for a while. Look for living organisms, such as insects, interacting with other organisms or with the environment. Describe and **record** any interactions you observe.

My observations: _____

5 Put wet paper towels in the aluminum pan, and use the garden trowel to scoop some soil onto them. Use a toothpick to sift through the soil. Be careful not to injure any living organisms with the toothpick.

6 **Record** what you **observe**, especially any interactions. Then return the soil to the plot of ground.

My observations: _____

Draw Conclusions

1. How did what you **predicted** compare with what you **observed**?

Answers will vary. Students may find fewer living organisms than they predicted or more pieces of rock and trash.

_____

2. What did you **observe** that showed living organisms interacting with one another or with the environment? Answers will vary. Students may observe such things as insects eating plants, worms moving soil, ants carrying bits of trash, and so on.

_____

3. **Scientists at Work** Scientists often use prior knowledge to **predict** what they might find or what might happen. What prior knowledge did you use to predict what you would find in the plot of ground? Answers will vary. Students may explain that they know that plants grow in soil, that insects eat plants, and so on.

_____

Investigate Further Sometimes you can **hypothesize** what interactions are occurring in an environment by **observing** what's in that environment. Choose an environment near your home or school. Observe what kinds of organisms live there, and hypothesize how they interact with one another and with the environment. Then **plan and conduct a simple investigation** to test your hypothesis.

_____

_____

_____

_____

Name _____

Date _____

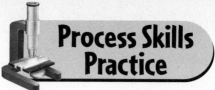

Predict

Scientists use what they already know to predict what they may find or what may happen. Careful observation helps them make a prediction rather than a guess.

Think About Predicting

Below is information about two different regions. Make predictions about the data by answering the questions that follow.

	Region I Temperate Grasslands	Region II Tropical Rain Forest
Soil conditions	porous soil, rich in organic matter	fragile soil
Vegetation	grasses and shrubs	tall, broad-leafed trees; multilevel canopy; sparse understory
Climate	short hot summers, long cold winters	tropical, hot throughout the year with rainy season
Annual rainfall	25–75 cm (10–30 in.)	200–400 cm (80–160 in.)

1. In which region would you be more likely to find animals that graze on grasses? Region I

2. In which region would you be more likely to find animals adapted to traveling along treetops? Region II

3. Which region would you predict could recover more quickly after a fire? Explain your answer. Accept reasonable answers. Students may say Region I would recover faster because it takes less time for grasses to grow back than it does for tall trees to grow back and because Region I contains fertile soil and the soil of Region II is fragile.

4. Predict which region would have the greater diversity of animals. Explain. Accept reasonable answers. Students may say Region II, because it has a greater diversity of plants and may provide food to more types of animals.

Reading Skills Practice

Make Generalizations

Read the selection. Then decide what generalization might be made about biomes and the plants and animals that live in them.

Climate and Habitats

Scientists classify the land surface of Earth into gigantic ecosystems called *biomes*. Biomes are determined by the climatic features of these ecosystems, especially temperature range and precipitation. Many biomes are named after their vegetation because plants determine what can grow and live in an area. The major biomes include tundra, coniferous forest, deciduous forest, tropical forest, grassland, scrub, and desert.

The borders of a biome are not always distinct, and some populations of plants and animals may be found on both sides of the border. Other populations, like monarch butterflies or Arctic terns, migrate long distances across biomes to reach the climatic conditions and communities they need in order to survive and reproduce.

Generalization:

Possible response: Not all biomes can support all plants and animals.

_____

_____

What Are Ecosystems?

Lesson Concept

An ecosystem consists of communities of living things and the environment in which they live.

Vocabulary

individual (B28)	**population** (B28)	**community** (B28)
ecosystem (B28)	**habitat** (B29)	**niche** (B29)

Use the vocabulary terms above as well as the terms listed below to complete the sentences about ecosystems.

temperature	**survival**	**density**	**rainfall**
soil conditions	**plants**	**limiting factor**	

1. A single organism in an environment is called an ____individual____.

2. A population has a role, or ____niche____, in its environment.

3. The sizes of animal populations are determined by the kinds and numbers of ____plants____ in an ecosystem.

4. Individuals of the same species make up a ____population____.

5. Populations of different organisms live together in a ____community____.

6. The ____soil conditions____, ____temperature____, and ____rainfall____ of an environment determine the types of plants that grow there.

7. In a healthy ecosystem, each population contributes to the ____survival____ of the other populations.

8. The amount of food is a ____limiting factor____ that affects population ____density____, or the number of individuals of a species in an ecosystem.

9. Communities and the environment make up an ____ecosystem____.

10. A ____habitat____ is a place where a population lives in an ecosystem.

What Eats What in Ecosystems

Materials

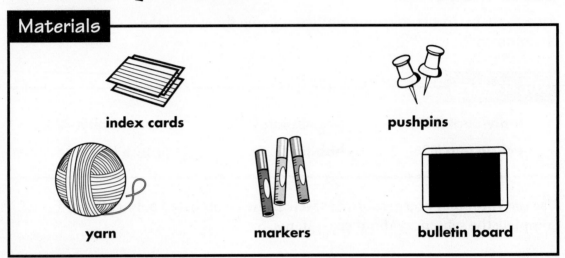

index cards

pushpins

yarn

markers

bulletin board

Activity Procedure

1 Your teacher will assign you an organism from a prairie ecosystem. Use an encyclopedia to find out what your organism eats. Then **classify** your organism into one of the following groups:

> plants
>
> meat-eating animals
>
> plant-eating animals
>
> animals that eat both plants and meat
>
> animals that eat dead organisms

2 Use markers to draw your organism or write its name on an index card.

3 Your teacher will now assign you to a class team. Each team will have at least one organism from each group listed above. With your teammates, **order** your team's cards to show what eats what in a prairie ecosystem.

4 When your team's cards are in order, pin them in a line on the bulletin board. Connect the cards with yarn to show what eats what—both within your team's group of organisms and between those of other teams.

Investigate Log

Draw Conclusions

1. When your team put its cards in **order**, what kind of organism was first?
plant

2. How would you **classify** the organism that came right after the first organism?
plant-eating animals or meat- and plant-eating animals

3. Scientists at Work When scientists **classify** things that happen in a particular order, it helps them understand how something works. Look again at your team's cards on the bulletin board. Could you classify or order them in any other way to explain what eats what in an ecosystem? Answers may vary, but students should realize that plants are always first in an ecosystem.

Investigate Further Find out what eats what in another ecosystem. If possible, use a computer to help you with your research. Then **hypothesize** about the flow of energy in that ecosystem. Then **plan and conduct a simple investigation** to test your hypothesis.

Students might choose to investigate a forest ecosystem or a freshwater ecosystem. They will find that all ecosystem food chains begin with plants.

_____

_____

_____

Name _____

Date _____

Process Skills Practice

Classify and Order

When you classify things, you put them into groups based on their
similarities. When you order these groups, you can see relationships
between the different groups.

Think About Classifying and Ordering

1. Read the descriptions of four groups of organisms. Then use the numbers
of the groups to classify the living things in the chart shown below.

Group 1 eats foodmakers   **Group 3** eats animals

Group 2 eats decaying things   **Group 4** makes its own food

Living Things	Group
Plant-eating mice	1
Grasses	4
Bacteria that break down animal wastes and dead organisms	2
Grass-eating voles	1
Worms that eat decaying grasses and berries and waste products of animals	2
Owls that eat weasels, mice, and voles	3
Shrubs that produce berries	4
Weasels that eat mice and voles	3

2. Order by what eats what from the living things listed. Start with the organism
that doesn't eat anything. Use each of these living things only once.

owl—grass—vole—waste-eating bacteria grass—vole—owl—waste-eating
bacteria

3. Can you see another relationship between these groups other than what eats
what? Accept reasonable answers. Students may say that animal size
increases as you move higher up the chain of what eats what.

Use Context to Determine/Confirm Word Meaning

Read the selection. Then complete the chart that follows.

What Do You Like to Eat?

One way scientists group organisms is to classify them according to what they eat. Some animals eat only plants. Deer, rabbits, and cows, for example, are considered *herbivores*. Other animals eat only meat. Lions, wolves, and killer whales are *carnivores*. These animals eat herbivores and other carnivores. Animals, including humans, that eat both plants and animals are *omnivores*.

Term	What It Might Mean	What It Means
herbivores	animals that eat only plants	animals that do not eat meat but eat only plants
carnivores	animals that eat only other animals	animals that eat only meat
omnivores	animals that eat both animals and plants	animals that eat both meat and plants

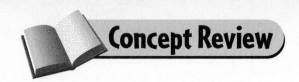
How Does Energy Flow Through an Ecosystem?

Lesson Concept

Energy starts to flow through an ecosystem when an organism uses the sun's energy to make food. Energy continues to flow when one organism eats another organism.

Vocabulary

producers (B34)   **consumers** (B34)   **food chain** (B35)

decomposer (B35)   **food web** (B36)   **energy pyramid** (B38)

Below is an energy pyramid and a list of organisms.
Write the names of the organisms where they
belong on the energy pyramid.

Grass   **Lion**
Vulture   **Antelope**

4. Vulture _____

3. Lion _____

2. Antelope _____

5. If a producer makes 1000 units of energy,
how many units of this energy can a
third-level consumer use?

1. Grass _____

1 unit of energy

6. What does it mean to say that an organism is a producer? An organism can
make its own food.

7. First-level consumers are called _____ herbivores _____, while second-
and third-level consumers are called _____ carnivores _____.

8. Is the energy pyramid more like a food chain or a food web? Explain.
It is more like a food chain because it shows only one set of organisms
consuming each other. No organism is consumed by more than one
other organism.

9. What kind of organism connects both ends of a food chain? a decomposer

Body Color

Materials

colored acetate
sheets: red, blue,
green, yellow

hole
punch

large
green
cloth

clock with
second
hand

Activity Procedure

1 Use the table on the next page. Use the hole punch to make 50 pieces from each of the acetate sheets. These colored acetate pieces will stand for insects that a bird is hunting.

2 **Predict** which color would be the easiest to find in grass. Predict which would be the hardest to find. **Record** your predictions.

My predictions: _____

3 Spread the cloth on the floor. Your teacher will randomly scatter the acetate "insects" over the cloth.

4 Each member of the group should kneel at the edge of the cloth. You will each try to pick up as many colored acetate "insects" as you can in 15 seconds. You must pick them up one at a time.

5 Total the number of acetate pieces of each color your group collected. **Record** the data in the table.

6 Put aside the "insects" you collected. Repeat Step 4 two more times. After each 15-second "hunt," **record** the number of acetate pieces of each color your group collected. After the third hunt, total each column.

Investigate Log

	Number of Insects Found			
	Red	**Blue**	**Green**	**Yellow**
Hunt 1				
Hunt 2				
Hunt 3				
Totals				

Draw Conclusions

1. Look at the data you **recorded** for each hunt. What color of acetate was collected least? Answers may vary, but green will probably be the least collected color for the first trial.

Were the results of each hunt the same, or were they different? Explain. The number of green pieces collected will probably increase with each trial.

2. **Compare** the results with what you **predicted**. Do the results match your prediction? Explain. Answers will vary, but students probably predicted that green insects would be the hardest to see and collect.

3. **Scientists at Work** Scientists often **gather data** before they **infer** a relationship between things. Based on the data you gathered, what can you infer about the survival chances of brown-colored insects in areas where grasses and leaves turn brown in the fall? Students should infer that brown insects would blend in with brown grass and leaves and have a better chance to survive.

Investigate Further Many insects have a body shape that allows them to blend in with their background. **Hypothesize** about what body shape might help an insect hide in a dead tree. Then **plan and conduct a simple experiment** to test your hypothesis.

_____

_____

_____

_____

Name _____

Date _____

Gather Data and Infer

One way to gather data is to observe objects or events. You can use the data to make inferences. You may need to gather more data to decide if your inference is correct.

Think About Gathering Data and Inferring

Abdul learned that periwinkles, small shelled organisms similar to snails, cling to rocks near the ocean shoreline. He spent a day at the shoreline gathering data about periwinkles on one cliff. He observed four types of periwinkles that were clinging to different levels of the cliff. He made a table to show the number of each type at each level.

Cliff Level	Periwinkle Type			
	Large Pink	Medium Blue	Small Pink	Large Gray
Splash zone (above or at high-tide level)	0	2	8	0
Upper shore (under water 6–12 hr a day)	1	5	3	3
Middle shore (under water 12–18 hr a day)	4	3	0	7
Lower shore (under water 18–24 hr a day)	7	1	0	1

1. What can Abdul infer about the lower shore? Smaller periwinkles don't live here. Only the large pink periwinkles appear to thrive here.

2. What inference can Abdul make about the splash zone? Accept reasonable answers. Students may say that large periwinkles don't live here.

3. What can Abdul infer about the different sizes of periwinkles on the cliff?
Accept reasonable answers. Periwinkle size increases as time under water increases. The time a periwinkle stays under water determines its size.

4. What other data could Abdul gather to support inferences he made?
Students may say Abdul could read more about periwinkles or go to other cliffs to observe more periwinkles.

Name _____

Date _____

Identify Supporting Facts and Details

Read the selection. Then complete the outline to show supporting details and facts.

Eucalyptus and the Koala

Eucalyptus trees are necessary for the survival of the koala. Unlike most other animals, which eat many different foods, the koala eats almost nothing but eucalyptus leaves. However, the koala requires a variety of eucalyptus leaves in its diet. It is becoming difficult for the koala to find the necessary assortment of trees to ensure its survival. Only in eastern Australia are there enough eucalyptus trees and the right climate for the koala.

It is estimated that 80 percent of the eucalyptus forests of eastern Australia have been cut down either for their wood or to make way for housing developments and farms. The remaining forests are not protected by law, and most are privately owned. These forests are where most koalas live, but the loss of their habitat is not their only threat. They also face injury or death from being hit by automobiles, being killed by other animals, and being poisoned by pesticides that seep into the waterways.

I. The Koala's Needs

    A. a variety of eucalyptus leaves _____

    B. the right climate _____

II. Threats to the Koala

    A. destruction of the remaining eucalyptus forests _____

    B. people _____

    C. other animals _____

    D. automobiles _____

    E. pesticides _____

Name _____

Date _____

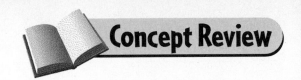

How Do Organisms Compete and Survive in an Ecosystem?

Lesson Concept

Organisms have various ways to compete for limited resources in ecosystems.

Vocabulary

competition (B42)	**symbiosis** (B45)
instinct (B46)	**learned behavior** (B46)

Fill in the chart below about how these organisms survive in their ecosystems.
Accept reasonable answers. The answers below are discussed in the student book.

Canada Goose	Cheetah	Raccoon
Resource It Must Share or For Which It Must Compete		
grains, water plants	zebras and antelopes	sea turtles' eggs
Adaptation That Helps It Compete		
body parts for flying	high speed for hunting	has paws to handle objects
Instinct		
mating for life, building shelters, migrating, eating grains and water plants	hunting prey, finding mates	finding mates, building shelter
Behavior It Might Learn		
hunting	hunting	hunting

Vanishing Habitats

Materials

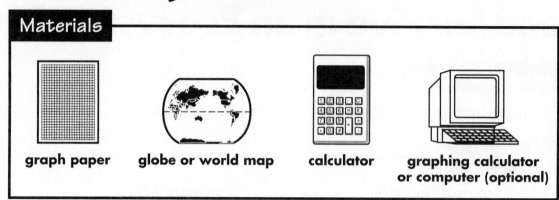

graph paper   globe or world map   calculator   graphing calculator or computer (optional)

Rain-Forest Area and Human Population In Ecuador				
Year	**1961**	**1971**	**1981**	**1991**
Rain forest (square km)	173,000	153,000	No data	112,000
Population (in millions)	5.162	7.035	No data	10.782

Activity Procedure

1 Locate Ecuador, a country in South America, on the globe or world map.

2 Study the table above. It shows the size of Ecuador's rain forests and the size of its human population between 1961 and 1991.

3 **Calculate** and **record** the changes in rain forest area for each period shown (1961–1971 and 1971–1991). Then calculate and record the changes in the population size for the same periods.

4 Using graph paper and a pencil, a graphing calculator, or a computer, make a double-bar graph that shows changes in forest area and population size for these periods.

Name _____

Draw Conclusions

1. **Compare** the two sets of data in the double-bar graph. What relationship, if any, do you **observe** between the growth of the human population and the amount of rain forest in Ecuador? As the human population increases, forest area decreases.

2. Based on the **data collected**, what can you **infer** about the size of Ecuador's human population and the area of its rain forests in 1981? In 1981, human population was about 8.909 million and the forest area was about 132,500 km².

3. According to the data, what do you **predict** the size of the rain forests in Ecuador would be in 2001 if the human population increases at the same rate as it has in the past? In 2001 the forest area should be about 92,000 km².

4. **Scientists at Work** Scientists often **interpret data** to help them **infer** what may happen. If the size of the rain-forest habitat keeps getting smaller, what can you infer about the populations of animals that live there? Further loss of habitat could lead to smaller populations of animals living in the rain forest.

Investigate Further Research the changes in the size of the human population over several decades in your area. Then make a graph of the changes. **Hypothesize** how these changes in the human population might have affected animal populations in your area. **Plan and conduct a simple investigation** to test your hypothesis.

Students might be able to obtain population data from their state government or wildlife data from their local Fish and Game Department.

_____

_____

_____

Interpret Data

Interpreting data involves using other skills, such as predicting and hypothesizing, to explain patterns or relationships in data. Interpretations may change when additional data is obtained.

Think About Interpreting Data

The table shows the number of individuals of different populations in two similar regions. Both regions were forests in 1995. Both became the sites of housing developments in 1999. On one site a network of forest areas was left between house lots. On the other site all the trees were removed, houses were built, and each lot was individually landscaped.

Forest Areas Left			Newly Landscaped		
	1995	2000		1995	2000
Owl	8	4	Owl	9	1
Bobcat	5	0	Bobcat	4	0
Fox	11	7	Fox	11	4
Beaver	7	2	Beaver	7	0
Rabbit	28	35	Rabbit	24	40
Deer	6	9	Deer	7	12
Skunk	4	7	Skunk	4	9

1. Which populations decreased at both sites? _owl, bobcat, fox, and beaver_

2. Which populations increased at both sites? _rabbit, deer, and skunk_

3. How do you explain the different impacts of the housing developments on the populations that increased and the populations that decreased?

   Possible responses include that habitats of predators were destroyed so their

   prey increased; some populations were able to adapt but others could not.

4. How would you use this data for planning another housing development?

   Possible answers: Leaving a network of forest is an improvement; any

   type of development will seriously harm some populations. Some students

   may suggest looking into ways of preserving habitats for animals.

Name _____

Date _____

Identify Cause and Effect

Read "Success Stories" on page B52. Then read the statements below that are taken from the selection. Underline the causes, and enclose the effects in parentheses.

During the 1940s people began using a poison called DDT to kill insects. One effect was the weakening of bald eagles' eggshells.

During the 1940s people began using a poison called DDT to kill insects. One effect was (the weakening of bald eagles' eggshells).

In 1972 the Environmental Protection Agency made the use of DDT illegal. Slowly, over many years, the bald eagle population has increased.

In 1972 the Environmental Protection Agency made the use of DDT illegal. Slowly, over many years, (the bald eagle population has increased).

A program of saving and restoring habitats began. Today there are more than 1,600 pairs of peregrine falcons in the wild.

A program of saving and restoring habitats began. Today there are (more than 1,600 pairs of peregrine falcons in the wild).

In 1982, scientists began breeding condors in captivity. Captive breeding is difficult, but some chicks hatched, grew to adulthood, and were released into the wild.

In 1982, scientists began breeding condors in captivity. Captive breeding is difficult, but (some chicks hatched, grew to adulthood, and were released into the wild).

What Is Extinction, and What Are Its Causes?

Lesson Concept

Extinction occurs when the last individual of a species dies. Extinction can happen naturally or be caused by human activities.

Vocabulary

exotic (B50)   **extinct** (B51)   **endangered** (B51)

threatened (B51)

Fill in the missing part in each cause-and-effect chain below. One column starts a sentence, while the other finishes the sentence.

Cause	Effect
1. Building new roads, homes, or buildings	reduces the size of a natural habitat.
2. A volcano or hurricane	can destroy an island habitat naturally.
3. Drought	kills producers in a food chain naturally.
Importing exotic species	**4.** brings diseases that kill native populations.
Strict hunting laws	**5.** may bring back populations of threatened or endangered species.
A change in an island habitat	**6.** may be permanent because there may be no other populations to replace lost organisms.
Using DDT in the 1940s	**7.** weakened bald eagle eggshells, causing fewer eagles to hatch. The bald eagle and peregrine falcon became endangered.
Restoring and saving peregrine falcon habitats has	**8.** increased the peregrine falcon population and removed it from the endangered species list.

Recognize Vocabulary

Write the letter of the definition in the right-hand column in the space in front of the term that it matches in the left-hand column.

_____ **1.** producers

_____ **2.** population

_____ **3.** food web

_____ **4.** consumers

_____ **5.** habitat

_____ **6.** exotic

_____ **7.** competition

_____ **8.** energy pyramid

_____ **9.** learned behaviors

_____ **10.** decomposer

_____ **11.** community

_____ **12.** ecosystem

_____ **13.** threatened

_____ **14.** individual

_____ **15.** instinct

_____ **16.** food chain

_____ **17.** niche

_____ **18.** endangered

_____ **19.** symbiosis

_____ **20.** extinct

A role of a population of organisms within a particular habitat

B community of organisms and their physical environment

C individuals of the same kind living in the same environment

D shows the relationships between many different food chains in a single ecosystem

E contest between organisms for limited resources

F species become this after the last individual in the population dies

G place in an ecosystem where each population lives

H consumer that breaks down tissues of decaying organisms

I all the populations of organisms living together in an environment

J behaviors animals are taught or acquire after birth

K living things that must eat to get energy

L single organism in an environment

M behavior an organism inherits

N likely to become endangered if it is not protected

O organisms that produce their own food through photosynthesis

P shows amount of energy available to pass from one level of a food chain to the next

Q shows how consumers in an ecosystem are connected to one another according to what they eat

R nonnative organisms

S having a population so small it is likely to disappear unless steps are taken to save it

T long-term relationship between different kinds of organisms

A Day in the Life of a Forest Animal

Narrative Writing—Story

Imagine that you are an animal that is part of a forest ecosystem. Write the story of one day in your life. Describe how you interact with living and nonliving things in your environment. Use the story map below to help you plan your narrative.

Character (animal):	**Setting (where the animal lives):**
In what part of the forest do you spend your day?	
On what other parts of the ecosystem do you depend for food?	
What other living and nonliving parts of the ecosystem help you?	
What parts of the ecosystem do you need to avoid, and why?	

Chapter 3 • Graphic Organizer for Chapter Concepts

Biomes

LESSON 1
LAND BIOMES

Type	plants—animals
1. Tropical rain forest	trees, birds, insects
2. Deciduous forest	deciduous trees, deer
3. Grassland	grasses, prairie dogs, bison
4. Desert	cacti, snakes, lizards
5. Taiga	evergreen trees, snowshoe hares
6. Tundra	small plants, caribous

LESSON 2
WATER ECOSYSTEMS

Ocean Ecosystems

1. Intertidal Zone

2. Near-shore Zone

3. Open-ocean Zone

Freshwater Ecosystems

1. ponds and lakes

2. rivers and streams

Mixed Ecosystem

estuaries

Biomes and Climates

Materials

**map of
North American
climate zones**

**map of
North American
biomes**

**markers or
colored pencils**

Activity Procedure

1 On the map of North American climate zones, color the different climates as shown in the table below.

North American Climate Zones		
Area	**Climate**	**Color**
1	More than 250 cm rain; warm all year	green
2	75–250 cm rain or snow; warm summer, cold winter	purple
3	20–60 cm rain or snow; cool summer, cold winter	blue
4	10–40 cm rain or snow; warm summer, cold winter	orange
5	Less than 10 cm rain; hot summer, cool winter	yellow
6	250 cm snow (25 cm rain); cold all year	brown

2 On the map of North American biomes, color the biomes as shown in the chart on the next page.

North American Biomes		
Area	**Biome**	**Color**
A	Tropical rain forest	green
B	Deciduous forest	purple
C	Taiga	blue
D	Grassland	orange
E	Desert	yellow
F	Tundra	brown

❸ Compare the green areas on the two maps. How does the area with a warm, wet climate compare to the area of tropical rain forest? Compare other biomes and climate zones that are colored alike.

Draw Conclusions

1. How do areas on the climate map **compare** to areas shown in the same color on the biome map? Areas on the climate map are very similar in size and shape to areas on the biome map.

2. Observe the maps. If an area is too wet to be a desert but too dry to be a forest, what biome would you expect to find there? grassland

3. Order the biomes from wettest to driest. tropical rain forest, deciduous forest, taiga, grassland, desert, tundra

4. Scientists at Work When scientists **compare** sets of data, they can **draw conclusions** about relationships between the data sets. Conifers are dominant plants of the taiga. Broad-leaved trees are the dominant plants of the deciduous forest. What conclusions can you draw about the water needs of conifers compared to those of broad-leaved trees? Taiga gets 20–60 cm of rain or snow; deciduous forest gets 75–250 cm of rain or snow. Conifers need less water than deciduous trees.

Investigate Further Use a computer to make a chart showing the climates of the six biomes and a map combining climate zones and biomes.

Name _____

Date _____

Compare

When you compare, you identify ways objects or events are similar or different.

Think About Comparing

Jessica made a chart to compare three different biomes in the United States.

	Desert	**Deciduous Forest**	**Grassland**
Climate	hot and dry summers, warm and dry winters	warm summers, cold winters, plenty of rain	hot summers with little rain; warm, wet springs and falls; cold winters
Vegetation	slow-growing plants that conserve water, like cacti and thorny shrubs	mostly trees and shrubs that shed leaves in fall, some grasses and flowers	mostly fast-growing grasses, some flowers, a few shrubs and trees
Animal adaptations	move to warmer or cooler locations during temperature changes, conserve water	hide in vegetation, fur is shed in spring and thickens before winter	can burrow or move fast, fur is shed in spring and thickens before winter, some can travel far

1. Which two regions have similar vegetation? Explain. _Deciduous forests and grasslands have the greatest amount of similar vegetation. Each has trees, shrubs, grasses, and flowers._

2. Jessica notices that grassland and forest animals have different ways of escaping danger. Why would animals need to run fast on grassland but hide in a forest? _Students may say that trees and shrubs would keep animals from being able to run. Grassland provides room to run. A forest provides places to hide._

3. Jessica knows that the fur of grassland animals grows thicker in winter. How do you think the thickness of fur on grassland animals that moved to a warmer place in the winter compares to the fur of animals that didn't move? Explain. _Students may say animals that moved to a warmer place had thinner fur. These animals didn't have to grow as much fur to stay warm._

Use with page B63.

Reading Skills Practice

Distinguish Fact and Opinion

Read the selection. Then identify each statement below as a fact or an opinion.

The Frozen Tundra

The word *tundra* means "barren land." The area north of the timberline is generally referred to as tundra. It is treeless, and the subsoil is permanently frozen. The Arctic tundra circles the North Pole. The Antarctic tundra is almost completely covered with ice.

There are not many animals that can survive in the harsh climate of the tundra. Lemmings, musk oxen, and polar bears, as well as caribou and snowy owls, make the tundra their home. Ducks and geese also live in the tundra.

The tundra has lakes, bogs, and streams. Most of the vegetation found there is mosses, grasses, and dwarf shrubs. The long winters and short summers bring about 14 inches of precipitation annually, keeping the soil waterlogged and frozen.

_____ People would be foolish to live in the tundra biome.

_____ The animals that live in the tundra must suffer from poor nutrition and frostbite.

_____ Some plants are able to survive the harsh climate of the tundra.

_____ Trees should be planted on the tundra to help with soil erosion.

_____ The tundra has a natural source of water.

What Are Land Biomes?

Lesson Concept

A biome is a large-scale ecosystem. There are many kinds of biomes, each with a different climate and organisms that have adaptations to live in it.

Vocabulary

biome (B64)	**climate zone** (B64)

Read the descriptions of the biomes below, and name each type of biome.

You'll find several layers of plants here. In the fall, people come to see the pretty leaves.

1. deciduous forest _____

Grains that feed people and animals grow here.

2. grassland _____

It can be very hot during the day and very cold at night.

3. desert _____

The trees are green year-round here. It is cold and has many mosquitoes.

4. taiga _____

When it's dark up here, everything is white.

5. tundra _____

Half of Earth's varieties of plant life are found here.

6. rain forest _____

Life in a Pond Community

Materials

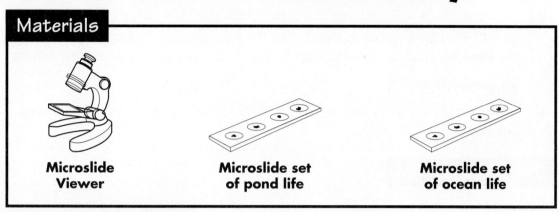

Microslide Viewer

Microslide set of pond life

Microslide set of ocean life

Alternate Materials

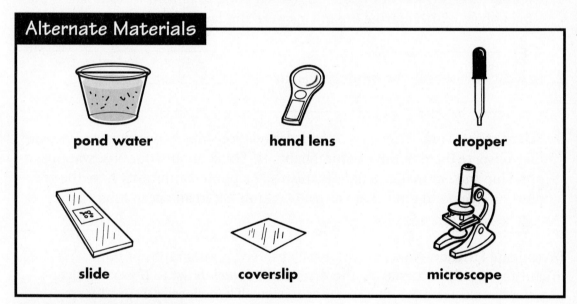

pond water

hand lens

dropper

slide

coverslip

microscope

Activity Procedure

Note: If microscopes are available, your teacher may provide an alternate procedure that you will follow to make a slide and observe a drop of pond water.

1 Put the "Pond Life" Microslide in the Microslide Viewer. **Observe** the first photograph, which shows the fish and plants found in a pond. **Record** your observations by making a drawing and writing a short description of these organisms. You may use the information on the Microslide card to help you with your description.

2 The other photographs in the set show microscopic life in a pond. **Observe** each of the organisms. Then **record** your observations by making a drawing and writing a short description of each organism.

❸ Classify each of the organisms as producer or consumer. **Record** this information on your drawings and in your descriptions.

❹ Now put the "Marine Biology" Microslide in the Microslide Viewer. **Observe** each of the organisms, but don't read the information on the Microslide card yet. **Predict** which of the organisms are producers and which are consumers.

My prediction: _____

❺ Now read the information on the Microslide card to see if your predictions were correct.

Draw Conclusions

1. **Compare** the two sets of organisms. Which pond organism was similar to the coral polyp? Which marine organisms were similar to the algae?
   the hydra; the phytoplankton

2. In what way were all the producers alike? They were all green. (They all had chlorophyll.)

3. **Scientists at Work** Scientists often **infer** relationships between organisms after they **observe** them in their natural habitats. Think about your observations of pond life and ocean life. What organisms in a pond community have the same position in a pond food chain as zooplankton has in an ocean food chain?
   amoeba and paramecium

Investigate Further Now that you have observed photographs of pond organisms, use the materials in the *Alternate Materials* list to **observe** a drop of water from a pond or other water ecosystem. Then **classify** as producers or consumers the organisms you observe. See page R3 for tips on using a microscope.
Students might collect water samples from a nearby pond, stream, large puddle, or the intertidal zone of an ocean. The drop can be observed under a microscope.

Name _____

Date _____

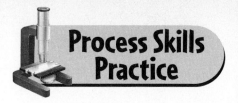

Infer

Inferring involves using logical reasoning to draw conclusions from observations.

Think About Inferring

Vladimir and his family just moved into their new home in Arkansas. He wrote a letter to his cousin Victor. In the letter he described the pond behind his home.

June 18

Dear Victor,

I love our new home! When you visit, we can go swimming in the pond behind our house. Today would be great for swimming. It's a hot, sunny day. It's 2:00 in the afternoon, and the thermometer says it's 82° Fahrenheit.

I'm looking out at the pond. I can see plants with roots in pond mud. They have long, thin stems and large, flat leaves floating on the pond's surface. Along the shore are clumps of tall grasslike plants with blades about a meter high. Lots of small bugs with long jointed legs walk on the surface of the water, more easily than I walk on the sidewalk. In the middle of the pond, six turtles are sitting on a log in a sunny spot. A female duck with five ducklings behind her is swimming by the turtles. I can hear buzzing and whirring from all the insects nearby.

I can't wait for your visit. Don't forget to bring your swim trunks!

Your cousin,
Vladimir

---

1. Victor knows that plants need to get sunlight to survive. What could Victor infer about the pond plants Vladimir observed? Accept reasonable answers. Students may say plants in the pond have to float or be tall enough to reach sunlight, because the water level may rise or fall.

2. Vladimir mentioned that many insects were walking on the pond's surface. Should Victor infer that the pond's surface where the insects were walking was calm or wavy? Explain. Victor should infer that the pond's surface was calm. Insects would probably have a hard time walking on rough water.

3. Victor is coming to see Vladimir in five weeks. What could Victor infer about what the pond will be like at that time? Accept reasonable answers. The water may be warmer. Not as many animals would be on the pond. The ducklings will be bigger or will not be there because they have flown away.

Name _____

Date _____

Summarize and Paraphrase a Selection

Read the selection. Then complete the outline below to identify supporting facts and details.

Cleaning Stations

Parasites can weaken an organism. To get rid of parasitic pests, some large fish can temporarily overcome their natural instinct to eat certain smaller fish that perform a helpful cleaning service to the larger fish. These smaller "cleaning fish" maintain regular "stations" that the larger fish visit. When the cleaner identifies itself to the larger fish through a series of body motions, it then can go safely about the business of picking off and eating dead skin and parasites from the body, teeth, and gills of its "customer."

The relationship is mutually beneficial. In fact, this relationship is so important to the health of the larger fish that it will travel to new areas of the ocean to search out a cleaning station if its regular station disappears.

I. **Parasites**

   A. can weaken an organism _____

   B. become food sources for smaller fish _____

II. **Cleaning Fish**

   A. set up regular stations for larger fish to visit _____

   B. eat dead skin and parasites from body, teeth, gills of larger fish _____

III. **Benefits to Both**

   A. food source for cleaning fish _____

   B. maintains health of larger fish _____

What Are Water Ecosystems?

Lesson Concept

Water ecosystems occur in fresh, salt, and brackish water.

Vocabulary

intertidal zone (B77)	**near-shore zone** (B77)
open-ocean zone (B77)	**estuary** (B80)

Use the terms below to label the parts of the picture.

fresh water	**open-ocean zone**	**intertidal zone**
near-shore zone	**estuary**	

fresh water   near-shore zone

estuary

intertidal zone ·   open-ocean zone

6. Where do near-shore zones get their nutrients, and in what form are these nutrients? Rivers that empty into the ocean dump dead organisms onto the ocean floor. _____

_____

7. Name three important roles of estuaries. They provide habitats for many organisms. Two-thirds of the world's fish and shellfish are harvested from estuaries. They prevent coastal flooding. They prevent shoreline erosion.

_____

_____

Name _____

Date _____

Recognize Vocabulary

| biome | climate zone | intertidal zone |
| near-shore zone | open-ocean zone | estuary |

Use the clues below to fill in the puzzle with the vocabulary terms.

Across

3. a saltwater ecosystem with calm waters; most nutrients provided by rivers

4. a place with similar yearly patterns of temperature, rainfall, and amount of sunlight

6. a large-scale ecosystem

Down

1. a saltwater ecosystem where breaking waves provide oxygen and nutrients

2. a saltwater ecosystem with very deep water

5. where a freshwater river empties into the ocean

Write Biome Poems

Expressive Writing–Poem

Write short poems describing three biomes. Describe the plants, animals, and climate of each biome. Each poem's lines should begin with the letters of the biome's name. Use the format below to make notes for your poems.

G _____

R _____

A _____

S _____

S _____

L _____

A _____

N _____

D _____

S _____

T _____

A _____

I _____

G _____

A _____

D _____

E _____

S _____

E _____

R _____

T _____

Chapter 4 • Graphic Organizer for Chapter Concepts

Protecting and Preserving Ecosystems

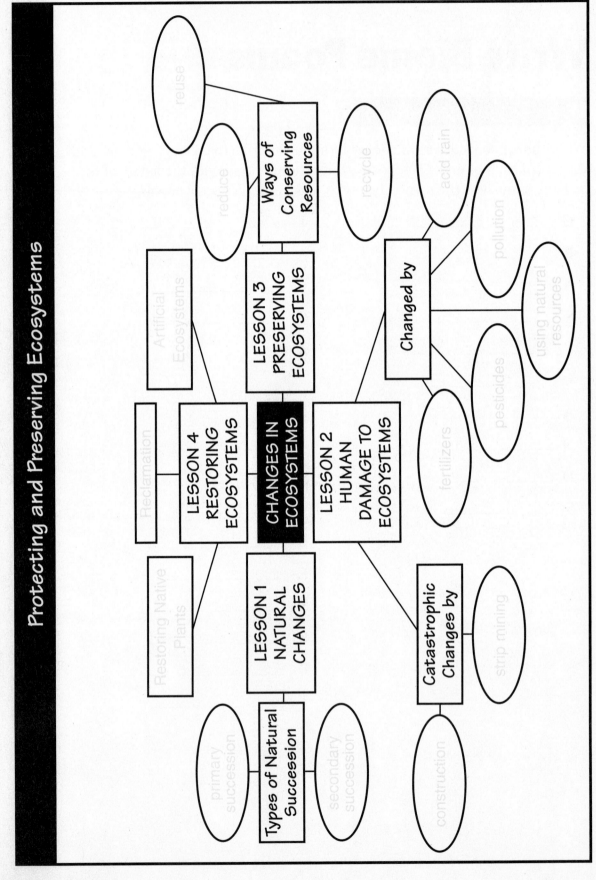

reuse

reduce

Ways of Conserving Resources

recycle

acid rain

pollution

using natural resources

Changed by

pesticides

fertilizers

Artificial Ecosystems

LESSON 3 PRESERVING ECOSYSTEMS

Reclamation

LESSON 4 RESTORING ECOSYSTEMS

CHANGES IN ECOSYSTEMS

LESSON 2 HUMAN DAMAGE TO ECOSYSTEMS

Restoring Native Plants

LESSON 1 NATURAL CHANGES

Catastrophic Changes by

strip mining

construction

primary succession

Types of Natural Succession

secondary succession

Name _____

Date _____

How a Pond Changes

Materials

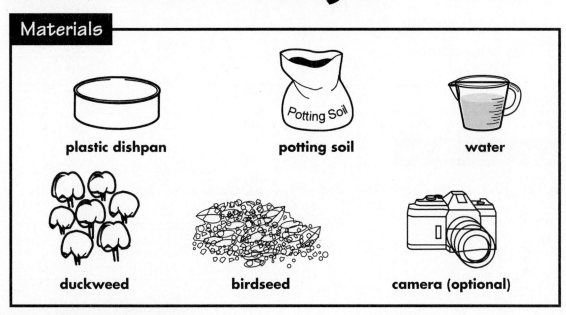

plastic dishpan	potting soil	water
duckweed	birdseed	camera (optional)

Activity Procedure

1 Spread a layer of potting soil about 5 cm deep in the dishpan. Now bank the soil about 10 cm high around the edges of the dishpan. Leave a low spot, with about 1 cm of soil, in the center of the pan.

2 Slowly pour water into the low area of the pan until the water is about 4 cm deep. You may have to add more water as some of it soaks into the soil. Place some duckweed on the "pond."

3 Sprinkle birdseed over the surface of the soil. Don't worry if some of the seed falls into the water. Do not water the seed. Take a photograph or draw a picture to **record** how your pond looks. Put your pond model in a sunny window.

My observations: _____

_____

4 After three or four days, **measure** and **record** the depth of the water. Take another photograph, or draw another picture. Then sprinkle more birdseed over the soil. Water the soil lightly.

My measurement: _____

5 After three or four more days, **observe** how your pond has changed. **Measure** and **record** the depth of the water. **Compare** your observations with the photographs you took or the pictures you drew.

My measurement: _____

My comparisons: _____

_____

_____

Draw Conclusions

1. Describe any changes in the pond during the week. How did the depth of the water change? Possible answers: The seed sprouted; much of the "pond" dried up; the pond filled in with dirt and seeds; the duckweed covered the pond.

2. **Compare** the changes in your model with those in a real pond. How are they the same? In both the model and a real pond, soil washes into the pond, the water dries up if there isn't any rain, and plants begin to grow at the edge of the pond.

How are they different? This process occurs much more slowly in a real pond.

3. **Scientists at Work** By **observing** the changes that occur while **they use models**, scientists can **infer** changes that might occur in nature. From what you observed in your model, what do you infer might happen to a real pond over time? A real pond might get smaller and eventually disappear as the water evaporates, the pond fills with soil, and plants begin to grow.

Investigate Further An actual pond ecosystem has a greater diversity of plants and animals than your model. **Make another model** that includes a greater variety of living things.

Name _____

Date _____

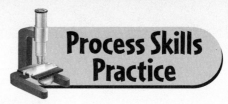

Use Models and Infer

When objects are very big or very small, or when processes take a long time or do not happen often, a mental or physical model can help you understand the process. You can use observations of models to make inferences.

Think About Using Models and Inferring

While planting a vegetable garden in his backyard, Mr. Koumjian decided to make a model of a region that has undergone a natural disaster. He did this by turning over the soil in one corner of the garden and leaving it unplanted. He wondered what would happen to this patch of soil if he didn't do anything to it. The garden was surrounded by a grass lawn. There were berry bushes and honeysuckle vines in another part of the yard, along with two apple trees and two pear trees.

1. Is Mr. Koumjian's garden patch a good model for an area left after a fire? Why or why not? Yes, because an area after a fire is bare with nothing growing on it; no, because the area hasn't been subjected to the heat and chemical reactions that occur during a fire. There are no charred remains left.

2. Is Mr. Koumjian's garden patch a good model for an area left after a flood? Why or why not? No, because a flood doesn't leave bare patches of soil.

3. Is Mr. Koumjian's garden patch a good model for an area left after a volcanic eruption? Why or why not? Yes, because a volcanic eruption leaves an area with nothing growing on it; no, because a volcanic eruption usually leaves lava or ash on the ground covering the soil.

4. How long will Mr. Koumjian have to observe his model to see the changes that occur in an area after a natural disaster? Accept reasonable answers. Possible answers: at least a year to see how all seasons affect the area, and several years to give life several growing seasons to return

5. Why do you think Mr. Koumjian chose to make this model instead of going to a place where there had been a natural disaster? Accept reasonable responses. Possible answers: It might be a long trip to an area where there had been a natural disaster; he wanted to observe the area every day for a long period of time.

Name _____

Date _____

Compare and Contrast

Read the selection. Then complete the chart by comparing and contrasting
Yellowstone National Park before and after the fires of 1988.

The Fires of 1988

Each summer most national parks experience forest fires that are caused by
lightning. The fires ignite tall trees and spread rapidly through the dried leaves,
branches, and underbrush. In 1988 Yellowstone National Park experienced the
worst series of forest fires in its history. The fires severely damaged the park and
decreased some of its wildlife populations. Grizzly bears, mountain sheep, elk,
bison, moose, many smaller animals, and more than 200 kinds of birds inhabit
Yellowstone Park, making it one of the world's largest wildlife sanctuaries.

Yellowstone rebounded quickly from the fires. The plant life in the burned areas
is now stronger than it was before the fire. Ash left in the soil also deposited
nutrients that, in turn, helped plant life flourish. Pine and fir trees, which make up
most of the forests of Yellowstone, are growing again. Lodgepole pines produce
cones that are opened only by the heat of a fire. When the cones open, they spread
their seeds and more new trees grow than before. Below-ground root systems were
not destroyed and have managed to regenerate new plant life. In these ways,
Yellowstone National Park actually benefited from the severe fires of 1988.

	Wildlife	**Trees**	**Other Plant Life**
Before Fires of 1988	larger populations of animals	abundant pines and firs	abundant forms of plant life
After Fires of 1988	smaller populations of animals	pines and firs growing back at rapid rate; more lodgepole pines than before	above-ground flora consumed by fires; below-ground root systems have been sustained

Use with page B94.

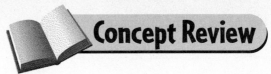

How Do Ecosystems Change Naturally?

Lesson Concept

Slow changes occur naturally in ecosystems every day. Quick changes, like fires, also occur naturally.

Vocabulary

succession (B92)   **pioneer plants** (B92)   **climax community** (B93)

Use the vocabulary terms above to complete the captions.

A Alder and willow trees can take root now. These trees have relatively slender trunks and grow quickly. They also add acids to the soil.

B Now the soil is deep enough to support the tall, sturdy hemlock and spruce trees. These trees are the _____. If left undisturbed, this forest could stay almost the same for thousands of years.

C Grasses and flowering plants begin to take root. The thick root structure of these plants anchors the soil as it deepens. These plants also attract insects, birds, worms, and small mammals that add wastes to the soil.

D In the early stages of _____, lichens form a thin layer of soil, which allows moss, a _____, to grow. Bits of organic matter and bird droppings become trapped in dense moss and add more nutrients to the deepening soil.

Write the letter of the caption above that goes with each picture below.

1. _____   **2.** _____   **3.** _____   **4.** _____

Name _____

Date _____

How Chemical Fertilizer Affects a Pond

Materials

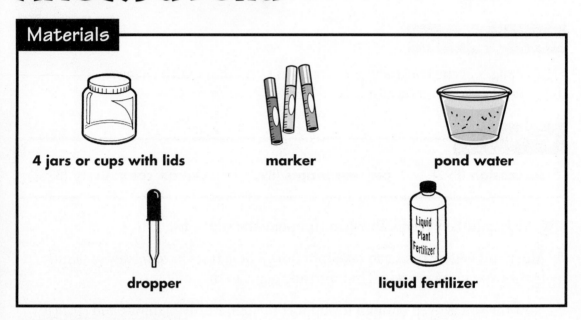

4 jars or cups with lids   marker   pond water

dropper   liquid fertilizer

Activity Procedure

1. Use the marker to label the jars 1, 2, 3, and 4.

2. Fill the jars with pond water.

3. Put 10 drops of liquid fertilizer in Jar 1, 20 drops in Jar 2, and 40 drops in Jar 3. Don't put any fertilizer in Jar 4.

4. Put the lids on the jars. Then place the jars in a sunny window.

5. **Observe** the jars every day for two weeks. **Record** your observations.

My observations: _____

_____

_____

_____

Draw Conclusions

1. What differences did you **observe** among the jars? Which jar had the most plant growth? Which had the least plant growth? How could you tell?

The jar with the most fertilizer had the most growth. The jar with no fertilizer had the least growth. The jar with the most growth is very green and cloudy.

2. As organisms die and decay, they use up the oxygen in the water. Which jar do you **infer** will eventually have the least oxygen? Students should infer that the jar with the most growth will eventually have the least oxygen.

3. When water ecosystems are contaminated by fertilizer, fish and other animal populations begin to die off. Why do you think this happens?

There is not enough oxygen in the water for the fish and other animals to breathe.

4. **Scientists at Work** When scientists **identify and control variables**, they can **observe** the effects of one variable at a time. What variable were you observing the effect of in this investigation? the amount of fertilizer in the water

What variables did you control? Possible answers include: size of water sample, type of water sample, amount of sunlight, and length of time sample sat in sunlight. Students may suggest others.

Investigate Further Some fertilizers contain additional chemicals that are supposed to kill weeds. **Hypothesize** about the effects of using these chemicals on a lawn. Then **plan and conduct a simple experiment** to test your hypothesis.

_____

_____

_____

_____

_____

Name _____

Date _____

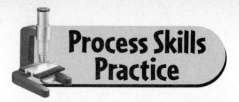

Identify and Control Variables

When you identify variables in an experiment, you pick out the factors that can be changed in a situation. You control variables in an experiment by changing one of the variables and keeping all the others the same.

Think About Identifying and Controlling Variables

Read the descriptions of each of the experiments below. Then, on the line below the description, identify the variables that affect the outcome of the experiment.

1. Fill each of three 1-quart glass jars with 2 inches of clay, 2 inches of sand, and 2 inches of potting soil. Put four earthworms in one jar, four ants in another jar, and no animals in the third jar. Observe the jars every day for a week. Make notes about the ways the contents of the jars change or stay the same. What is the variable in this experiment and what could you learn by controlling it?

   type of organism in the jars: earthworms, ants, or nothing; the effect of

   certain organisms on soil

2. Fill two aluminum baking pans of the same size with a layer of potting soil 3 inches deep. Plant grass seed in one of the pans. Place both pans in a sunny location, and water both pans with the same amount of water every two days. After the grass has grown to a height of 3 inches, prop up one end of both pans on a block or brick 1 to 2 inches high. (Both pans should be propped up on blocks of the same height.) Then place an empty pan in front of the lower end of each pan containing soil. Slowly pour one half-gallon of water into the higher end of each pan. Measure how much water and soil runs off into each of the empty pans. What is the variable in this experiment, and what could you

   learn by controlling it? grass; the effect of plants on soil erosion due to water

3. Place four identical leafy green houseplants in a sunny spot. Each plant should be in a 2-inch pot, be the same height (about 4 inches), and have about the same number and size of leaves. Label the pots *A*, *B*, *C*, and *D*. Water each pot with 8 ounces of water every day. Water Plant A with plain water. Add 1 teaspoon of distilled white vinegar to the water for Plant B every day. Add 1 tablespoon of distilled white vinegar to the water for Plant C every day. Add 3 tablespoons of distilled white vinegar to the water for Plant D every day. Observe the plants each day, making notes on their appearances. What is the variable in this experiment, and what could you learn by controlling it?

   the amount of vinegar or acid in the plant water; the effect of differing

   amounts of vinegar on plant growth

Reading Skills Practice

Draw Logical Conclusions

Read the selection. Then draw logical conclusions about the introduction of a non-native species to an ecosystem.

Another Threat to Ecosystems

   People are not the only threat to the balance of ecosystems. The introduction of non-native species of plants or animals to an ecosystem can also pose a serious threat. Sometimes the non-native species compete with the native species for the same resources. Non-native species also may prey on one or more of the native species they find in their new environment. For example, the brown tree snake was accidentally brought to Guam on airplanes after World War II. The snakes ate the native birds, leading ten native species of birds to become extinct. In the United States, the American chestnut tree was nearly driven to extinction by the introduction of a fungus called the chestnut blight. As a result, seven species of moths and butterflies that fed only on chestnut trees now may be extinct. Introducing non-native species to an environment can cause the extinction of native species in that environment.

Suppose alligators have just been introduced into an ecosystem that has many rivers, lakes, and other waterways. What could be the impact of this?

Many species of fish and other wildlife and domesticated animals might be lost because of the introduction of the alligator.

_____

_____

_____

How Do People Change Ecosystems?

Lesson Concept

Human activity can change ecosystems. Some ecosystems can recover from the changes, while other ecosystems are altered forever.

Vocabulary

pollution (B99)	**acid rain** (B99)

Complete the sentences below by writing the letter of a phrase from the chart.

A	paper products damage forest ecosystems and destroy habitats	**E**	corn, barley, wheat, or oats reduces the diversity of life
B	nitrogen oxides and sulfur dioxide that mix with water vapor and cause acid rain	**F**	strip mining, all the communities and many nonliving parts of an ecosystem are destroyed
C	roads, homes, schools, and office buildings, habitats for other organisms are destroyed	**G**	destroy habitats completely or change conditions so much that natural communities can't survive
D	kill unwanted plant and animal pests can damage natural ecosystems	**H**	birds, fish, and other water animals

1. Replacing the natural producers in a grassland ecosystem with ___E___.

2. Using pesticides and herbicides to ___D___.

3. As human communities grow and people build ___C___.

4. Cutting down trees to make wood and ___A___.

5. Energy stations and motor vehicles give off ___B___ .

6. Runoff from acid rain kills ___H___.

7. When topsoil and rock layers are removed in the process of ___F___.

8. Large-scale construction projects on fragile ecosystems may ___G___.

Name _____

Date _____

What Happens in a Landfill

Materials

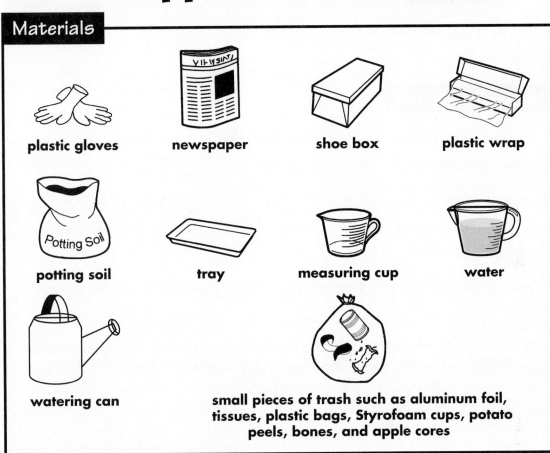

plastic gloves

newspaper

shoe box

plastic wrap

potting soil

tray

measuring cup

water

watering can

small pieces of trash such as aluminum foil,
tissues, plastic bags, Styrofoam cups, potato
peels, bones, and apple cores

CAUTION   ## Activity Procedure

1. Make a chart listing ten different items of trash. Allow space in your chart to **record** observations you will make later.

2. **CAUTION** **Put on the plastic gloves.** Spread newspaper on your work surface. Choose the ten items of trash listed on your chart to put in the model landfill. Lay the trash on the newspaper.

3. Now prepare the model landfill. First, line the shoe box with plastic wrap. Then put a layer of potting soil on the bottom of the box.

4. Take the pieces of trash from the newspaper and place them on top of the soil. Then cover the trash completely with another layer of soil.

5. Set the model landfill on the tray. Use the watering can to sprinkle the surface of the soil each day with 50 mL of water.

6 After two weeks, put on plastic gloves and remove the top layer of soil. **Observe** the items of trash, and **record** your observations.

My observations: _____

_____

_____

Draw Conclusions

1. Did you **observe** anything starting to decay? What items decayed the most? What items decayed the least? Animal and plant matter decays quickly. Plastics and aluminum do not decay at all.

2. Things that decay are said to be *biodegradable*. What items in your trash are biodegradable? plant and animal matter and paper

3. What do you **infer** might eventually happen to trash that is not biodegradable? Nothing, because it would never decay.

4. Scientists at Work Scientists often **draw conclusions** based on observations made while **using a model**. From your observations of a model landfill, what conclusions can you draw about using paper trash bags instead of plastic trash bags? Students might conclude that paper bags are better because they decay in landfills and plastic bags don't.

Investigate Further   Hypothesize how quickly trash in landfills would decay if it were all biodegradable. **Plan and conduct a simple experiment** to test your hypothesis.

_____

_____

_____

_____

_____

_____

Name _____

Date _____

Using a Model to Draw Conclusions

Using a model involves making or using a representation of a process or structure to better understand how the process works. Examples of models include maps, diagrams, three-dimensional representations, and computer simulations.

Think About Using a Model to Draw Conclusions

The table below is a simple model showing how many plastic bags Mark would save in a year by using the same bag to carry things from the store instead of getting a new bag two times a week. Each cell lists a month and the number of bags Mark will save by the end of that month if he starts carrying a bag on January 1. Study the model, and answer the questions to draw a conclusion.

January:	8	April:	34	July:	60	October:	86
February:	16	May:	42	August:	68	November:	94
March:	24	June:	50	September:	76	December:	104

1. How many bags would Mark save in a year? _____ 104 _____

   How did the model help you reach that conclusion? _by showing clearly how_
   the number of bags used adds up each month

2. Suppose three of Mark's friends think he has a good idea and decide to carry their own bags. These friends buy things about as often as Mark does. Use multiplication to figure out how many bags Mark and his three friends would

   save in a year. _416_____

3. Another friend decided to follow Mark's example, but half the time he forgot to take his bag to the store. About how many bags would this friend save?
   50–52 bags

4. From this mathematical model, draw a conclusion about reusing plastic bags.

   Use the information to argue for or against Mark's practice. _Answers will_
   vary but may state that a habit that doesn't involve a lot of inconvenience,
   even if practiced inconsistently, can reduce the use of resources.

Use Prefixes and Suffixes to Determine Word Meanings

The suffix -*tion* can mean "the act of" or "the result of." Several words in Lessons 3 and 4 have this ending. Reread both lessons, and notice the -*tion* words in the chart below. In the second column of the chart, write what you think the words mean. Then write in the third column their dictionary meanings.

Vocabulary Terms Ending with -*tion*	What Word Might Mean	What Word Does Mean
conservation	the act of protecting something	a careful preservation and protection of something
preservation	the act of preserving something	the act of keeping safe from injury, harm, or destruction
reclamation	the act of reclaiming something	the act or process of reclaiming
consumption	the act of consuming something	the act or process of consuming something
pollution	the result of polluting something	the act of polluting, especially by environmental contamination with human-made waste
construction	the act of constructing something	the process, act, or manner of constructing something

Use with page B105.

How Can People Treat Ecosystems More Wisely?

Lesson Concept

People can treat ecosystems more wisely by reducing pollution, protecting ecosystems, and conserving resources.

Vocabulary

conserving (B104) **reduce** (B104) **reuse** (B105) **recycle** (B105)

Listed below are several things Carla does to treat ecosystems wisely. After each behavior, tell what resource she is reducing the use of, reusing, or recycling. Some behaviors may accomplish more than one of these goals.

1. Carla rides her bike to the library instead of riding in a car.
   reduces use of oil and reduces air pollution from auto emissions

2. Instead of buying a new CD, Carla asks Bob if she can borrow his CD.
   reduces use of energy and resources to manufacture, package, and sell the CD

3. Carla's neighbor, Ms. Esposito, has a yard sale to sell used books, CDs, clothes, and other items. Carla buys a used chair to put in her living room.
   reuses items that would be discarded; reduces use of energy and resources to manufacture, package, and sell items; reduces items being thrown away

4. Instead of turning the thermostat to a higher setting, Carla puts on a sweater and a pair of thick socks to keep warm in the winter. reduces use of oil, electricity, or gas to heat buildings

5. Carla needs notebook filler paper for class. She buys paper made from postconsumer waste paper. reduces number of trees that must be cut to make new paper products; recycles a resource to make a new product

6. Carla buys organically grown oranges from the farmers' market to make marmalade. reduces use of pesticides and fertilizers, which protects soil resources and food webs

Investigate Log

How Waste Water Can Be Cleaned

Materials

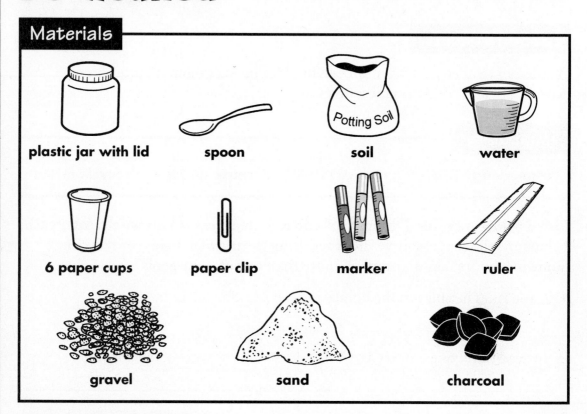

plastic jar with lid	spoon	soil	water
6 paper cups	paper clip	marker	ruler
gravel	sand	charcoal	

Activity Procedure

1 Put several spoonfuls of soil in the jar. Then fill the jar with water and put the lid on.

2 Shake the jar for 15 sec. Then put the jar aside for about 5 min. A process called *sedimentation* is taking place in the jar. It is the first step in waste-water treatment. **Observe** the water in the jar. **Record** your observations.

My observations: _____

_____

3 Unbend the paper clip. Use it to punch 10 small holes each in the bottoms of 3 paper cups. Using the marker, label the cups *A*, *B*, and *C*.

4 Using the spoon, put a 2.5-cm layer of gravel in Cup A. Put a 2.5-cm layer of sand and then a 2.5-cm layer of gravel in Cup B. Put a 2.5-cm layer of charcoal, and then a 2.5-cm layer of sand, and finally a 2.5-cm layer of gravel in Cup C.

5 Put each cup with holes inside a cup without holes. Label the outer cups *A*, *B*, and *C* to match the inner cups. Then carefully pour equal amounts of water from the jar into each set of cups. Try not to shake the jar as you pour. A process called *filtering* is taking place in the cups. It is the second step in waste-water treatment.

6 Separate each set of cups, allowing all the water to drain into the outer cups. **Observe** the water in the outer cups. **Record** your observations.

My observations: _____

_____

Draw Conclusions

1. What did you **observe** happening during sedimentation?

Large particles of soil settled to the bottom of the jar.

2. What combination of materials did the best job of filtering the water?

the combination of charcoal, sand, and gravel

3. What materials do you **infer** might not be filtered out of waste water?

Answers may include harmful organisms and materials dissolved in water, such as salt or poisonous chemicals.

4. Scientists at Work Scientists must **identify and control variables** when they **experiment**. In a real waste-water treatment plant, what variables might affect the filtering process? Possible answers: The water might contain materials that require different filtering materials; each step in the filtering process may require more materials; the filtering process may take more time.

Investigate Further Hypothesize what filter would best clean water that is "polluted" with food coloring. **Plan and conduct a simple experiment** to test your hypothesis.

_____

_____

_____

_____

_____

_____

Experiment

When you experiment, you design procedures for gathering data. An experiment tests a hypothesis under conditions in which variables are controlled or manipulated.

Think About Experimenting

Experiments must be designed carefully so the people running the experiment will know the meaning of the experiment's outcome. Everything that happens in an experiment can affect the outcome. Something the experimenter doesn't notice—like a 2 degree difference in temperature—could have an impact on what happens. That's why experiments must be repeated over and over, with the same results, before experimenters have proved anything. The first step, however, is to design an experiment to test the thing about which the experimenter wants to learn.

Read the problem that follows, and then design an experiment that will help you find the solution to the problem.

Rachael plants native bushes and flowers in her yard to attract insects, birds, and other creatures native to her ecosystem. She doesn't use pesticides in her garden. One year, however, she notices small black bugs on a berry bush. She has read about people using soap or garlic on plants to get rid of pests, but she doesn't know how much to use or which would be more effective. She has five bushes of this type, in three different sunny locations in her yard. Design an experiment for Rachael that would let her test these remedies. Possible answer: Spray one bush with water only, one bush with 1 teaspoon soap per cup of water, one bush with 1 tablespoon soap per cup of water, one bush with 1 teaspoon crushed garlic per cup of water; and one bush with 1 tablespoon crushed garlic per cup of water; observe all carefully.

_____

_____

_____

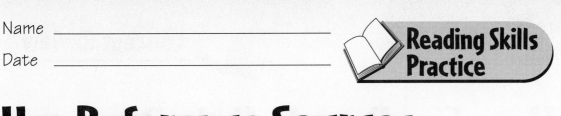

Use Reference Sources

Read the selection on strip-mine reclamation. Then use reference sources to find more information on strip mining and on how the land is reclaimed.

Strip-Mine Reclamation

People need resources such as coal and copper. Open-pit mining and strip mining often are the most efficient ways to obtain these resources.

However, in a strip mine, the top layers of soil must be removed in order to obtain the coal and other minerals. This process leaves enormous pits in the land that can lead to soil erosion and mudslides. Rain washes the chemicals from mine wastes into streams which then become contaminated. These changes upset the balance of many natural habitats.

Today, companies that dig mine strips must save the soil that is removed during mining. When they have finished with the mine, the saved soil is used to refill part of the pit. More soil then is added to fill the pit completely. Trees, flowers, and grass are planted to control erosion. Over time, other plants and animals return.

Information I discovered:

_____

_____

_____

_____

_____

_____

Reference sources I used:

_____

_____

_____

_____

Name _____

Date _____

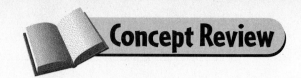

How Can People Help Restore Damaged Ecosystems?

Lesson Concept

People can help restore damaged ecosystems by rebuilding them.

Vocabulary

reclamation (B110)   **wetlands** (B111)

Fill in the chart below to describe some of the typical problems found in damaged ecosystems and the solutions people have used.

Ecosystem	Problems	Solutions
River	high levels of poisons, like PCBs, in the bodies of fish; other forms of pollution	require treatment of waste water before it is dumped in the river
Wetlands	wetlands drained and used for farming or other types of development	rebuild wetlands and protect remaining wetlands
Backyard	pollution from fertilizers and pesticides gets into groundwater and also kills animals	plant native grasses, flowers, and bushes that require smaller amounts of water, fertilizers, and pesticides

Use with page B113.

Recognize Vocabulary

succession	**pioneer plants**	**climax community**	**pollution**
acid rain	**conserving**	**reduce**	**reuse**
recycle	**reclamation**	**wetlands**	

Fill in the blanks below with the vocabulary terms above to complete the paragraphs about protecting ecosystems.

Even if most of the plants in an ecosystem are destroyed, hardy _____ pioneer plants _____ will return and begin to grow, building up the soil and attracting animals. Over time, through natural _____ succession _____, the area will change. The last stage of these slow changes occurs when a _____ climax community _____ is achieved. If no disasters occur, this ecosystem will remain unchanged for thousands of years. Unfortunately, _____ pollution _____ from human activities like manufacturing can kill organisms and break food chains. Activities like manufacturing, generating electricity, and operating motor vehicles produce gases that mix with water vapor in the atmosphere and fall back to Earth as _____ acid rain _____.

We can all work to protect ecosystems by buying fewer things and using less energy. Instead of throwing things away, _____ reuse _____ them a second or third time. Do you really need a fresh plastic bag every time you buy something? If you don't need a bag when you buy something, don't get one. If everyone did this, we would _____ reduce _____ the number of plastic bags we throw away. A lot of towns and cities encourage people to _____ recycle _____ newspapers, glass, and plastics.

It's not hard to think of things that individuals and communities can do if they care about _____ conserving _____ resources. There are many inspiring stories about people who work together on _____ reclamation _____ projects to restore damaged ecosystems. If everybody did just a little, it would help protect our ecosystems and preserve our resources.

Writing Practice

Write a Community Speech

Imagine that the government of your city or town has proposed building a landfill in your community. Some people support the proposal. Others oppose it. Think about your opinion. Write a speech expressing your opinion, to be given at a community meeting. Include supporting details that are based on what you have learned about landfills and waste management. Use the outline below to help you plan your speech.

State your opinion.
State reasons.   **Reason 1:**
Reason 2:
Reason 3:
Restate your opinion or call for action.

Chapter 1 • Graphic Organizer for Chapter Concepts

Changes to Earth's Surface

LESSON 1
SURFACE PROCESSES THAT CHANGE LANDFORMS

1. weathering _____
2. erosion _____
3. deposition _____

THE AGENTS THAT CAUSE LANDFORMS TO CHANGE

4. water _____
5. wind _____
6. ice _____
7. gravity _____

LESSON 2
PROCESSES THAT BEGIN IN EARTH'S INTERIOR

1. mountain building _____
2. volcano formation _____
3. earthquakes _____

LESSON 3
STAGES IN CONTINENTAL DRIFT

1. Pangea _____
2. Gondwana-Laurasia _____
3. present Earth _____

EVIDENCE FOR CONTINENTAL DRIFT

4. similar rock layers _____
5. similar fossils _____

Name _____

Date _____

How Water Changes Earth's Surface

Materials

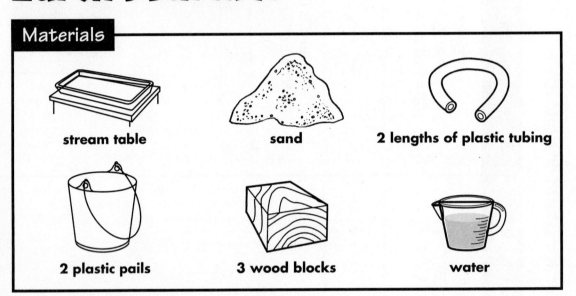

stream table

sand

2 lengths of plastic tubing

2 plastic pails

3 wood blocks

water

Activity Procedure

1. Place the stream table on a classroom table. Make sure the front end of the stream table is even with the edge of the table. Put the stream-table support under the back end of the stream table.

2. Fill the stream table with sand.

3. Using two fingers, make a path, or channel, down the middle of the sand.

4. Connect one end of one length of tubing to the front of the stream table. Let the other end of the tubing hang over the edge of the table. Place an empty pail on the floor under the hanging end of the tubing.

5. Place the other pail on two wood blocks near the raised end of the stream-table channel. Fill this pail $\frac{3}{4}$ full of water.

6. Put the second length of tubing into the pail, and fill it with water.

7. Start the water flowing through the tube from the pail to the stream table by lowering one end of the filled tube.

8. **Observe** any changes the water makes to the sand in the stream table. **Record** your observations.

9. Place the third wood block on top of the support under the stream table. Repeat Steps 7 and 8.

Name _____

Draw Conclusions

1. In which setup was the speed of the water greater? the second setup

_____

2. In which setup did you **observe** greater movement of sand from the channel?

the second setup

_____

3. **Scientists at Work** Scientists learn by **observing**. What did you learn about the way water can change the land by observing the channel in the stream table?

Flowing water moves soil and makes stream channels wider.

Water that flows faster digs deeper and can remove more soil.

Investigate Further Hypothesize what would happen if you replaced the sand with soil. **Experiment** to test your hypothesis.

_____

_____

_____

_____

_____

Observe

You observe by using your senses to see, hear, smell, and feel the world around you.

Think About Observing

Think about the things you see every day that may have been changed by moving water or ice. You may observe the dirt and gravel that pile up at the end of the street or the holes in the street that have to be repaired every year. What kinds of changes have you seen? Fill in the chart below with your observations and the possible causes for them. Two examples have been provided.

Observation	Possible Cause
1. Roots of plants growing on the side of a drainage ditch have been exposed.	1. Rushing water during heavy rain has washed soil away from the roots.
2. Bits of gravel have piled up under the downspout that comes from the roof.	2. Rainwater has washed bits of gravel off the roof shingles.
3.	3.
4.	4.
5.	5.
6.	6.

1. What do you think would happen if rain continued to wash away the soil in Observation 1 on the chart? Possible answers: The plants would lose their grip on the soil and be washed away; the ditch would get wider; more roots would be exposed.

2. What do you think would happen to the roof in Observation 2? The shingles would eventually wear away.

3. How do you think the scenes you observed will change over the passing of many years? Answers will depend on the student's observations. _____

_____

Use Reference Sources

Read the selection. Then look up the vocabulary terms in a dictionary, and write the part of speech and the definition for each.

Earthquakes and Their Damage

The damage caused by earthquakes depends on several *factors*. One factor is the amount of energy released during the earthquake. Generally, the more energy released, the more *extensive* the damage. Another factor is the population *density* in the affected area. Heavily populated areas often suffer more damage from an earthquake than do less populated areas. A third factor is the types of structures in the affected area. Buildings, bridges, and elevated highways that are not specially reinforced for earthquakes often are damaged during even moderate quakes. Another factor is the land underlying the area. Some soils *collapse*, or turn to quicksand, causing much damage.

Vocabulary Term	Part of Speech	Definition
factors	noun	circumstances that bring about a result
extensive	adjective	having wide or considerable extent
density	noun	the quantity per unit area
collapse	verb	to fall down or fall to pieces

Concept Review

What Processes Change Landforms?

Lesson Concept

The action of water, wind, ice, and gravity break down Earth's crust and change landforms.

Vocabulary

landforms (C6)   **weathering** (C7)   **erosion** (C7)

deposition (C7)   **mass movement** (C9)

Answer each question with one or more complete sentences.

1. Most of the time, changes to landforms are slow. What are some examples of very fast changes? _Possible answers include a hurricane washing away a beach, a volcano erupting and enlarging an island, or a mudslide filling in part of a lake._

2. What are two landforms that can be caused by glaciers? _Terminal moraines and U-shaped valleys can be caused by glaciers._

3. Why has wind erosion shaped so many landforms in the American Southwest? _There is very little plant life to hold the soil in place, so the dry soil is picked up and blown against the rocky landforms by the wind._

4. Name three kinds of mass movement. _Three kinds of mass movement are mudslides, landslides, and creep._

5. How is a river delta formed? _Sediments are picked up and carried away by the river. When the river slows down as it empties into the ocean, it deposits the sediments. They build up and eventually form a delta._

Journey to the Center of Earth

Materials

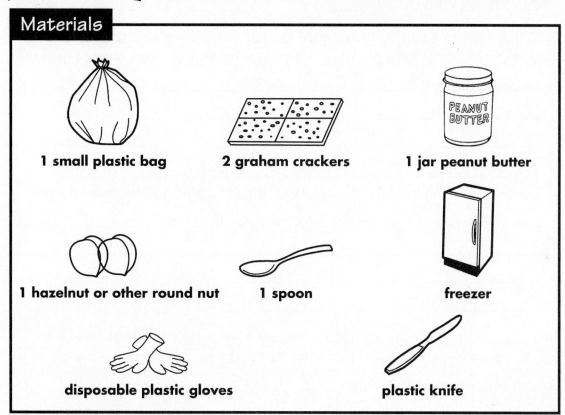

1 small plastic bag

2 graham crackers

1 jar peanut butter

1 hazelnut or other round nut

1 spoon

freezer

disposable plastic gloves

plastic knife

Activity Procedure

1 Put the graham crackers in the plastic bag. Close the bag and use your hands to crush the crackers into crumbs. Then set the bag aside.

2 Put on the plastic gloves. Use the spoon to scoop a glob of peanut butter from the jar and put it in your gloved hand. Place the nut in the center of the peanut butter. Cover the nut with more peanut butter until there is about 2.5 cm of peanut butter all around the nut. Using both hands, roll the glob of peanut butter with the nut at its center into a ball.

3 Open the bag of crushed graham crackers, and roll the peanut-butter ball in the graham cracker crumbs until the outside of the ball is completely coated.

4 Put the ball in the freezer for about 15 minutes. Remove the ball and cut into your model with the plastic knife. **Observe** the layers inside. You might want to take a photograph of your model for later review.

Name _____

Draw Conclusions

1. The peanut-butter ball is a model of Earth's layers. How many layers does Earth have in this model? _three_____

2. Which layer of Earth do the crushed graham crackers represent? Why do you think your model has a thick layer of peanut butter but a thin layer of graham cracker crumbs? _the crust; the mantle (peanut butter) is thicker than the crust_

   _____

   _____

3. **Scientists at Work** Scientists can see and understand complex structures better by **making models** of them. What does the model show about Earth's layers? What doesn't the model show about Earth's layers? _It shows how many_ _layers Earth has, the shapes of the layers, and the relative thickness of the_ _layers. The model does not show what Earth's layers are made of._

   _____

Investigate Further Some geologists, scientists who study the Earth, say that Earth's center is divided into a soft outer part and a hard inner part. How could you **make a model** to show this? _____

_____

_____

_____

_____

Name _____

Date _____

Make and Use Models

Sometimes making a model can give you a better understanding of a
process. This is especially so when you are trying to understand an
Earth process, which takes millions of years to occur.

Think About Making and Using Models

Suppose you are using biscuit dough to model the movement of
Earth's surface. First you would roll the dough flat and cut two blocks
out of it. Those blocks would model two opposing plates of Earth's
crust. Suppose you put them together as shown and push them against
one another. Then think of trying to slide them past one another.

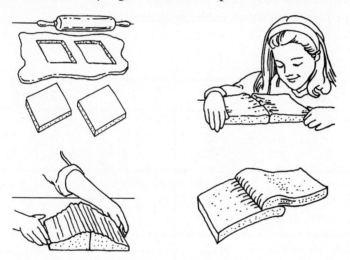

1. What is the dough modeling when the two blocks are pushed together?
It models the formation of mountain ranges. Some students may recognize
that it also models subduction zones.

2. What do you think happens when you try to slide the blocks of dough past one
another? What do you think this models? The dough blocks will probably stick
and resist sliding past one another. This models how pieces of Earth's crust
and mantle stick together. When the dough blocks then slide past each
other, they model earthquakes.

3. You have seen how this model is similar to Earth's surface, or crust. How is this
model different? The dough is soft, but Earth's crust is made of solid rock.

Use with page C13.

Identify Cause and Effect

Read the selection. Then complete the cause-and-effect chart below.

Mount St. Helens

    Scientists studied Mount St. Helens before, during, and after the 1980 eruption. As early as 1975, scientists predicted that Mount St. Helens probably would erupt before the year 2000. On March 20, 1980, a series of small earthquakes alerted scientists that the volcano was becoming active. In the following weeks, small eruptions of ash and steam occurred. These eruptions signaled the possibility of a large eruption. On May 18, when the big explosion occurred, over 100,000 acres of land were destroyed. Scientists kept a careful record of events. In the days that followed the eruptions, scientists took measurements and watched for signs of returning life.

Cause	Effect
a series of small earthquakes	alerted scientists that the volcano was becoming active
small eruptions of ash and steam	signaled the possibility of a large eruption
the big explosion occurred	destroyed over 100,000 acres of land

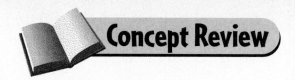
What Causes Mountains, Volcanoes, and Earthquakes?

Lesson Concept

Earth has three layers. The outer layer, or crust, is broken into tectonic plates. The movement of the plates results in mountains, volcanoes, and earthquakes.

Vocabulary

crust (C14)	**mantle** (C14)	**core** (C14)	**plate** (C15)
magma (C16)	**volcano** (C16)	**earthquake** (C18)	**fault** (C18)

Choose from the vocabulary list, and add the missing words to the paragraph below. Use each vocabulary term only once.

The _____ core _____ is Earth's center and its hottest layer. It is divided into two parts. The outer section is molten rock. Great pressure keeps the inner section solid. The middle layer of Earth is called the _____ mantle _____. It is made of molten rock called _____ magma _____. This molten rock sometimes reaches Earth's upper layer through openings called _____ volcanoes _____. The molten rock is called lava when it flows on Earth's surface. The outermost layer of Earth is called the _____ crust _____. It is made of many _____ plates _____ that float on the soft rock below them. When these pieces of Earth's surface crash together or scrape against one another, the release of energy causes an _____ earthquake _____. The places where pieces of Earth's crust move can bend or break. These breaks can become _____ faults _____.

Investigate Log

Movement of the Continents

Materials

3 copies of a world map

scissors

globe or world map

Glue
glue

3 sheets of construction paper

Activity Procedure

1. Cut out the continents from one copy of the world map.

2. Arrange the continents into one large "supercontinent" on a sheet of construction paper. As you would with a jigsaw puzzle, arrange them so their edges fit together as closely as possible.

3. Label the pieces with the names of their present continents, and glue them onto the paper.

4. Use a globe or world map to locate the following mountains: Cascades, Andes, Atlas, Himalayas, Alps. Then draw these mountains on the supercontinent.

5. Use your textbook to locate volcanoes and places where earthquakes have occurred. Put a *V* in places where you know there are volcanoes, such as the Cascades. Put an *E* in places where you know that earthquakes have occurred, such as western North America.

6. Repeat Steps 1–5 with the second copy of the world map, but before gluing the continents to the construction paper, separate them by about 2.5 cm. That is, leave about 2.5 cm of space between North America and Eurasia, between South America and Africa, and so on.

7. Glue the third world map copy onto a sheet of construction paper. Then place the three versions of the world map in order from the oldest to the youngest.

Name _____

Investigate Log

Draw Conclusions

1. Where do the continents fit together the best? _Possible answers: the western_ _edge of Africa and the eastern edge of South America; the bulge of Africa_ _and the curve of the eastern coast of North America_ _____

   _____

2. Where are most of the mountains, volcanoes, and earthquake sites in relation to the present continents? Why do you think they are there?
   Most are at the edges of the present continents, near plate boundaries. ____

   _____

3. **Scientists at Work** Scientists **use models**, such as maps, to better understand complex structures and processes. How did your models of Earth's continents

   help you **draw conclusions** about Earth's past? _The continents were once_ _joined and have slowly moved to their present locations._ _____

   What limitations did your models have? _The map doesn't show how the_ _continents moved or how fast they moved._ _____

Investigate Further Hypothesize about the fact that the continents do not fit together exactly. Then **plan and conduct a simple experiment** to test your

hypothesis. _____

_____

_____

_____

_____

Make a Model

Making a model can help you understand an object or a process. You use models to find out about things all the time. When you use a map, you are using a model of a specific geographic area.

Think About Making a Model

In the space below, draw a map that someone could use to get from your house to your school. Show special landmarks, such as large buildings, trees, or other objects, that a person could use as help in following your map.

[blank box]

1. Write a paragraph telling someone how to get from your house to your school.

_____

_____

_____

_____

2. Do you think someone could use your map and get from your house to school without reading the paragraph you wrote? Students could test it by exchanging with other students. The second student could describe how to get from the house to the school.

3. Is your map a good model of the process of getting from your house to school? Why or why not? If it is a good model, you'll need almost no verbal instructions.

4. What could you do to make your map more accurate? Answers will depend on the map drawn but may include: draw it to scale, add color, indicate compass directions, or put in more landmarks.

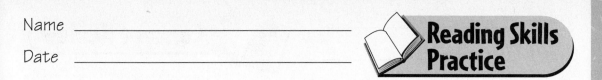
Arrange Events in Sequence

Read the selection. Then write, in correct order, the steps by which we get salt from rocks.

Where Does Salt Come From?

Did you know that some of the salt we eat comes from rocks? Salt may be taken from evaporated sea water, but it also comes from underground deposits called *rock salt*. The source of salt is brine, which is salty water from lakes or seas. The underground salt is what remains of seas that evaporated millions of years ago.

Salt that comes from rocks is mined. To purify it into crystals, it is dissolved in water to form brine. Then the brine is placed in pans to allow the water to evaporate and the salt to crystallize.

Step 1:

Salt is mined from rocks .

_____

_____

Step 2:

The salt is dissolved in water to form brine.

_____

_____

Step 3:

The brine is placed in pans to allow the water to evaporate and the salt

to crystallize.

_____

Name _____

Date _____

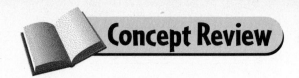

How Has Earth's Surface Changed?

Lesson Concept

Earth's surface features have changed over millions of years.
Fossils help scientists learn about plants and animals of the past.

Vocabulary

continental drift (C22)   **Pangea** (C22)   **fossils** (C23)

Review the concepts in Lesson 3 by answering the following riddles.

1. At my deepest point, I'm a mile-deep slice into Earth's history—and a very
popular tourist attraction. What am I? Grand Canyon

2. There are continents, and then there is . . . SUPERCONTINENT! I don't wear a
cape, but I once included all the land on Earth. What am I?
Pangea

3. We were left behind a long time ago, but today we can tell you a lot about
Earth's history. What are we? fossils

4. In observing rock layers, I am usually found on the bottom. What am I?
the oldest layer

5. Scientists have found fossils on the tops of mountains. What do they infer?
that the area was once covered by water

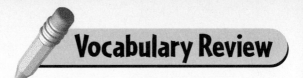
Recognize Vocabulary

Listed below are the vocabulary terms from this chapter. Match the terms in Column A with the definitions in Column B by writing the letter of the correct definition in the space next to the term.

Column A

_____ **1.** landform

_____ **2.** weathering

_____ **3.** erosion

_____ **4.** deposition

_____ **5.** mass movement

_____ **6.** crust

_____ **7.** mantle

_____ **8.** core

_____ **9.** plate

_____ **10.** magma

_____ **11.** volcano

_____ **12.** earthquake

_____ **13.** fault

_____ **14.** continental drift

_____ **15.** Pangea

_____ **16.** fossils

Column B

A the downhill movement of rock and soil because of gravity

B molten rock from Earth's mantle

C Earth's hottest layer; the center layer of Earth

D the process of breaking rock into soil, sand, or other tiny pieces

E a shaking of the ground caused by the sudden release of energy in Earth's crust

F an opening in Earth's crust through which lava flows

G the layer of rock beneath Earth's crust

H the process of dropping, or depositing, sediment in a new location

I the theory of how Earth's continents move over its surface

J the process of moving sediment from one place to another

K According to theory, this was a "supercontinent" that contained all of Earth's land about 225 million years ago.

L a rigid block of crust and upper mantle

M the remains or traces of past life found in Earth's crust

N the outer layer of Earth made of solid rock

O a physical feature of Earth's surface

P a place where pieces of Earth's crust move

Write the History of a River

Informative Writing–Report

Imagine that you are a tour leader at a natural history museum. Choose a river in your area or state, and write a report on the history of that river. Imagine that you will be giving the report to museum visitors as they view a large map of the river. Add details to the topical outline below to help you plan your report. Attach a hand-drawn or photocopied map of the river to your finished report.

Name of the river _____

I. The Course of the River
  A. The source
    1. _____
    2. _____
  B. The mouth
    1. _____
    2. _____

II. The Age of the River
  A. Landforms that identify the river's age
    1. _____
    2. _____
  B. How the river's course has changed over time
    1. _____
    2. _____

III. The River's Impact on the Land
  A. _____
    1. _____
    2. _____
  B. _____
    1. _____
    2. _____

Chapter 2 • Graphic Organizer for Chapter Concepts

Rocks and Minerals

LESSON 1
MINERALS

How They Form

1. in the mantle
2. at or near the surface
3. from mineral-rich water

Mineral Properties

1. streak
2. luster
3. hardness

How They Are Used

1. jewelry
2. coins
3. metal containers
4. plaster
5. construction materials

LESSON 2
ROCKS

Three Types

1. **Name** igneous

   Form when melted rock
   hardens

   Three examples pumice,
   obsidian, granite

2. **Name** sedimentary

   Form when sediments are
   compressed and hardened

   Three examples siltstone,
   conglomerate, limestone

3. **Name** metamorphic

   Form when other rocks are
   changed by heat and pressure

   Three examples schist, gneiss,
   slate

LESSON 3
THE ROCK CYCLE

Definition the process in which
rocks are changed from one form to
another

Processes Involved

1. weathering
2. erosion
3. heat
4. pressure
5. melting
6. compaction
7. cementation

Mineral Properties

Materials

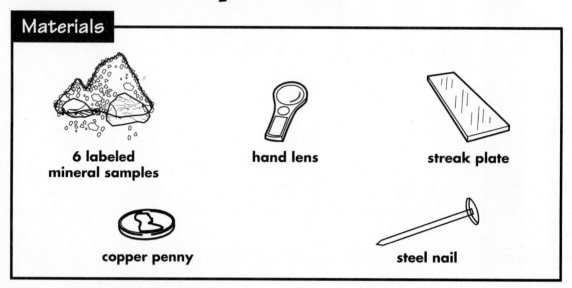

6 labeled mineral samples

hand lens

streak plate

copper penny

steel nail

Activity Procedure

1 Use the chart on the next page.

2 Use the hand lens to **observe** each mineral. Describe the color of each sample. **Record** your observations in the chart.

3 Use each mineral to draw a line across the streak plate. What color is the streak each made? **Record** your observations.

4 **CAUTION** **Use caution with the nail, it is sharp.** Test the hardness of each mineral by using your fingernail, the copper penny, and the steel nail. Try to scratch each mineral with each of these items. Then try to scratch each sample with each of the other minerals. **Record** your observations in the chart.

5 **Classify** the minerals based on each property you tested: color, streak, and hardness. Make labels that list all three properties for each mineral.

Name _____

Mineral Sample	Color of the Mineral Sample	Color of the Mineral's Streak	Things that Scratch the Mineral
A talc	light green, white, or gray	white	penny, fingernail, nail, all other samples
B quartz	clear, milky white, rose, violet, smoky, or gray	none	none of the objects or other mineral samples
C fluorite	usually light purple	white	quartz, feldspar, magnetite, pyrite
D feldspar	white, salmon pink, or clear	white	quartz
E magnetite	usually black	black	quartz
F pyrite	yellow-gold	greenish-black	quartz

Draw Conclusions

1. How are the minerals you tested different from each other?

They vary in color, hardness, and streak.

2. Which of the minerals you tested is the hardest? Explain your choice.

Quartz is the hardest because none of the objects or other minerals listed

can scratch it.

3. Scientists at Work Scientists **classify** things so it is easier to study them. How

do you think scientists classify minerals? Scientists classify minerals

according to their properties. Students may also say that minerals are

classified on the basis of their hardness.

Investigate Further Obtain five other unknown mineral samples. Determine the hardness, color, and streak of each. **Classify** all of the mineral samples after testing

the new samples. _____

_____

Name _____

Date _____

Classify

When you classify things, you put them into groups based on how they are alike. One way to classify minerals is to group them with other minerals that have similar properties, such as color.

Think About Classifying

After Ling had finished doing a streak test for several minerals, his teacher gave him a chart that listed different properties of other minerals. He compared each mineral and saw that some of them had similar properties. He also noticed that some of the minerals did not have similar properties.

Name of the Mineral	How Common the Mineral Is	How Hard the Mineral Is
Silver	Very rare	Fairly soft
Borax	Rare	Soft
Quartz	Very common	Hard
Diamond	Very rare	Extremely hard
Sulfur	Rare	Soft
Galena	Very common	Soft
Salt (halite)	Very common	Soft
Turquoise	Rare	Very hard

1. How could Ling classify the minerals in the chart? He could classify them by commonness or hardness.

2. Ling has a piece of turquoise. Which of these minerals would scratch the turquoise? Which minerals could the turquoise scratch? Explain.
   The diamond would scratch the turquoise, because diamond is harder than turquoise. The turquoise could scratch all the minerals except the diamond, because all the other minerals are softer than turquoise.

3. If you had to choose some of these minerals to sell to a rock shop, which ones would you choose and why? Accept reasonable answers. Students may pick the rarer minerals, because they are more valuable. Students may pick common minerals, because they are easier to find.

Use Reference Sources

Use a dictionary to look up the origins of the words *sedimentary*, *igneous*, and *metamorphic*. The origin is noted in brackets before the definition. Then find how the words describe the three types of rock formations. Be careful—*sedimentary*, *igneous*, and *metamorphic* are adjectives. You will need to refer to the noun or verb entry, which is where you will find the word's origin. Note the noun or verb form with the origin.

Sedimentary rock is formed from plant, mineral, and animal matter that settles out of water. Shale, made of compressed mud, and limestone are the most common types of sedimentary rock.

Noun or Verb and Word Origin:

Noun is *sediment*; origin is *sedēre* – "to sit, sink down."

Origin relates to *sedimentary rock*: The origin of the word is "to sit or sink," and sedimentary rock is formed from deposits of minerals that sit or sink and become compressed.

Igneous rock is formed from volcanic activity either near Earth's surface or deep below, crystallizing magma into rocks such as granite.

Noun or Verb and Word Origin:

Verb is *ignite*; origin is *ignis* – "fire."

Origin relates to *igneous rock*: The origin of the word is "fire," and igneous rock is formed from volcanic activity that makes magma, which then solidifies into rock.

Metamorphic rock is rock that is changed by chemical or physical means, such as heat or pressure. Marble is metamorphic rock that was once limestone.

Noun or Verb and Word Origin:

Noun is *metamorphosis*; origin is *metamorphosis* – "to transform."

Origin relates to *metamorphic rock*: The origin is "transform," and metamorphic rock is rock that has been transformed by heat or pressure.

What Are Minerals?

Lesson Concept

Minerals are Earth's materials that have never been alive. They may be formed in the mantle or the crust.

Vocabulary

mineral (C36)   **streak** (C37)   **luster** (C37)   **hardness** (C37)

Answer the questions about minerals below.

1. Where and how do minerals form? Give three different examples.

Accept reasonable answers. Possible answers: Some minerals such as diamonds form in Earth's mantle; other minerals such as calcite form at or near Earth's surface; and some such as galena form in hot, mineral-rich water below Earth's surface.

2. Define three different properties of minerals, and give examples of each one.

Streak is the color of the powder left behind when you rub a mineral against a white tile. Accept all reasonable examples. Luster is the way the surface of a mineral reflects light. Metals have a metallic luster; diamonds have a brilliant luster. Hardness is the ability of a mineral to resist scratching. Accept all answers from the investigation or from the Mohs scale.

3. In the space below, draw a picture of the kitchen in your home. Point out four different uses of minerals there.

Drawings could include copper in electric wires or pans, gypsum in plasterboard, salt in food, aluminum in foil, and iron in steel cookware.

Name _____

Date _____

Identifying Rocks

Materials

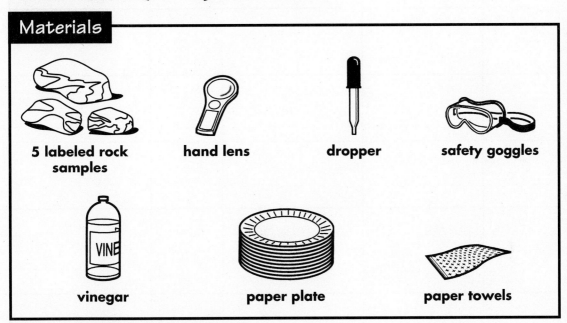

5 labeled rock samples   hand lens   dropper   safety goggles

vinegar   paper plate   paper towels

Activity Procedure

1 Use the chart on the next page.

2 Use the hand lens to **observe** each rock. What color or colors is each rock? **Record** your observations in your chart.

3 Can you see any grains, or small pieces, making up the rock? Are the grains very small, or are they large? Are they rounded, or do they have sharp edges? Do the grains fit together like puzzle pieces? Or are they just next to one another? **Record** your observations under *Texture* in your chart. Draw a picture of each rock in the *Picture* column.

4 **CAUTION** **Put on your safety goggles.** Vinegar bubbles when it is dropped on the mineral calcite. Put the rock samples on the paper plate. Use the dropper to put a few drops of vinegar on each rock. **Observe** what happens. **Record** your findings.

5 **Classify** your rocks into two groups based on how the rocks are alike.

Name _____

Rock Sample	Color	Texture	Picture	Bubbles When Vinegar Added
1 sandstone	brown, reddish, or gray, depending on sand color	may have round or jagged grains stuck together		probably not
2 limestone	usually white or gray, may be colored	may have small rounded or jagged grains		yes
3 conglomerate	usually brown with pebbles of many colors	large pebbles stuck together		probably not
4 granite	usually light rocks with pink, white, and black mineral crystals showing	medium to large grains of different-colored minerals		no
5 gneiss	usually a dark rock with lighter bands	medium to large grains of different-colored minerals		no

Draw Conclusions

1. What properties did you use to **classify** your rocks? Possible answers: color, texture, or whether calcite is present

2. How does your classification system **compare** with those of two other students? Classification systems will likely be similar, although students may differ on the defining characteristic chosen.

3. **Scientists at Work** One way scientists **classify** rocks is by how they formed. Choose one rock and **hypothesize** how you think it might have formed. Accept reasonable answers.

Investigate Further Plan and conduct a simple experiment to test this **hypothesis:** Color is one of the best properties to use to identify rocks.

_____

_____

Name _____

Date _____

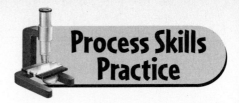

Classify

When you classify rocks, you put them into groups based on how the rocks are alike.

Think About Classifying

Malcom's teacher gave him a picture of four rocks, like the ones shown below. Malcom classified the rocks based on what they look like. Then he made a chart showing his classification.

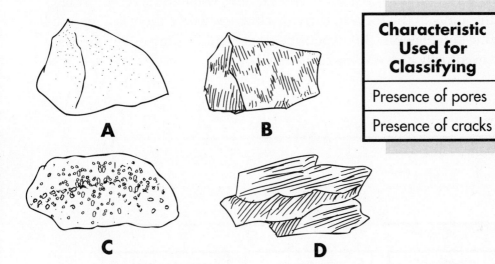

Characteristic Used for Classifying	Rocks in the Group
Presence of pores	A and C
Presence of cracks	B and D

1. Malcom based his classification on the types of breaks in the rocks. What other features could he use to classify these rocks? Accept reasonable answers. Possible answer: Rocks could be classified by bright or dark colors.

2. What tests could he do to help classify the rocks? Accept reasonable answers. Possible answers include testing streak or hardness, or dropping vinegar on each rock.

3. Gabbro is a kind of rock made up of a few light-colored minerals sprinkled in with mostly dark-colored minerals. Basalt is a kind of rock made up of tiny pieces of these same types of minerals. Which rocks in the picture would you classify as gabbro? Which would you classify as basalt? Explain your reasoning for each decision. Rock C is most likely gabbro because it has large pieces of minerals in it. Rock B is basalt because it has small bits of minerals mixed with a few light flecks.

Use with page C41.

Summarize a Selection

Read the selection below. Then supply the main idea and summarize the supporting details.

Frosty Break-Ups

Weathering breaks the rocks on Earth's surface into smaller pieces. One of the processes that breaks up rocks is called *frost wedging*. Frost wedging is a mechanical process, meaning that it involves a physical, not a chemical, change. Rainwater seeps into the cracks in rocks and expands when it freezes, putting pressure on the joints in the rock. In extreme climates, where there is a repeated cycle of freezing and thawing, this expansion puts extreme pressure on the rock joints, which eventually give way and split apart.

Main Idea: Frost wedging is a weathering process that breaks apart rocks.

Supporting Detail:

Frost wedging is a mechanical process.

Supporting Detail:

Rainwater seeps into the cracks in rocks and expands when it freezes.

Supporting Detail:

After repeated freezing and thawing, the rocks split apart because of extreme pressure on the rock joints.

Name _____

Date _____

What Are Rocks?

Lesson Concept

Rocks are made up of one or more minerals. They are classified as igneous, sedimentary, or metamorphic.

Vocabulary

rock (C42)	**igneous rock** (C42)
sedimentary rock (C44)	**metamorphic rock** (C46)

Fill in the missing parts of the chart. Some blanks will need more than one word.

Type of Rock	How Rock Forms	Examples
Igneous rock	From melted rock that hardens	Basalt_____: made of feldspar and pyroxene in hardening lava.
		Granite_____: made of feldspar, quartz, and mica in cooling magma_____.
Sedimentary rock	From pieces of rock that are squeezed or stuck together	Conglomerate: made of _____ pieces of rock _____ as big as boulders _____ or as small as peas.
		Limestone_____: made of calcite, sometimes from seashells.
		Shale: Made of sediments that are very small _____.
Metamorphic rock	From rock that has undergone great heat and pressure	Marble: Formed from limestone _____ that was squeezed and heated.
		Slate_____: Formed from shale exposed to great pressure.

Use with page C47.

The Rock Cycle

Materials

3 pieces of modeling clay, each a different color

small objects—pieces of aquarium gravel, fake jewels, and a few pennies

2 aluminum pie pans

Activity Procedure

1 The small objects stand for minerals. Press the "minerals" into the three pieces of clay. Each color of clay with its objects stands for a different igneous rock.

2 Now suppose that wind and water are weathering and eroding the "rocks." To **model** this process, break one rock into pieces (sediments) and drop the pieces into one of the pie pans (a lake).

3 Drop pieces from the second rock on top of the first rock layer. Then drop pieces of the third rock on top of the second layer. Press the layers together by using the bottom of the empty pie pan. What kind of rock have you made?

4 Squeeze the "sedimentary rock" between your hands to warm it up. What causes the rock to change? Which kind of rock is it now?

Investigate Log

Draw Conclusions

1. How did the igneous "rocks" change in this investigation ? They underwent
"weathering" and "erosion" to change from igneous to sedimentary rocks.
Then they were changed into metamorphic rocks by heat and pressure.

_____

_____

2. What might weathering and erosion do to a metamorphic rock?
Pieces of it might be deposited and form a sedimentary rock.

_____

_____

3. **Scientists at Work** Scientists often **make a model** to help them understand
processes that occur in nature. What process did your hands represent in
Step 4 of the activity? the pressure and sticking together that occur as
sediment layers build up on a lake bottom

_____

_____

Investigate Further Plan and conduct a simple experiment to test this
hypothesis: Any type of rock can be changed into any other type of rock by
natural processes within the Earth.

_____

_____

_____

_____

Process Skills Practice

Make a Model

Making a model can help you understand processes that are hard to observe because they occur over a very long time in nature.

Think About Making a Model

Gabe read about sedimentary rocks forming from pieces of rock dropped by moving water. He read that small sediments are carried farther and are dropped later than larger sediments are. He made a model to try to see how this worked.

Gabe put small pebbles, coarse sand, and mud in a large jar and filled the jar with water. He shook the jar for several minutes, until the water was cloudy and gray. Then he set the jar on a table. He started observing the jar ten minutes later and continued making observations every five minutes for the next twenty-five minutes.

Number of Minutes	Height of the Sediment	Observations
10	4 centimeters	The water is very cloudy, and pebbles have all settled to the bottom of the jar.
15	5 centimeters	The sediment layer is still cloudy.
20	7 centimeters	The sand is beginning to settle on the bottom of the jar.
25	10 centimeters	The sand has settled some more, but the clay particles are still floating in the water.

1. Based on what he had read, what do you think Gabe expected would happen with his model? He probably expected to see the pebbles settle out first, then the sand, and then the silt and clay from the mud.

2. Did Gabe's model show what he was interested in learning about? Explain. Accept reasonable answers. Possible answer: Yes, because the pebbles settled first, the sand was settling, and the silt had not yet begun to settle.

3 How is Gabe's model not like a river? It is not like a river in that water is allowed to settle and does not flow continually, as a river does.

Name _____

Date _____

Use Prefixes and Suffixes to Determine Word Meanings

Read the sentences below. Then fill in the chart with each word's meaning based on its context in the sentence. The meanings of the prefixes c*om*– and *con*– are *with*, *together*, and *jointly*.

Matter from plants, animals, and minerals becomes *compacted* during the formation of sedimentary rocks.

A *conglomerate* is a sedimentary rock that contains round bits of rocks and minerals.

The compacted material in sedimentary rock eventually becomes *condensed*.

Metamorphic rock can change forms repeatedly, but it must melt *completely* to become igneous rock.

Word	Meaning
compact	tightly joined
conglomerate	made with many parts
condense	with denseness
complete	with totality

What Is the Rock Cycle?

Lesson Concept

Rocks change from one kind to another in the rock cycle.

Vocabulary

rock cycle (C52)

**Complete the captions for each of the pictures below
to describe parts of the rock cycle.**

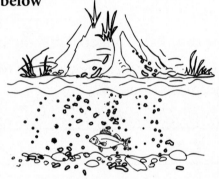

1. Heat and pressure change

sedimentary rock to

metamorphic rock.

2. Igneous rock is eroded and

deposited at the bottom of

the river, eventually forming

sedimentary rock.

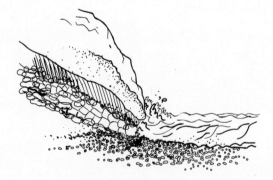

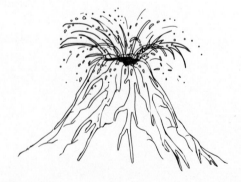

3. _Lava_ cools and hardens as it flows

into the ocean. The new _igneous_

rock is weathered and eroded by

waves.

4. Completely melted rock erupts

from a volcano and hardens to

form _igneous_ rock.

Use with page C53.

Recognize Vocabulary

Write the letter of the best answer on the line.

mineral	streak	hardness
luster	rock	sedimentary rock
igneous rock	metamorphic rock	rock cycle

___E___ **1.** a solid material, formed in nature, with particles arranged in a repeated pattern

___F___ **2.** a material made up of one or more minerals

___C___ **3.** the way the surface of a mineral reflects light

___B___ **4.** rocks that form when melted rock hardens

___I___ **5.** the color of powder left behind when you rub a mineral against a white tile

___D___ **6.** rocks that have been changed by high heat or very high pressure

___G___ **7.** the changes rocks go through as they change back and forth from igneous to sedimentary to metamorphic rock

___H___ **8.** rocks that form when layers of rock particles are squeezed or stuck together

___A___ **9.** a mineral's ability to resist being scratched

A hardness

B igneous rocks

C luster

D metamorphic rocks

E mineral

F rock

G rock cycle

H sedimentary rocks

I streak

Name _____

Date _____

Write About Earthquakes

Informative Writing–Explanation

Write and illustrate a booklet for children living in places where earthquakes are common. Explain what causes earthquakes. Give advice about how to stay safe during an earthquake. Make notes and sketches in the bookmap below to help you plan your booklet.

Cover	Title Page		
	1	2	3
4	5	6	7
8	9	10	11
12	13	14	15

Use with pages C58–C59.

Chapter 3 • Graphic Organizer for Chapter Concepts

Weather and Climate

LESSON 1
WEATHER FACTORS

Atmosphere

1. troposphere _____
2. stratosphere _____

Air Pressure

1. low pressure—warmer air _____
2. high pressure—cooler air _____

Humidity

Precipitation

Water Cycle

evaporation ↑
condensation ↓

Clouds

1. cirrus _____
2. cumulus _____
3. stratus _____
4. cumulonimbus _____

LESSON 2
WIND CAUSES

The Sun's Uneven Heating
of Earth causes

1. some energy to be absorbed by _____
   the atmosphere

2. some energy to be reflected _____
   back by Earth

3. some energy to be absorbed by _____
   Earth

Types of Winds

1. local winds _____
2. prevailing winds _____

Types of Fronts

1. cold front _____
2. warm front _____

LESSON 3
CLIMATE

Average of All Weather Over Time

Climate Zones

1. polar _____
2. tropical _____
3. temperate _____
4. mountain _____
5. desert _____

Climate Changes

1. El Niño _____
2. greenhouse effect _____
3. global warming _____

Measuring Weather Conditions

Materials

weather station

Activity Procedure

1 Use the Weather Station Daily Record chart below to **record** the date, the time, the temperature, the amount of rain or snow, the wind direction and speed, and the cloud conditions each day for five days. Try to **record** the weather conditions at the same time each day.

2 Place the weather station in a shady spot, 1 m above the ground. **Record** the temperature.

3 Be sure the rain gauge will not collect runoff from any buildings or trees. **Record** the amount of rain or snow (if any).

4 Be sure the wind vane is located where wind from any direction will reach it. **Record** the wind direction and speed. Winds are labeled with the direction from which they blow.

Weather Station Daily Record					
Date					
Time					
Temperature					
Rainfall or snowfall					
Wind direction and speed					
Cloud condition					

5 Describe and **record** the cloud conditions by noting how much of the sky is covered by clouds. Draw a circle and shade in the part of the circle that equals the amount of sky covered with clouds.

6 Use the temperature data to make a line graph showing how the temperature changes from day to day.

Draw Conclusions

1. Use your Weather Station Daily Record to **compare** the weather conditions on two different days. Which conditions were about the same? Which conditions changed the most? Students might note differences in temperature, amount of rain or snow, wind direction and speed, and cloud conditions.

_____

_____

2. From the **data** you **gathered** in this activity, how might scientists use weather data to **predict** the weather? Possible answer: Scientists might look for trends in weather conditions and use the data to predict the weather.

_____

_____

3. **Scientists at Work** Scientists learn about the weather by **measuring** weather conditions and **gathering data**. What did you learn by measuring the amount of rain your area received during the week of your observations? Students should realize that the total amount of rain an area receives may come from only one or two storms.

_____

Investigate Further Find a newspaper weather page, and note the temperatures in various cities throughout the United States. **Hypothesize** why there are different temperatures in different cities. **Plan and conduct a simple investigation** to find out.

_____

_____

_____

_____

Name _____

Date _____

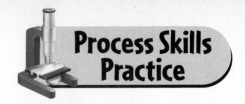

Measure and Collect Data

Measurements are a kind of observation. You measure when you use a tool, such as a thermometer, a clock, or a ruler.

Think About Measuring and Collecting Data

When you measure, you are actually comparing. For example, if you measure a rope and find that the rope is 1.5 m long, you are comparing the length of the rope to a standard length. The standard is, in this case, the meter. If you weigh the rope and find that it weighs 20 newtons, you are comparing the rope to a standard weight, the newton. Of course, it's important to use the right measuring unit, too. For example, you wouldn't measure a 5-m rope in kilometers. You would use meters. Think about setting a new standard for measuring lengths as shown below.

thumb   span   cubit

pace

1. Which of these units would you use to measure the length of a swimming pool?
the cubit or pace
_____

2. Which would you use to measure your height? the span or possibly the cubit
_____

3. How many spans equal a cubit? Answers will depend on the size of each
student's hands and arms, but it should be about two or three.

4. Why do you think no one uses a measuring system like this one?
It's not standard. Hand and arm sizes differ from person to person, so no one
would know exactly how much you were talking about. You wouldn't be able to
make a reliable comparison.

5. How could you make this measuring system work as a standard?
Choose one person, and use his or her arm, hand, thumb, and pace as
the standard.

Summarize and Paraphrase a Selection

Read the selection. Paraphrase the information in the chart, listing facts about clouds. Then use the information to write a summary.

Clouds

Clouds can be categorized in several ways. One way is by appearance. Another way is by how they are formed. When clouds are categorized by appearance, they can be grouped into three main types: *high clouds*, *middle clouds*, and *low clouds*. These types are classified by altitude. Clouds that are categorized by formations are divided into four main groups. There are two types of *layer clouds*: those formed by regularly rising air and those formed by turbulent air. *Cumuliform clouds* are formed by a process called *penetrative convection*, during which air currents heat and rise or cool and sink. *Orographic clouds* are formed by air rising over mountainous or hilly areas.

Facts About Clouds
There is more than one way to categorize clouds.
Clouds can be categorized by appearance or by how they are formed.
The three types of clouds categorized by appearance are grouped by altitude.
These clouds are called high clouds, middle clouds, and low clouds.
There are four types of clouds that are categorized by formation.
Clouds categorized by formation are layer clouds (2 kinds), cumuliform clouds, and orographic clouds.

Clouds can be categorized by appearance or formation. Three types of clouds are categorized by appearance, and they are grouped by altitude. Four types of clouds are categorized by formation, based on the air currents that created them.

Name _____

Date _____

How Can You Observe and Measure Weather Conditions?

Lesson Concept

Weather conditions such as temperature, air pressure, humidity, wind speed and direction, and precipitation can be observed and measured.

Vocabulary

atmosphere (C64)   **air pressure** (C65)   **humidity** (C65)

precipitation (C65)   **evaporation** (C67)   **condensation** (C67)

Answer each question with one or more complete sentences.

1. Where in the atmosphere does most weather occur? Most weather occurs in the troposphere.

2. Why does most weather occur only in one layer of the atmosphere? Most of the water in the atmosphere is in the troposphere. Therefore, that is where the clouds form and weather occurs. Also, there is not enough air above the troposphere.

3. What is the largest source of water for the water cycle? The ocean is the largest source of water for the water cycle.

4. Fog is actually a cloud that is low enough to touch the ground. What kind of cloud is fog? Fog is made of stratus clouds that are near the ground.

5. What are you measuring when you measure air pressure? You are measuring the weight of the atmosphere.

6. Why do people measure atmospheric conditions? When they measure atmospheric conditions, they can predict what the weather will be.

7. If you see cumulus clouds in the sky, what type of weather are you likely to have? Cumulus clouds usually mean fair weather, but they can also produce light rain or snow.

Use with page C69.

The Sun's Energy Heats Unevenly

Materials

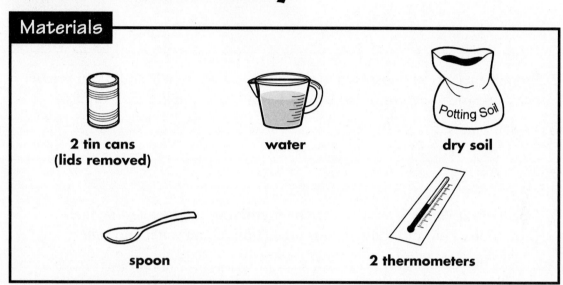

2 tin cans (lids removed)

water

dry soil

spoon

2 thermometers

Activity Procedure

1 Fill one can about $\frac{3}{4}$ full of water and the other can about $\frac{3}{4}$ full of soil.

2 Place one thermometer in the can of water and the other in the can of soil. Put the cans in a shady place outside. Wait for 10 minutes, and then **record** the temperatures of the water and the soil.

3 Put both cans in sunlight. **Predict** which of the cans will show the faster rise in temperature. **Record** the temperature of each can every 10 minutes for 30 minutes. In which can does the temperature rise faster? Which material— soil or water—heats up faster?

4 Now put the cans back in the shade. **Predict** in which of the cans the temperature will drop faster. Again **record** the temperature of each can every 10 minutes for 30 minutes. In which can does the temperature drop faster? Which material—soil or water—cools off faster?

5 Make line graphs to show how the temperatures of both materials changed as they heated up and cooled off.

Draw Conclusions

1. How did your results match your predictions? Which material—water or soil—heated up faster? Which cooled off faster? Predictions will vary, but results should show that the can of soil heated up faster and cooled off faster than the can of water.

_____

2. From the results you **observed** in this investigation, which would you **predict** heats up faster—oceans or land? Which would you predict cools off faster? Explain. Based on the results students should predict that land heats up faster and cools off faster than oceans.

_____

3. **Scientists at Work** Scientists learn by **predicting** and then testing their predictions. How did you test your predictions about water and soil? The predictions were tested by measuring the temperatures of water and soil as they heated up and cooled off.

_____

Investigate Further Hypothesize how fast materials, such as moist soil, sand, and salt water, heat up and cool off. **Plan and conduct a simple experiment** to test your hypothsis. _____

_____

_____

_____

_____

Name _____

Date _____

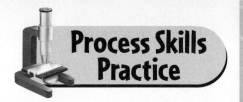

Predict

When you predict, you make a statement about what you think will happen. To make a prediction, you think about what you've observed before. You also think about how to interpret data you have.

Think About Predicting

Robert wanted to see if he could predict the weather if he knew which way the wind was blowing and whether the barometer was rising or falling. He decided to find out. All through the winter, he kept records of wind direction, air pressure, and the weather that followed his observations. Then he made this chart.

Wind Direction (From)	Barometer	Weather
varies	neither rising nor falling	pleasant weather, no changes in temperature
south, changing to southeast	falling	wind picks up, rain after a few hours
southeast, changing to northeast	falling	windy and colder
east, changing to northeast	falling slowly	rain the next day
east, changing to northeast	falling rapidly	wind increases, and it snows
south, changing to southwest	rising slowly	the skies clear, and the sun comes out
southwest, changing to west	rising rapidly	the skies clear, and it gets really cold

1. Using Robert's chart, what kind of weather would you predict if the wind is from the southwest and the barometer is neither rising nor falling?

   pleasant weather, no temperature change

2. Using Robert's chart, what kind of weather would you predict if the barometer is rising and the wind direction has changed from the south to the southwest?

   clearing and sunny

3. The wind direction has changed from the east to the northeast, and the barometer is falling fast. Using Robert's chart, what kind of weather would you predict?

   wind and snow

Use with page C71.

Name _____

Date _____

Identify Supporting Facts and Details

Read the selection. Then complete the chart below.

Santa Ana Winds

    Santa Ana winds are well known to the people of southern California. The winds are known not for their cooling breezes but for their destructive capabilities. Named after the Santa Ana Mountains of Southern California, the Santa Ana winds are common during autumn. These winds are formed when air moves across the Mojave Desert and then over and through the San Gabriel, San Bernadino, and San Jacinto Mountains. The air that comes down the mountains is extremely warm and dry and can easily spread small fires begun by careless campers or set on purpose. Often everything in the path of the fires is destroyed, including homes and businesses. The winds are so strong and the air is so dry that the fires can destroy many acres of vegetation and homes before firefighters have a chance to stop them.

Main Idea	Santa Ana winds are known for their destructive capabilities.
Supporting Details	The air coming down the mountains is extremely warm and dry. A careless camper can start a fire in the area. The Santa Ana winds can whip a small fire into a huge blaze within minutes.

What Causes Weather?

Lesson Concept

Changes in air pressure, caused by uneven heating of Earth's surface and the air above it, cause the wind to blow. There are local winds and prevailing winds.

Vocabulary

local winds (C73)	**prevailing winds** (C73)
air mass (C75)	**front** (C76)

You know that within an air mass, weather conditions like temperature, humidity, and air pressure are similar. The interaction of air masses produces weather systems. A weather system can be a storm, very cold air, or pleasant, sunny weather. Weather systems are moved by prevailing winds from west to east across the United States.

1. Suppose weather conditions in your area are hot and dry. Do you think local winds are blowing toward the center of the hot area or away from it? Explain. _Local winds are probably blowing toward the center of the hot area. As the hot air rises, it forms an area of low pressure. Air moves from areas of higher pressure to lower pressure._

2. In which general direction is the air mass in Question 1 most likely to move? Why? _It will most likely move from west to east because of the prevailing winds._

3. Suppose it is raining today in Ohio and Michigan. What kind of weather would you expect to find in New York state tomorrow? _rain_

4. What causes prevailing winds? _uneven heating of large parts of the atmosphere and the rotation of Earth_

Local Weather Conditions

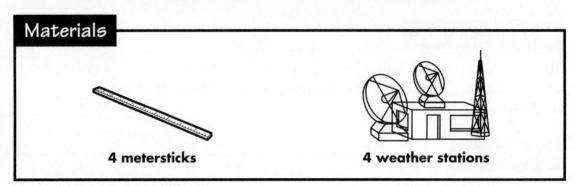

4 metersticks　　　　　　　　**4 weather stations**

Activity Procedure

1 Use the table below.

Local Weather Conditions

Location	Temperature	Wind Direction	Wind Speed
1			
2			
3			
4			

2 Choose four locations near your school to study. Select different kinds of locations, such as a shady parkway, a sunny playground, a parking lot on the south side of your school, and a ball field on the north side. For the same time on any given day, **predict** whether the temperature, wind direction, and wind speed will be the same or different at the different locations.

3 At the chosen time, four people should each take a meterstick and a weather station to a different one of the selected locations. Use the meterstick to locate a point 1 m above the ground. **Measure** and **record** the temperature at that point. Use the weather station to determine the wind direction and speed, too. Record the data in your table.

4 Make a double-bar graph to show the temperatures and wind speeds recorded at all the locations. Write the wind direction at each location on the appropriate wind-speed bar.

Name _____

Draw Conclusions

1. Use your table to **compare** the temperature, wind direction, and wind speed at the different locations. What differences, if any, did you find? What conditions were the same? _Answers may vary. Students should note differences in temperature, wind direction, and wind speed for some of the locations._

_____

_____

2. Local weather conditions affect the organisms that live in a location. Do you think wind speed or temperature is more likely to affect living organisms? Explain. _Answers may vary. Temperature will have a more direct effect, but wind speed could also affect how hot or cold an area is._

_____

_____

3. Based on your investigation, how would you define the phrase *local weather conditions*? _Possible answer: "weather conditions in a small area"_

_____

_____

_____

4. Scientists at Work Scientists learn about local weather conditions by **comparing** weather data from different locations. **Draw conclusions** about local weather conditions, based on the locations you studied.

Students should realize that many different local weather conditions can exist in a small area.

_____

_____

Investigate Further What other factors, in addition to temperature, wind direction, and wind speed might affect local weather conditions? **Hypothesize** about a factor that might affect local weather conditions. Then **plan and conduct a simple experiment** to test your hypothesis. _____

_____

_____

_____

_____

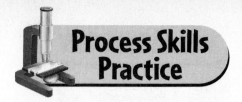

Process Skills Practice

Compare and Draw Conclusions

When you compare objects or events, you look for what they have in common. You also look for differences between them.

Think About Comparing and Drawing Conclusions

Earth's climates can be grouped into five major climate zones. In this activity you can compare three of those climate zones. Use the map and the descriptions of three world climates to answer the questions below.

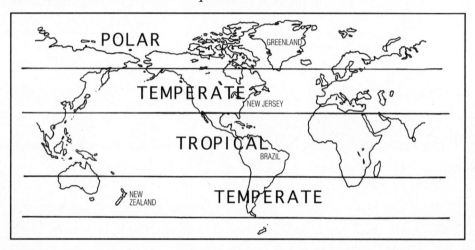

Polar climates are the world's coldest. Winter temperatures fall below $-50°C$.

Temperate climates have four seasons a year, with a warm or hot summer and a cool or dry winter. Average daily temperatures range between $-3°C$ in the winter and $18°C$ in the summer. These areas have an average amount of precipitation.

Tropical climates are found in most of Earth's rain forests and savannas. These areas have an average daily temperature of $27°C$ and high rainfall.

1. Do you think the climate of Brazil is similar to or different from that of Greenland? Explain. _Brazil and Greenland have very different climates._
Greenland is in a polar zone; Brazil is in a tropical zone.

2. Do you think the climate in New Zealand would be very different from the climate in New Jersey? _Probably not; both are in temperate zones and are_
about the same distance from the equator; therefore, they have similar
climates.

Draw Logical Conclusions

Read the selections below. Then answer the questions, using the information provided to draw logical conclusions.

New Shoes

Ryan's family lives in southern Georgia, where the weather is warm enough in winter that there is rarely any snow. In November, Ryan's mother tells him it is time to go shopping for new shoes. The store they go to sells sports shoes and warm boots. Which type of shoes would Ryan be more likely to buy, and why?

Ryan would be more likely to buy sports shoes. Since there is rarely snow in

southern Georgia, he would have little use for warm boots.

How Does Your Garden Grow?

Petra and her family live in the northwestern part of the United States. The weather there is often rainy. Petra decides that she is going to plant a garden. When she goes to the store to buy seeds, she sees that some seeds are better suited for growing in dry climates and some seeds are better suited for growing in wet climates. Which seeds do you think Petra would buy, and why?

Petra would be more likely to buy the seeds that grow better in wet climates

because her area receives a large amount of rain.

_____

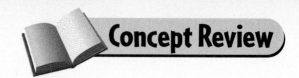

What Is Climate and How Does It Change?

Lesson Concept

Climate is the average of all weather conditions through all seasons over a period of time. Earth's climate has changed over time as average temperatures have risen and fallen. Human activities can affect climate.

Vocabulary

climate (C80)	**microclimate** (C80)	**El Niño** (C83)
greenhouse effect (C84)	**global warming** (C84)	

Fill in the chart with information from your textbook and answer the questions.

Climate Zones	Summer Temp.	Winter Temp.	Precipitation	Where Found?
Polar	cool	cold	snow	near North and South Poles
Mountain	cool	cold	snow	on top of high mountains
Temperate	warm to hot	cool to cold	average	most land between tropical and polar regions
Tropical	hot	hot	heavy rain	most land around the equator

1. Which climate zones are coldest? _polar and mountain_____

2. Which climate zone is wettest? _tropical_____

3. Which climate zone shows the most variation over a year? _temperate_____

4. How did putting information in a chart help you compare the climate zones?
   Possible answers include that it made it easier to see differences.

Recognize Vocabulary

Listed below are scrambled vocabulary terms. Use the clues to unscramble them. Write the unscrambled terms on the lines provided.

1. D S L O W N L C I A
(2 words)

_____ local winds _____

horizontal movement of air resulting from local changes in temperature

2. N N O L E I
(2 words)

_____ El Niño _____

short-term change in climate occurring around the Pacific Ocean every two to ten years

3. S T R P O E M H A E

_____ atmosphere _____

blanket of air surrounding Earth

4. O I R L C E I M M A T C

_____ microclimate _____

the climate of a very small area

5. A E M T C L I

_____ climate _____

the average of all weather conditions through all seasons over a period of time

6. P C E I I O N P T A T R I

_____ precipitation _____

rain or snow

7. I I P N S V A G L N W I R E D
(2 words)

_____ prevailing winds _____

global winds that blow constantly from the same direction and cover a large part of Earth's surface

8. B G L W A L M O G I R N A
(2 words)

_____ global warming _____

an abnormally rapid rise in Earth's average temperature caused by excess carbon dioxide in the atmosphere

9. A S R R E R I S U P E
(2 words)

_____ air pressure _____

the weight of air

10. Y H M I I U T D

_____ humidity _____

water or moisture in the air

Name _____

Date _____

Write a Diamante About Climate

Expressive–Poem

Choose a climate zone that is different from the climate zone where you live. Write a diamante poem about that climate zone. In your poem, include details about the kinds of vegetation and weather you can find in the climate zone. Use the idea web and the diamante format below to help you plan your poem.

Word Web

> **Climate Zone**
>
> _____

> **vegetation**   **weather**

Diamante Format

_____

_____

_____

_____

_____

Chapter 4 • Graphic Organizer for Chapter Concepts

Exploring the Oceans

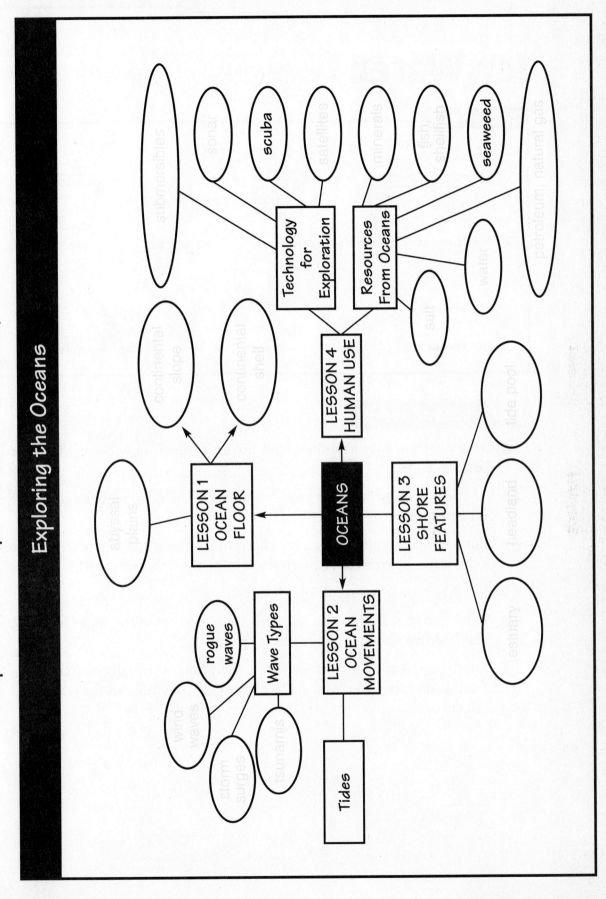

Icy Water

Materials

2 plastic measuring cups   **marker**   **ice cubes**   **water**

spoon   **salt**   **thermometer**

Activity Procedure

1 Make a copy of the chart shown on the next page. You will use it to **record data** you collect.

2 Use the marker to label the cups A and B. Fill each cup with ice cubes. Then add equal amounts of water to each cup.

3 Wait 5 minutes, and then use the thermometer to measure the temperature of the water in each cup. Record these temperatures in a chart.

4 Stir two heaping spoonfuls of salt into cup B.

5 Wait 2 minutes, and then measure the temperature of the water in each cup again. Record these temperatures in the chart.

6 Repeat Steps 4 and 5 two more times. Each time, stir to dissolve the salt in cup B, and then measure and record the temperature of the water in each cup.

Name _____

Date _____

Investigate Log

Water Temperature			
Cup A		**Cup B**	
Spoonsful of Salt	**Temperature**	**Spoonsful of Salt**	**Temperature**
0		0	
0		2	
0		4	
0		6	

Draw Conclusions

1 **Compare** the final temperatures of the two cups of water. What happened to the temperature of the salt water as more salt was added to cup B? The more salt that was added to Cup B, the lower the water temperature became.

2 Based on your results, **predict** the temperature at which the water in cup B will freeze. Possible response: The higher the salinity, the lower the freezing point of the water.

3 **Scientists at Work** Scientists record the temperature and measure the salinity of ocean water in the North Atlantic and Arctic Oceans. The Arctic Ocean tends to be less salty, on average, than the Atlantic Ocean. Scientists use this information to predict when winter temperatures will cause certain harbors and ports to freeze. Explain why cold winter temperatures will affect the formation of harbor ice differently in the two oceans. If temperatures are the same in both oceans, ice will form in the Arctic before it forms in the Atlantic because of the Arctic's lower salinity.

4 **Investigate Further** **Hypothesize** how the amount of salt in water affects the temperature at which the water will freeze. Then **plan and conduct a simple experiment** using varying amounts of salt dissolved in water to test your hypothesis. Remind students to write their hypotheses as *if . . . then* statements and to analyze their hypotheses based on the scientific evidence they obtain while they carry out the activity. Be sure students identify both the control and the variables in their investigations.

Name _____

Date _____

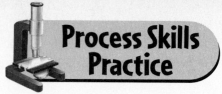

Process Skills Practice

Compare

Comparing involves identifying similar and different characteristics of objects or events. After you compare data, you can **predict** what might happen in similar situations. Study the chart below to answer the questions.

Variations of Surface Salinity with Latitude

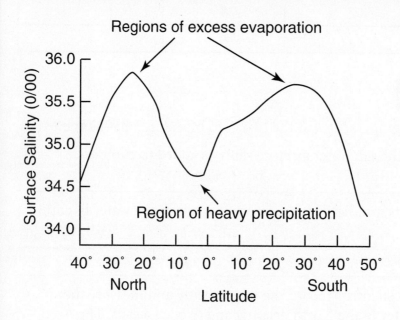

1. In what latitudes of Earth is evaporation the greatest? in the region of 20°N and 30°N and between 20°S and 40°S.

2. How would evaporation affect the salinity of the ocean? In the areas where there is greater evaporation, the salinity would be higher than in areas where there is not as much evaporation.

3. Where is the area of heaviest precipitation? 0°–10°N

4. What could you **predict** about the salinity of the ocean in areas of heavy precipitation? I predict that in areas with heavy precipitation the salinity of the ocean water will be lower.

Use with page C95.

Use Prefixes and Suffixes to Determine Word Meaning

The suffixes *-est* and *-er* are used to show comparison. The suffix *-er* is used to compare two things or two groups. The suffix *-est* is used to compare three or more things or groups. Read the selection. Then list words that contain the suffixes *-est* and *-er*. Determine what is meant by the word and its suffix.

The World's Oceans and Seas

Oceans are vast bodies of water that usually separate continents. The Pacific Ocean, which is the largest and deepest, lies between America and Asia and covers more than one-third of the globe. The others, in descending order of size, are the Atlantic, Indian, and Arctic Oceans. The Arctic Ocean lies between the land masses around the North Pole and is largely covered by ice. Seas, bays, and gulfs are smaller bodies of water that lie between islands and land masses. Some, such as the Caspian and Dead Seas, are entirely surrounded by land and are not seas but large lakes.

Terms Ending in *-est* or *-er*	What's Being Compared?
largest	superior in size to all oceans
deepest	superior in depth to all oceans
smaller	less in size than another ocean

What Are the Oceans Like?

salinity (C97)	**water pressure** (C97)

Fill in the blank with the word that better completes the sentence.

1. The oceans' _____ salinity _____ varies, depending on the climate of the region.

2. At the average depth of the oceans, the _____ water pressure _____ is 380 atmospheres.

Answer the following questions. Use complete sentences.

3. How much of Earth's surface is covered with the salty water that makes up the oceans and seas? Almost 71 percent of Earth's surface is covered with salty water.

4. How does climate influence the salinity of the oceans? If an area is warm and dry, evaporation combined with little rainfall increases salinity. In colder areas less evaporation and melting snow and ice decrease salinity.

5. Does the ocean floor have features that are the same as or different from the features found on continents? How are the features the same or different? The features on the ocean floor are the same as those found on continents. Ocean floor features include mountains, valleys, volcanoes, and plateaus.

Waves

Materials

rectangular pan   water   straw

Activity Procedure

1 **Make a model** of the ocean by half-filling the pan with water.

2 Place your straw near one side of the pan, and gently blow across the surface of the water. What happens?

3 **Observe** the height and speed of the waves you make. **Record** your observations.

4 Repeat Step 2 several times, blowing a little harder each time. What do you **observe** about the waves you make? **Record** your observations.

Investigate Log

Draw Conclusions

1. Use your observations to describe a relationship between how hard you blow and the height and speed of the waves. _The harder you blow, the faster the_ _waves move and the bigger they are._

_____

2. From what you observed in this activity, what can you **infer** about the cause of waves on oceans and other bodies of water? _Waves are caused by wind._

_____

_____

3. **Scientists at Work** Scientists often **use models** to learn about things they cannot **observe** directly. What did your model help you observe about waves? _Waves are caused by wind; more wind causes faster and larger waves;_ _waves move in the direction the wind is blowing._

_____

Investigate Further **Hypothesize** how high the waves on a pond, a lake, or the ocean can be on a calm day or on a stormy day. Then **plan and conduct a simple**

experiment to test your hypothesis. _Hold a class brainstorming session to_ _develop a hypothesis to use as the basis for the experiment._

_____

_____

_____

Name _____

Date _____

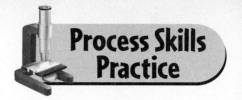

Observe

You observe when you use your senses to note the properties of an object or event. You can observe directly, or you can use instruments such as microscopes or hand lenses.

Think About Observing

When you observe something, you often ask questions about what you are observing. Observing then leads to other process skills, such as measuring, comparing, recording data, inferring, or drawing conclusions. Beneath the drawing below, you will see that some conclusions have been drawn. What can you observe in the drawing that would help you reach those conclusions?

Conclusion	Observation
1. It is either morning or evening.	The sun is low in the sky.
2. It is dark under the water.	The diver is using a light.
3. The diver does not have to come to the surface to breathe and can probably stay underwater for a long while.	The diver has an air tank on his back, and air bubbles are coming from his face, indicating he is breathing underwater.

Compare and Contrast

Read the selection that follows. Use the information to complete the chart that compares and contrasts the ocean currents.

Ocean Currents

Some ocean currents are part of the West Wind Drift. One of these currents is the Benguela Current, a Southern Hemisphere current that flows north along the coast of Africa through the South Atlantic Ocean. Another Southern Hemisphere current that is part of the West Wind Drift is the Antarctic Circumpolar Current. This current, which flows from west to east, circles Antarctica. Both of these currents are affected by prevailing winds and underwater land features.

Benguela and Antarctic Circumpolar Currents

Similarities	Differences
Both are West Wind Drift currents.	Benguela Current flows north. Antarctic Circumpolar Current flows west to east.
Both are in the Southern Hemisphere.	Benguela Current is in the South Atlantic Ocean. Antarctic Circumpolar Current circles Antarctica.
Both are influenced by prevailing winds and underwater features.	Benguela Current flows along the coast of Africa. Antarctic Circumpolar Current circles Antarctica.

How Do Ocean Waters Move?

Lesson Concept

Ocean waters move as waves, currents, and tides. Most waves are caused by wind. Currents are caused by prevailing winds and differences in water temperature. Tides are caused by the gravitational pull of the sun and the moon.

Vocabulary

wave (C102)	**current** (C104)	**tide** (C106)

Choose the short answer that best completes each sentence below.

1. Most of the movement of water on the ocean's surface is caused by _____.

  A waves   **B** currents   **C** tides

2. Earthquakes and volcanoes cause _____.

  A some of the biggest waves   **B** some of the strongest currents   **C** tropical storms

3. A stream of water that flows through the ocean like a river is called a _____.

  A rogue wave   **B** tsunami   **C** current

4. The Gulf Stream is a surface current that _____.

  A strikes the shore at an angle   **B** carries warm water to cold regions   **C** is a cold, deep-ocean current

5. Surface currents are caused by _____.

  A differences in water temperature   **B** long ridges of sand that form near the shoreline   **C** prevailing winds

6. Deep-ocean currents are caused by _____.

  A differences in water temperature   **B** long ridges of sand that form near the shoreline   **C** prevailing winds

7. Tides are caused by _____.

  A powerful deep-ocean currents   **B** the pull of gravity from the sun and the moon   **C** prevailing winds

Use with page C107.

Name _____

Date _____

The Effect of Waves on a Beach

Materials

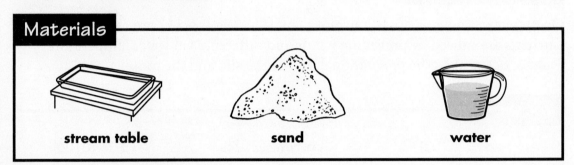

stream table   sand   water

Activity Procedure

1 Use sand to **make a model** of a beach at one end of the stream table. The beach should have a gentle slope.

2 Slowly add water to the stream table until it is about half full. Try not to disturb the beach.

3 Make a wave by lifting the sand end of the stream table about 2 cm above the tabletop and then dropping it. What do you **observe** about the beach and the water? Repeat this several times. **Record** your observations.

4 Repeat Steps 1–3, but this time build a beach that is much steeper than the first one. **Record** your observations.

Name _____

Draw Conclusions

1. Use your observations to explain how waves affect a beach. The beach
erodes and the water becomes tan or brown in color as it mixes with the
eroded sand.

2. Does the slope of the beach matter? Explain. Yes, the beach with the gentle
slope will not erode as fast as the beach with the steep slope.

_____

3. Scientists at Work Scientists often **make a model** to study how natural
processes work. How did your model help you **observe** how waves affect a
beach? The model demonstrates how waves might move sand or dirt to and
from the beach.

_____

What couldn't you observe about wave action with your model?
The model couldn't show wave action over a long period of time.

_____

_____

Investigate Further If possible, study the shore of a pond, a lake, or an ocean in
your area. What do you **observe** about the shore? **Hypothesize** how waves affect
the shore. **Plan and conduct a simple experiment** to test your hypothesis.

_____

_____

_____

_____

Name _____

Date _____

Use a Model

Sometimes the best way to investigate a process is to make and use a model. This is especially true when you want to take a closer look at large-scale Earth processes such as ocean currents.

Think About Using a Model

You have already learned that Earth's rotation causes ocean currents to bend to the right in the Northern Hemisphere and to the left in the Southern Hemisphere. You can model this effect with a very simple experiment. Suppose you are riding on a carousel and you have a tennis ball in your hand. You toss the ball to a friend who is standing in the grass beside the carousel.

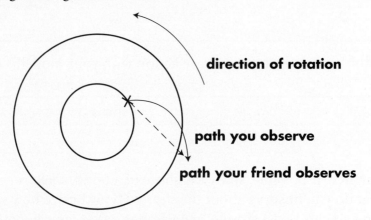

direction of rotation

path you observe

path your friend observes

× = **Your position on the carousel**

1. Does the path of the ball seem curved to your friend? No _____

2. Why does the path seem curved to you? You are moving with the carousel, and the ball is not. Accept any answer that expresses this concept.

_____

3. Has some force acted on the ball to make its path curve? Explain.

No, the carousel has rotated beneath the path of the ball, which makes the path seem curved to someone on the carousel.

4. How is this model like Earth and the ocean currents? How is it different?

The rotation of Earth is like the rotation of the carousel. Earth is much bigger and has land masses in the path of the ocean currents, which redirect the currents. Accept all reasonable answers.

Predict Probable Future Actions and Outcomes

Mining Coral Reefs

Many people in developing countries often can earn money only by gathering materials from nearby ecosystems and making products to sell. This practice eventually can destroy an ecosystem. For example, many people from Sri Lanka, an island country off the coast of India, harvested coral to sell as souvenirs to tourists. The Sri Lankan government, concerned about the destruction of the reef and about the thousands of people who relied upon the reef for income, decided to ban reef mining and to compensate the people for their lost income.

Read the selection. Then consider what might have happened to the coral reef off the coast of Sri Lanka if the Sri Lankan government had not stepped in and stopped the selling of the coral. It is probable that the entire ecosystem would have been destroyed, along with the sea life and plant life in the area of the coral reef.

By stopping the selling of coral, how might the future of the coral reef now be different? The coral reef in that area now probably will thrive and remain intact for future generations to enjoy.

How Do Oceans Interact with the Land?

Lesson Concept

The shore is changed by waves, currents, and human activities. Waves erode beaches and cliffs, longshore currents deposit material along the shore, and human-made structures affect the natural process of shore change.

Vocabulary

shore (C110)   **headland** (C111)   **tide pool** (C111)

jetty (C112)

Ocean waves, ocean currents, and human activity all have an effect on the shore. Read this list of things that can be done to the shore. Decide whether each one is the result of waves, currents, or human activity. Mark the effects of waves with a *W*. Mark the effects of currents with a *C*. Mark the effects of human activity with an *H*.

_____C,W_____ **1.** beach material being pushed along the shore

_____H_____ **2.** structures built to block longshore currents

_____W_____ **3.** rock along the shore slowly dissolved by a weak acid

_____C_____ **4.** the formation of sand spits by beach material that has been pulled sideways

_____H_____ **5.** jetties building up the beach by catching sand

_____W_____ **6.** the bottom of a cliff eroding, causing the cliff to break apart and fall into the ocean

_____H_____ **7.** structures built to protect beaches from erosion

_____W_____ **8.** pebbles and small rocks loosened through water pressure and carried out to the ocean

_____C,W_____ **9.** the formation of a new beach or the addition of material to an existing beach

How Scientists Measure Ocean Depths

Materials

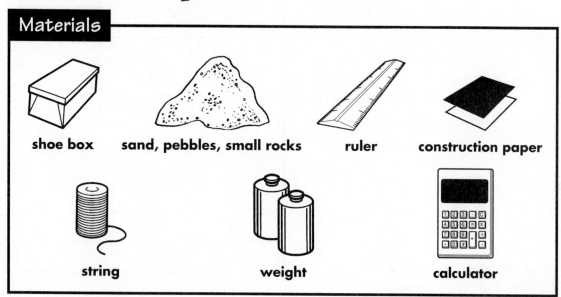

shoe box   sand, pebbles, small rocks   ruler   construction paper

string   weight   calculator

Activity Procedure

1 **Make a model** of the ocean floor by pouring sand and pebbles into the shoe box. Then scatter a few small rocks on top of the sand.

2 Cut a piece of construction paper large enough to cover the top of the box. This will stand for the sea surface.

3 With a pencil and ruler, draw a grid on the paper 4 squares wide by 8 squares long. Number the squares 1 through 32, and tape the lid onto the box. Tie the weight to a piece of string about twice as long as the box is deep.

4 Make a hole in the first square in any row and lower the weighted end of the string until the weight just touches the ocean floor.

5 Hold the string at sea level. **Measure** the length of string you pinched off to find the depth of the ocean. **Record** your measurement. Repeat Steps 4 and 5 for the remaining squares in that row.

6 Use the Sonar Data table on page WB216. The "Time" is the number of seconds it takes for a sound to travel from a boat to the bottom of the ocean and back to the boat.

Investigate Log

7 Use a calculator to multiply the Location 1 time by 1500 m/s (the speed of sound in water). Then divide the product by 2. This number is the depth of the water in meters at Location 1. This one has been done for you.

8 Repeat Step 7 for each location in the table. Then make a line graph of the depths. The graph will be a profile of the ocean floor.

Sonar Data		
Location	**Time (s)**	**Depth (m)**
1	1.8	1350
2	2.0	1500
3	3.6	2700
4	4.5	3375
5	5.3	3975
6	2.3	1725
7	3.1	2325
8	4.6	3450
9	5.0	3750
10	5.2	3900

Draw Conclusions

1. Why do you think scientists today use sonar rather than weighted ropes to **measure** the depth of the ocean? Sonar is more accurate; sonar takes less time; weighted ropes aren't always long enough to reach the bottom.

2. When using sonar, why must you divide each product by 2 to calculate the depth of the water? Sound waves must travel from the boat to the bottom of the ocean and then the same distance back again.

3. **Scientists at Work** How could a scientist use sonar to **measure** the size of large objects on the ocean floor? by comparing data from several spots, looking for places where the depth is less

Investigate Further How could you find the depth of a pond, lake, or river? **Plan and conduct a simple investigation** to find out. _____

Name _____

Date _____

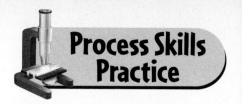

Measure

When you measure something, you are determining what its length, weight, volume, or some other quality is. You do this by using measuring standards, such as meters, inches, grams, or pounds.

Think About Measuring

Olden is a world where there are no roads, cars, airplanes, or any type of modern transportation. The only way to get from one place to another on Olden is by walking. The people who live there have no idea how big their world is. They have no idea what a mile or a kilometer is. They measure distance by the amount of time it takes to walk from one place to another.

1. Assuming that it takes you about one hour to walk two miles, how would you tell someone living on Olden that you live one mile away from school?
You would say you live one half-hour from school.

2. How would you describe the distance between New York and Chicago, which is about 800 miles? The rate is 2 miles per hour. Formula: distance divided by rate (2). The answer: 400 hours.

3. Finish the table by filling in the Olden units of distance (that is, time) between New York and the cities listed in the left column.

	Miles	Olden Units
Cincinnati to New York	600	300 hours
Indianapolis to New York	700	350 hours
Little Rock to New York	1300	650 hours
Las Vegas to New York	2500	1250 hours

4. Scientists on Earth use a unit called a light-year to measure the distances between the stars. Light travels about 186,000 miles in one second. What do you think a light-year is? Students should understand that a light-year is a measure of distance, not time. It is the distance light travels in one year.

_____

Distinguish Fact and Opinion

Light-Producing Fish

As the depths of the oceans are explored, scientists have discovered that many deep-ocean creatures, such as some species of squids, fish, jellyfish, and crustaceans, produce light. This ability is called bioluminescence. Other creatures, such as the firefly, also exhibit this unusual ability.

Bioluminescence is an adaptation that serves a variety of important functions. Some organisms use the light they produce to attract or recognize a mate. Others use it to locate prey or deter predators.

Read the selection. Then determine whether the statements below are facts or opinions.

_____ Deep-ocean organisms probably have this light-producing ability because of a change in their natures or habitats.

_____ I believe that only marine animals that have bioluminescence should be studied by scientists.

_____ Bioluminescence serves many vital functions.

_____ Fireflies are probably the only non-sea animals with bioluminescence.

How Do People Explore the Oceans and Use Ocean Resources?

Lesson Concept

A wide range of technology is used to explore the ocean, including scuba equipment, submersibles, satellites, and sonar. The oceans contain valuable natural resources, such as fish, petroleum, minerals, and sea water.

Vocabulary

scuba (C117) **sonar** (C117) **submersible** (C117) **desalination** (C120)

Match the dates in the left column with the events in the right column. Write the letter of the event that matches each date in the space next to the date.

____D____ 1690

____F____ 1872

____B____ 1912

____I____ 1942

____G____ 1956

____A____ 1960

____C____ 1977

____H____ 1986

____E____ 1987

A Jacques Piccard and Donald Walsh go down to the deepest place in the Pacific Ocean (10, 920 m) in the *Trieste II*.

B The RMS *Titanic* strikes an iceberg in the North Atlantic and sinks to the bottom of the ocean.

C Scientists in *Alvin* discover hot springs deep under the ocean. The springs come from vents in the ocean floor over volcanically active areas.

D Sir Edmund Halley, an English astronomer, builds a diving bell that traps air for divers to use.

E *Nautile* brings up some objects from the *Titanic* wreck.

F Six scientists spend more than three years at sea on the voyage of the HMS *Challenger*.

G Allyn Vine convinces the United States government that scientists need deep-diving vessels that can hold small crews.

H *Alvin* is used to explore the wreckage of the sunken RMS *Titanic*.

I French explorer Jacques Cousteau invents an aqua-lung that allows a diver to move about freely under water to a depth of about 100 m.

Recognize Vocabulary

Look at the vocabulary terms in the box. Choose the term that best fits each phrase. Write your answers on the lines. Use each term only once.

wave	salinity	water pressure	current
tide	shore	headland	tide pool
jetty	scuba	submersible	sonar
desalination			

1. up-and-down movement of surface water   *wave*

2. area where the ocean and land meet and interact   *shore*

3. stream of water that flows through the ocean   *current*

4. the rise and fall in ocean level   *tide*

5. saltiness of water   *salinity*

6. pool of water found along a rocky shoreline   *tide pool*

7. process of hard rock being left after softer rock has eroded   *headland*

8. weight of water pressing on an object   *water pressure*

9. wall of rock that sticks out into the ocean   *jetty*

10. process of removing salt from sea water   *desalination*

11. self-contained underwater breathing apparatus   *scuba*

12. reflected sound waves   *sonar*

13. small underwater vehicle   *submersible*

Name _____

Date _____

Write a Marine Center Brochure

Informative Writing—Description

Imagine that you work for a marine science center. For the center's brochure, find or draw pictures of three important ocean resources. Write a detailed description of each resource, telling why it is important. Use the idea web below to help you plan your writing.

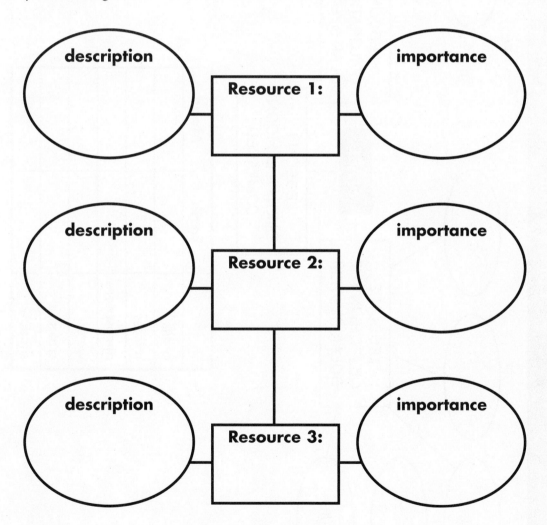

Name _____ Date _____

Chapter 1 • Graphic Organizer for Chapter Concepts

Earth, Moon, and Beyond

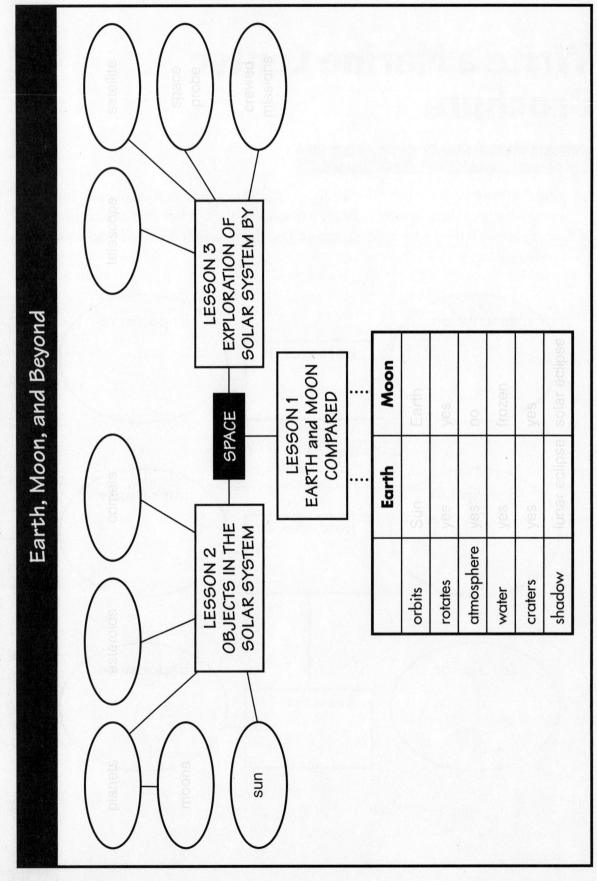

satellite

space probe

crewed missions

telescope

LESSON 3
EXPLORATION OF SOLAR SYSTEM BY

SPACE

LESSON 1
EARTH and MOON COMPARED

comets

asteroids

LESSON 2
OBJECTS IN THE SOLAR SYSTEM

planets

moons

sun

	Earth	Moon
orbits	Sun	Earth
rotates	yes	yes
atmosphere	yes	no
water	yes	frozen
craters	yes	yes
shadow	lunar eclipse	solar eclipse

Date _____

The Moon's Craters

Materials

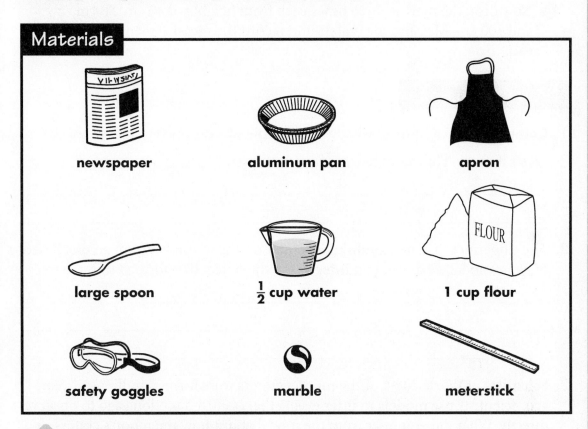

newspaper

aluminum pan

apron

large spoon

$\frac{1}{2}$ cup water

1 cup flour

safety goggles

marble

meterstick

Activity Procedure

1 Use the following table.

Trial	Height	Width of Craters
1	20 cm	
2	40 cm	
3	80 cm	
4	100 cm	

2 Put the newspaper on the floor. Place the pan in the center of the newspaper.

3 Use a large spoon to mix the water and flour in the aluminum pan. The look and feel of the mixture should be like thick cake batter. Now lightly cover the surface of the mixture with dry flour.

4 **CAUTION** **Put on the safety goggles and apron** to protect your eyes and clothes from flour dust. Drop the marble into the pan from a height of 20 cm.

5 Carefully remove the marble and **measure** the width of the crater. **Record** the measurement in the table. Repeat Steps 4 and 5 two more times.

6 Now drop the marble three times each from heights of 40 cm, 80 cm, and 100 cm. Measure the craters and record the measurements after each drop.

Draw Conclusions

1. **Compare** the height from which each marble was dropped to the size of the crater it made. How does height affect crater size? _The greater the height,_ _the wider the crater._

2. The Copernicus (koh•PER•nih•kuhs) crater on the moon is 91 km across. Based on your model, what can you **infer** about the object that formed this crater? _The object came from a great distance or it was very large._

3. **Scientists at Work** Most of the moon's craters were formed millions of years ago. Scientists **use models** to **infer** events that occurred too long ago to **observe** directly. What did you infer from the model about how the moon's craters formed? _The moon's craters formed when its surface was hit by objects_ _from space._

Investigate Further Hypothesize how using larger or smaller marbles would affect the size and shape of the craters. **Plan and conduct a simple experiment** to test your hypothesis. _____

_____

_____

_____

_____

_____

Infer

You infer when you use logical reasoning to draw conclusions based on observations. An inference based on logical reasoning and observation is always valid, even though it may not be correct.

Think About Inferring

Imagine you are in a spacecraft flying over the surface of an unexplored planet that is about the same size as Earth. Crewless probes have reported that the planet is composed of material that is common to both the moon and Earth. You are the first human to see this planet. Looking down through thin, moving clouds, you notice that there are craters and a lot of areas that look like the maria of the moon. Most of the craters look worn and old, but a few have high, sharp sides and look new. Some of the craters have steam rising from them and are surrounded by a plain made of fresh material. Others are in rougher areas and are surrounded by material that has been thrown out over the ground. You also notice very large fields of what look like sand dunes.

1. From your observations of the new planet, what can you infer about how the craters were formed? Explain. The craters were formed by impacts and also by volcanic action. The material thrown from some of the craters is a sign of impact; the steam rising from other craters could be from volcanic action. The maria are probably fields of lava from volcanoes.

_____

2. What can you infer about life on this planet? There probably isn't any. If there is, it will be adapted to life in an extremely dry climate.

_____

_____

_____

3. What can you infer about weather on this planet? There probably isn't any rain, but you can infer from the existence of sand dunes and moving clouds that there are probably winds, maybe even strong winds.

_____

_____

Distinguish Fact and Opinion

Read each factual statement below. Change each statement to an opinion statement, and write the statement in the chart below. Responses will vary.

Eclipses

Fact	Opinion
During a total solar eclipse, the moon completely covers the sun.	During a total solar eclipse, scientists believe that the moon completely covers the sun.
A solar eclipse can be seen from only a limited part of Earth.	A solar eclipse probably can be seen from only a limited part of Earth.
A lunar eclipse occurs when the full moon passes through Earth's shadow.	People believe that a lunar eclipse occurs when the full moon passes through Earth's shadow.
In most calendar years, there are two lunar eclipses.	In most calendar years, there are probably only two lunar eclipses.
Between 1901 and 2000 there was a total of 228 eclipses.	It is believed that between 1901 and 2000, there was a total of 228 eclipses.

Name _____

Date _____

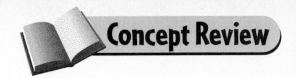

How Do Earth and the Moon Compare?

The moon revolves around Earth. The Earth-moon system revolves around the sun. Both Earth and the moon rotate on axes and have day-night cycles. Many features on Earth and the moon are different, but some landforms occur on both.

revolve (D6)	**orbit** (D7)	**rotate** (D7)
axis (D7)	**eclipse** (D8)	

Select words from the box below to label the diagram. Watch out! Not every word in the box can be used to label the diagram, so you'll have to pick and choose.

lunar mare	gibbous	orbit	moon	full moon
day-night cycle	sun	Earth	eclipse	crater
quarter moon	half moon	axes	revolve	rotation

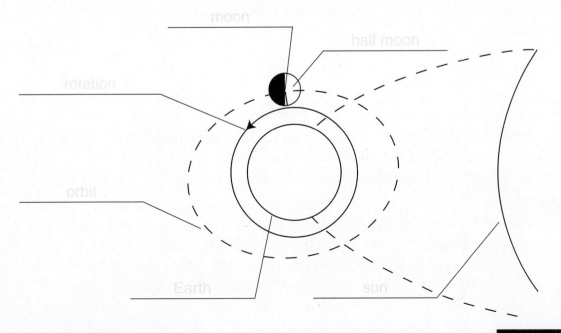

How Earth, the Moon, and the Sun Move Through Space

Materials

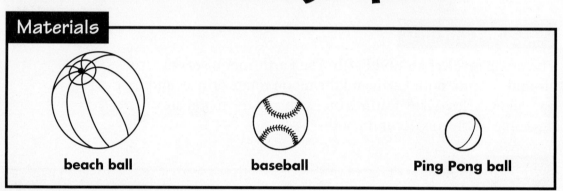

beach ball   baseball   Ping Pong ball

Activity Procedure

1 You will work in a group of four to **make a model** of the sun, Earth, and the moon in space. One person should stand in the center of a large open area and hold the beach ball over his or her head. The beach ball stands for the sun. A second person should stand far from the "sun" and hold the baseball overhead. The baseball stands for Earth. The third person should hold the Ping Pong ball near "Earth." The Ping Pong ball stands for the moon. The fourth person should **observe** and **record** what happens.

2 The real Earth moves around the sun in a path like a circle that has been pulled a little. This shape, called an *ellipse* (ee•LIPS), is shown below.

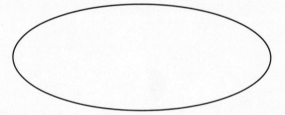

For the model, Earth should move around the sun in an ellipse-shaped path. Earth should also spin slowly as it moves around the sun. The observer should **record** this motion.

3 While Earth spins and moves around the sun, the moon should move around Earth in another ellipse-shaped path. The moon should also spin once as it moves around Earth. The same side of the moon should always face Earth. That is, the moon should spin once for each complete path it takes around Earth. The observer should **record** these motions.

Name _____

Draw Conclusions

1. Your model shows three periods of time—a year, a month, and a day. Think about the time it takes Earth to spin once, the moon to move around Earth once, and Earth to move around the sun once. Which period of time does each movement stand for? Earth moving once around the sun—a year; the moon moving once around Earth—a month; Earth spinning around once—a day.

_____

_____

_____

2. Compare the movements of the moon to the movements of Earth.

Possible answers: The moon and Earth spin at different speeds; the moon orbits the Earth, while Earth orbits the sun; the same side of the moon is always facing Earth.

_____

_____

_____

3. Scientists at Work Scientists often **make models** to show **time and space relationships** in the natural world. However, models can't always show these relationships exactly. How was your model of Earth, the moon, and the sun limited in what it showed? Possible answer: Earth did not spin exactly 365 times as it moved around the sun once.

_____

_____

_____

Investigate Further Plan and conduct a simple investigation to test this **hypothesis:** The amount of sunlight reaching Earth changes as Earth moves around the sun.

_____

_____

_____

_____

_____

_____

Use Time and Space Relationships

Time relationships tell you the order of events. Space relationships tell you about locations of objects. Understanding these relationships can help you make accurate models.

Think About Using Time and Space Relationships

Suppose you are a space traveler from Earth and you have just discovered a new solar system. You want to make an accurate map for those who will follow you. Answer these questions to plan your map. Use a separate sheet of paper if you need more space.

1. Think about mapping a new solar system. What space relationships will you show? Answers should include where the new system is relative to Earth and what the relative distances of the new planets and star are from each other.

2. Seven large objects orbit a single star. Three of them have smaller objects orbiting them. What do the locations of the orbits tell you about the objects? The seven objects orbiting the star are planets; the other smaller objects are moons.

3. One of the seven larger orbiting objects is very close to the star. Three are a little farther away. Three are very far away. In which group are you most likely to find a planet to colonize? Explain. In the second group; the first is too close to the star; the third group is too far away.

4. Why is it important to show the locations of the planets accurately? Answers should include: you don't want those who follow you to get lost, you don't want them to go to the wrong planet, or you want to be able to find your own way back again. Accept all reasonable answers.

5. What would happen if you made a mistake in showing the locations of some of the planets or moons? Answers should include: colonists may believe they are in the wrong solar system, or colonists may try to colonize the wrong planet. Accept all reasonable answers.

Compare and Contrast

Read the selection. Then complete the chart by comparing and contrasting asteroids and comets.

Asteroids and Comets

Although they may seem similar, asteroids and comets are very different. Asteroids are small, rocky bodies that can be as big as small planets or as small as basketballs. Most of our solar system's asteroids are found between the orbits of Mars and Jupiter in a place called the Asteroid Belt. Some scientists believe that billions of years ago a large planet tried to form between Mars and Jupiter but was prevented from doing so by Jupiter's gravitational forces. The asteroids in the Asteroid Belt are thought to be pieces of that failed planet. Some asteroids even have other asteroids that orbit them like miniature moons.

Comets are rocky and icy bodies that have been compared to dirty snowballs. Unlike asteroids, most of which are located between Mars and Jupiter, comets orbit the sun from well beyond the orbit of Pluto. Usually the core of a comet is smaller than an asteroid. When a comet nears the sun, its icy core melts, forming clouds of gas, ice, and dust. The sun's energy then turns these clouds into comet tails that can measure several million kilometers in length.

	Appearance	**Size**	**Orbit**
Asteroids	small rocky bodies; perhaps left over from formation of planets	some as large as small planets; others as small as a basketball	most located between the orbits of Mars and Jupiter
Comets	balls of ice and rock covered by clouds	core is smaller than an asteroid	located much farther from the sun than are asteroids

The Cycles in Our Solar System

Lesson Concept

Earth rotates on its axis once every 24 hours. The position of Earth in its orbit and the tilt of its axis cause the change of seasons in the Northern and Southern Hemispheres. The solar system contains many bodies that orbit the sun, including planets and their moons, asteroids, and comets.

Vocabulary

solstice (D15)   **equinox** (D15)   **planets** (D17)

asteroids (D17)   **comets** (D17)

Identify the following events as occurring either during a solstice (S) or during an equinox (E). Some events may involve both occurrences.

___S___ **1.** The beginning of winter.

___S,E___ **2.** The beginning of a different season.

___E___ **3.** The hours of daylight and darkness are equal.

___S___ **4.** The day with the most daylight in the Northern Hemisphere.

Choose the answer that best completes the statement.

___B___ **5.** Some _____ are almost the size of small planets.

    A comets
    B asteroids
    C hemispheres

___C___ **6.** In our solar system there are nine _____.

    A asteroids
    B comets
    C planets

___A___ **7.** Balls of ice that often have clouds surrounding them are _____.

    A comets
    B planets
    C asteroids

Make Your Own Telescope

Materials

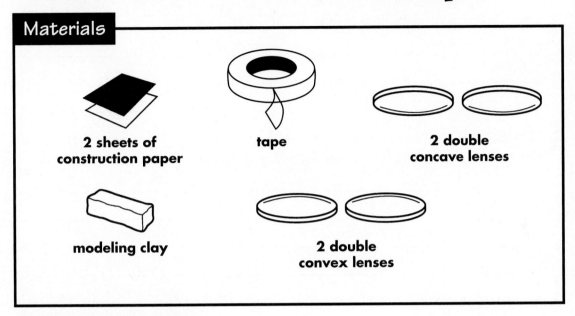

2 sheets of construction paper

tape

2 double concave lenses

modeling clay

2 double convex lenses

Activity Procedure

1 Roll and tape a piece of construction paper to form a tube that is slightly larger in diameter than the lenses. Then make a second tube that is just enough larger in diameter that the first tube will fit snugly inside it.

2 Slide most of the small tube into the larger tube.

3 Place one of the lenses in one end of the smaller tube, and use modeling clay to hold it in place. This lens will be the eyepiece of the telescope.

4 Place the other lens in the far end of the larger tube. Use clay to hold it in place. This lens will be the objective lens, or the lens closest to the object being viewed through the telescope.

5 Choose several distant objects to view with your telescope. You might look at a tree or distant building. **CAUTION: Do not look at the sun with your telescope. You can seriously damage your eyes.** Slide the smaller tube in and out until the object you are viewing comes into focus.

6 **Observe** each object twice, first using only your eye and then using the telescope. **Record** your observations by making two drawings that show how the object appears when viewed with and without the telescope.

7 Repeat steps 5 and 6 using your telescope. Make two drawings of each object, showing how it appears both with and without the telescope.

Name _____

Draw Conclusions

1. **Compare** each set of drawings. How does the appearance of each object change when viewed through the telescope? How does the use of the telescope affect your ability to observe details in those objects? Objects viewed through the telescope appear larger than when viewed without the telescope. Details are more easily noticed with the telescope.

_____

2. In which of the objects could more details be seen with the telescope than with the eyes alone? In which of the objects, if any, were details not more visible? Students may respond that a tree, when viewed with the telescope, appears to have more detail. A building may be too large to see clearly with the telescope.

_____

3. **Scientists at Work** Scientists use many kinds of telescopes to **observe** objects in space. Some telescopes use curved mirrors instead of lenses to make objects appear larger. How is your model telescope limited for use in studying objects in space? The model telescope is not powerful enough to view objects in space, and the lenses appear to bend.

_____

Investigate Further Plan and conduct a simple experiment to test this **hypothesis:** The curved surfaces of a lens bend the light rays that pass through it. In their hypotheses, students should note that light traveling through their lenses appears to bend.

_____

_____

_____

Name _____

Date _____

Observe

There is always something happening around us. Sometimes we do not realize how much we observe of our surroundings.

Think About What You Saw

How aware are you of your surroundings? On the lines provided below, write a list of selected events or items you saw during the day. In the next column, write what you thought about what you observed.

What I Saw	What I Thought
Answers will vary.	Answers will vary

Name _____

Date _____

Draw Logical Conclusions

Read the selection. Complete the chart by writing a logical conclusion based on the statements.

Space Stations

A space station is a satellite made by humans that revolves in a fixed orbit. It is a center for scientific observations and experiments. Spacecraft are refueled and satellites are launched from it.

Skylab was the first successful space station. It was launched May 14, 1973, by NASA. Astronauts were able to observe the sun and the comet Kohoutek. *Skylab* left orbit earlier than expected and entered Earth's atmosphere in 1979.

The space station *Mir* was launched February 20, 1986. It was designed to be a permanent laboratory and living space. Like *Skylab*, it was used for experiments, to refuel spacecraft, and to launch satellites. In 2001 *Mir* was brought back to Earth by the Russian government in a controlled crash.

The United States, Russia, and 14 other nations are planning to work together on the *International Space Station*. Technology from *Mir* will be used on the station.

Information	Conclusion
Spacecraft are refueled and satellites are launched from a space station.	Possible answer: By providing for the launching and refueling of spacecraft, a space station could help scientists in their attempts to further explore the universe.
As the first successful space station, *Skylab* enabled astronauts to observe the sun and the comet Kohoutek.	Possible answer: Because of the work on *Skylab*, scientists have information about the sun and the comet Kohoutek that they can use in future studies of the universe.
The United States, Russia, and 14 other nations are planning to work together on the International Space Station, *Alpha*.	Possible answer: Because 16 countries have agreed to work on *Alpha*, it could be a very successful project.

Name _____

Date _____

How Have People Explored the Solar System?

Lesson Concept

People have studied objects in space since ancient times. They began by using their unaided eye and then the telescope. Today they also use satellites and space probes. In the future, people may live and work on space stations and moon bases.

Vocabulary

telescope (D23)   **satellite** (D23)   **space probe** (D24)

Write the letter of an event next to the year it occurred.

___D___ 900

___F___ 1609

___H___ 1668

___I___ 1936

___A___ 1957

___C___ 1961

___G___ 1969

___B___ 1977

___E___ 1981

A The Soviet Union launches *Sputnik 1*, the first artificial satellite.

B *Voyager I* and *Voyager II* space probes are launched. They have sent back pictures of Jupiter, Saturn, Uranus, and Neptune and are traveling beyond the solar system.

C The Mercury program sends the first Americans into space.

D Mayan people build an observatory for viewing the stars and planets at Chichén Itzá, in Mexico, around this date.

E Beginning of the use of space shuttles to lift heavy cargoes into orbit; to provide labs for scientific research in space; and to launch, bring back, and repair satellites

F Galileo uses a telescope to observe four moons orbiting Jupiter.

G American astronaut Neil Armstrong is the first person to walk on the moon.

H Sir Isaac Newton designs a telescope that uses a mirror as well as lenses to produce sharper images than those produced by Galileo's telescope.

I The first radio telescope is built and detects radio waves coming from objects in space.

Recognize Vocabulary

Read the following sentences. On each line, write the letter for the word or phrase that could be substituted for the vocabulary term in italics.

_____C_____ **1.** In 1609 Galileo used a *telescope* to observe craters on the moon.

    A artificial satellite

    B robot vehicle used to explore space

    C instrument that makes distant objects appear nearer

_____A_____ **2.** As it travels around the sun, Earth *rotates*.

    A spins on its axis

    B travels in a closed path

    C moves in an ellipse

_____A_____ **3.** Earth's *axis* travels through its North Pole and South Pole.

    A imaginary line that passes through Earth's center

    B elliptical path that Earth travels around the sun

    C shadow that Earth casts over the moon at some points in its orbit

_____B_____ **4.** Gravity makes the Earth-moon system *revolve* around the sun.

    A spin on its axis

    B travel in a closed path

    C face the sun as it moves

_____A_____ **5.** A total lunar *eclipse* lasts more than two hours and can be seen from any place on Earth that is facing the moon.

    A passage through Earth's shadow

    B trip around Earth in an elliptical path

    C volcanic eruption that leaves pools of dark lava on the moon

_____C_____ **6.** Planets, asteroids, and comets *move* around the sun.

    A circle

    B spin

    C revolve

_____A_____ **7.** Earth's *orbit* around the sun is an ellipse, a shape that is nearly but not quite circular.

    A path as it revolves

    B imaginary line that passes through the center and the poles

    C shadow cast that causes an eclipse

Writing Practice

Expressive Writing

Pretend that you are spending a week on the Space Station, *Alpha*.
Write an E-mail message to a family member or friend, describing
what you are seeing and doing. Use the chart below to plan the
message.

Send an E-Mail from Space

Heading
To:
Date:
Subject:
Greeting
Dear _____
Body of message
Closing
Your _____
_____
Your E-mail address: _____ @spacestationalpha.space

Chapter 2 • Graphic Organizer for Chapter Concepts

The Sun and Other Stars

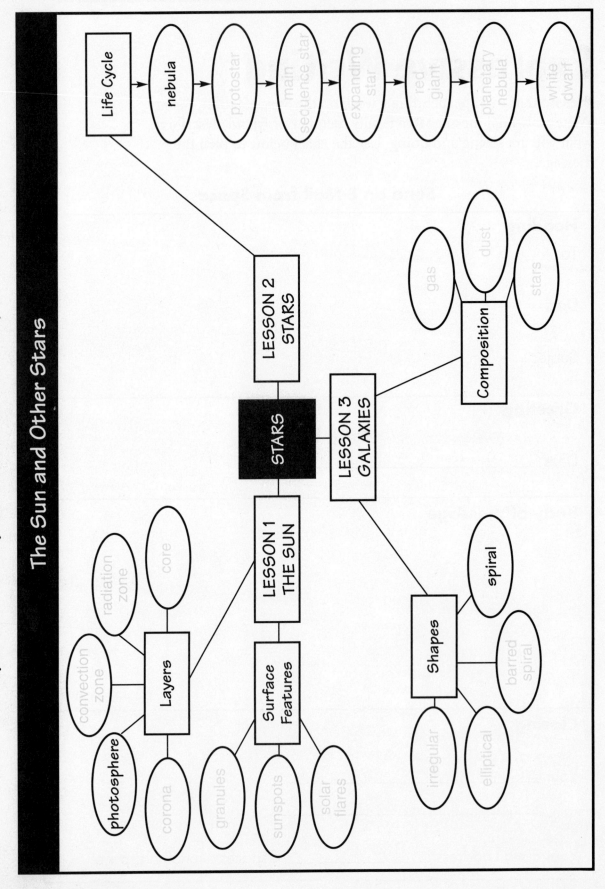

Sunspots

Materials

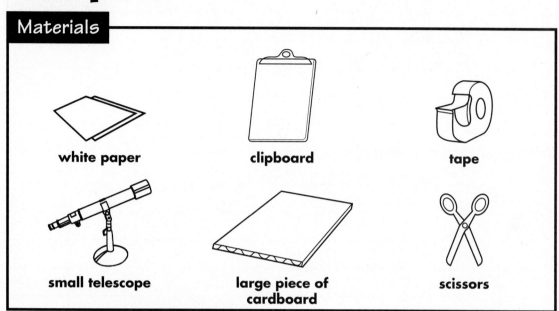

white paper

clipboard

tape

small telescope

large piece of cardboard

scissors

CAUTION ## Activity Procedure

1. **CAUTION** **Never look directly at the sun. You can cause permanent damage to your eyes.** Fasten the white paper to the clipboard. Tape the edges down to keep the wind from blowing them.

2. Center the eyepiece of the telescope on the cardboard, and trace around the eyepiece.

3. Cut out the circle, and fit the eyepiece into the hole. The cardboard will help block some of the light and make a shadow on the paper.

4. Point the telescope at the sun, and focus the sun's image on the white paper. **Observe** the image of the sun on the paper.

5. On the paper, outline the image of the sun. Shade in any dark spots you see. The dark spots are called *sunspots*. **Record** the date and time on the paper. **Predict** what will happen to the sunspots in the next day or two. *Note:* Since the image of the sun on the paper is reversed, any movement you **observe** will also be reversed. For example, movement from east to west, or from right to left on the image, represents movement from west to east on the sun.

6. Repeat Step 5 each sunny day for several days. **Record** the date, the time, and the positions of the sunspots each day.

Name _____

Draw Conclusions

1. How did the positions of the sunspots change over several days?

The sunspots should have moved across the paper from right to left until

reaching the left side of the image.

_____

_____

_____

2. What can you **infer** from the movement of sunspots? Since sunspots move

across the sun's surface from west to east, right to left on the paper, students

can conclude that the sun rotates from west to east.

_____

_____

_____

3. Scientists at Work Scientists **draw conclusions** from what they **observe**. Galileo was the first scientist to observe that a sunspot takes about two weeks to cross from the left side of the sun's surface to the right side. Two weeks later, the sunspot appears on the left side of the sun's surface again. From this information, what conclusions can you draw about the time it takes the sun to make one complete rotation? about four weeks

_____

_____

Investigate Further Hypothesize whether sunspots change in size. **Plan and conduct a simple investigation** to test these hypotheses.

_____

_____

_____

_____

_____

_____

Name _____

Date _____

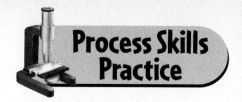

Draw Conclusions

Drawing conclusions involves the use of other process skills, such as observing. Unlike inferences, conclusions are usually based on much more data and should be tested repeatedly.

Think About Drawing Conclusions

In ancient times two astronomers were watching sunspots. The first astronomer concluded the spots were planets orbiting the sun. The second astronomer watched the sunspots more closely than the first. He noticed the spots changed shape as they approached the edge of the sun's image. They became compressed and then seemed to disappear. The second astronomer concluded the spots were part of the sun's surface.

1. Why do you think the two astronomers came to such different conclusions?

The second astronomer was basing his conclusion on more data: his

observations that the spots changed shape. Accept any reasonable answer.

2. What other data could the astronomers have gathered to support their

conclusions? Answers may include counting the number of sunspots visible

at each observation, noticing that the number of sunspots visible from

observation to observation changes, or noticing that some sunspots are not

spherical in shape (as planets are).

3. Astronomers over the ages have kept records of sunspots. The following is a graph showing the appearance of sunspots from 1900 to 2000. What

conclusions can you draw from the graph? Possible answers: sunspots appear

in cycles, there were a lot of sunspots in the late 1950s, or the sunspot cycle

is about 11 years in length. Accept all reasonable answers.

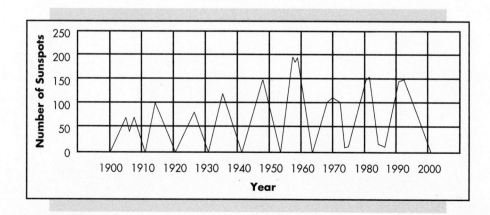

Identify Cause and Effect

Read the selection. Then complete the chart to show the causes of the uneven heating of Earth.

Uneven Heating by the Sun

Earth is heated by energy from the sun. However, the sun doesn't heat all of Earth's regions evenly. One reason for the uneven heating is the angle at which the sun's rays strike Earth's surface. When sunlight hits Earth at an angle of 90°, the sunlight covers the smallest possible area. But when sunlight hits Earth at an angle smaller than 90°, the same amount of light spreads out over a larger area. When this happens, each part of the area gets less energy. In addition, light loses some of its energy as it travels through air. When the sun is directly overhead, light travels the shortest distance through the atmosphere before reaching Earth's surface. The smaller the angle the light makes, the farther it has to travel through the atmosphere. More of its energy is absorbed or reflected before it reaches Earth's surface.

What Happens
(Effect)

uneven heating of Earth's surface
_____

Why it Happens
(Causes)

the different angles at which the sun's energy strikes Earth
_____

the distance the sun's light has to travel to Earth's surface
_____

What Are the Features of the Sun?

Lesson Concept

The sun is the source of almost all the energy on Earth. The sun has layers and visible surface features.

Vocabulary

photosphere (D41)   **corona** (D41)   **sunspot** (D42)

solar flare (D42)   **solar wind** (D42)

Vocabulary terms and other words from this lesson are listed in the chart below. Choose the correct term for each blank attached to a part of this diagram of the sun.

| corona | core | solar flare | convection zone |
| solar wind | photosphere | sunspot | radiation zone |

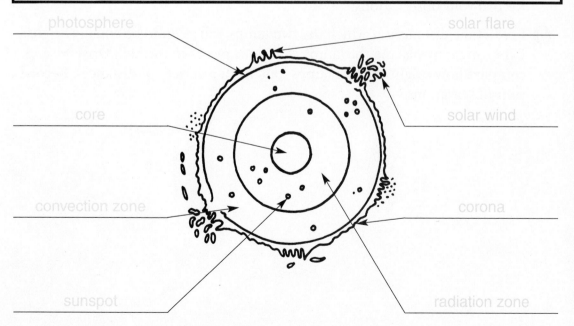

Name _____

Date _____

The Brightness of Stars

Materials

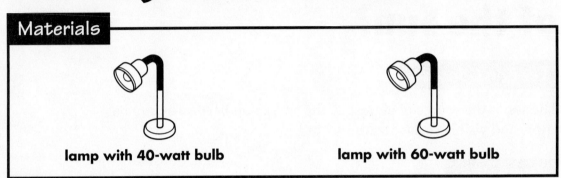

lamp with 40-watt bulb   lamp with 60-watt bulb

Activity Procedure

1 Place the two lamps near the middle of a darkened hall. Turn the lamps on.

2 **Observe** the lamps from one end of the hall. **Compare** how bright they look. **Record** your observations.

3 Move the lamp with the 60-watt bulb to one end of the hall. **Observe** and **compare** how bright the two lamps look from the other end of the hall. **Record** your observations.

4 Now place the lamps side by side at one end of the hall. Again **observe** and **compare** how bright the two lamps look from the other end of the hall. **Record** your observations.

5 **Predict** the distances at which the two lamps will seem to be equally bright. **Experiment** by placing the lamps at various places in the hall. **Observe** and **compare** how bright the two lamps look from a variety of distances. **Record** your observations.

Draw Conclusions

1. What two variables did you test in this experiment? how bright the light actually is and how far it is from the observer

_____

_____

2. From what you **observed**, what two factors affect how bright a light appears to an observer? distance and brightness

_____

_____

3. **Scientists at Work** Scientists often **draw conclusions** when **experimenting**. Use the results of your experiment to draw conclusions about how distance and actual brightness affect how bright stars appear to observers on Earth.

Possible answer: If two stars have the same brightness, the star that is farther away appears less bright than the nearer star. If a dimmer star is closer, it can look as bright as a brighter star that is farther away.

_____

_____

_____

Investigate Further Why can't you see stars during the day? **Plan and conduct a simple experiment** to test this **hypothesis**: Stars don't shine during the day.

_____

_____

_____

_____

_____

Name _____

Date _____

Experiment and Draw Conclusions

You draw conclusions after you have experimented and collected data.
Drawing conclusions is usually the last step in an investigative process.
When you draw a conclusion, you pull together what you have learned
from observation or experimentation.

Think About Experimenting and Drawing Conclusions

You are involved in a search for extraterrestrial
intelligence. You build a gigantic radio antenna
on top of the highest building near your home.
You let it scan the sky, hoping someone on another
planet is sending signals to Earth. After you
experiment with your antenna, you begin
gathering data and drawing conclusions.

1. You receive a burst of radio noise, called static, at the same time every day. You
   suspect it's coming from a local radio station. Can you draw any conclusions?

   Explain. _You probably can't draw any conclusions yet because you don't_
   have enough data.

2. You notice the radio noise is coming from a fixed point in the sky and is
   actually a series of pulses. If you keep your antenna aimed at that spot, the
   pulses continue without stopping. Can you draw any conclusions? Explain.
   The source of the pulse is not the radio station; the pulse is probably coming
   from outer space. You still don't have enough data to conclude what it is.

3. You aim a telescope at the source of the pulses and see a small white star. Can
   you draw any conclusions? Explain. _You can conclude that the signal source_
   could be the white star. You still don't have enough data to conclude what the
   pulse is.

4. You check a star map. The star you have been observing is a pulsar, which is a
   star that spins very, very fast and sends out a radio signal as it spins. Can you
   draw any conclusions? Explain. _You have enough data now to conclude that_
   your signal is from a pulsar and not from extraterrestrial intelligence.

Arrange Events in Sequence

The Big Dipper

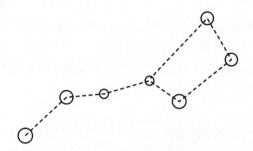

The illustration above shows the star pattern called the Big Dipper, part of the constellation Ursa Major. It is made up of many named stars, but its main stars are Dubhe, Merak, Phecda, Megrez, Alioth, Mizar, and Alkaid. If you look at Ursa Major carefully, you will see the outline of a cup-like square with a handle, or a dipper. Trace the cup and its handle.

Now look at the full illustration of the Ursa Major. Some say that it resembles a bear (*Ursa Major* in Latin means "Big Bear"). Others call it the Plough, Charlie's Wain, or the Wagon. Using another color, trace the outline of the entire Big Dipper.

Look at the illustration again. Trace over the line between Merak and Dubhe. Then extend that line until it is about five times its original length. At that point you will have located Polaris, or the North Star.

Now arrange the seven major stars that make up the Big Dipper in correct sequence, starting at the handle's end.

Alkaid, Mizar, Alioth, Megrez, Dubhe, Merak, Phecda

_____

_____

How Are Stars Classified?

Lesson Concept

Stars are classified by absolute magnitude, surface temperature, size, and color. Stars change from nebula to protostar to main-sequence star to expanding star to red giant to planetary nebula and white dwarf. Most stars are main-sequence stars.

Vocabulary

magnitude (D46)   **main sequence** (D47)

Match the star type in Column A with its description in Column B by writing the letter of the correct description next to the star type.

Column A

_C_ main-sequence star

_F_ nebula

_G_ red giant

_A_ expanding star

_B_ planetary nebula

_E_ protostar

_D_ white dwarf

Column B

A An object with the mass of the sun shines for billions of years. Then, as its hydrogen runs low, it starts to get bigger.

B The star's atmosphere expands a million times.

C After several million years, the temperature at the center of the object gets hot enough to release various kinds of energy.

D The object continues to shine dimly for billions of years as it slowly cools.

E Attracted to each other by gravity, the particles squeeze together. The object grows, gets hotter, and starts to glow.

F A star begins within a huge cloud of hydrogen, helium, and tiny particles of dust.

G The star may expand to 100 times its former size.

Name _____

Date _____

The Sun's Location in the Milky Way Galaxy

Materials

scrap paper

Activity Procedure

1. Make about 70 small balls from scrap paper. These will be your "stars."

2. On a table, **make a model** of the Milky Way Galaxy. Arrange the paper stars in a spiral with six arms. Pile extra stars in the center of the spiral. Use fewer stars along the arms.

3. Look down at the model. Draw what you **observe**.

4. Position your eyes at table level. Look across the surface of the table at the model. Again, draw what you **observe**.

5. Look at the photographs at the bottom of page D55. One is of a spiral galaxy viewed from the edge. The other shows the galaxy viewed from the "top." **Compare** the pictures you drew in Steps 3 and 4 with the photographs of a spiral galaxy. Then look at page D54. **Observe** the photograph of a ribbon of stars. This is our view of the Milky Way Galaxy from Earth. Using your drawings and the photographs, **infer** where in the Milky Way Galaxy the sun is.

Name _____

Draw Conclusions

1. Suppose the sun were located "above" the Milky Way Galaxy. What view of the galaxy might we see from Earth? _We would see the arms of the spiral Milky Way Galaxy._

   _____

   _____

2. If the sun is in one of the arms, what view might we see of the galaxy then? _We would see the Milky Way Galaxy as a ribbon of stars._

   _____

   _____

3. From your drawings and the photographs of a spiral galaxy, where in the Milky Way Galaxy do you **infer** the sun is? _The sun is in one of the arms of the spiral Milky Way Galaxy. The side view students drew looks like the view from Earth._

   _____

   _____

   _____

4. **Scientists at Work** Scientists often **infer** when **using models** like the one you made. How did your model of the Milky Way Galaxy help you infer the sun's location in the galaxy? _A model helps you draw the Milky Way Galaxy from several points of view._

   _____

   _____

   _____

Investigate Further Observe the Milky Way Galaxy in the night sky. You will need a clear, dark night, far away from city lights. Binoculars or a telescope will help you see some of the fainter stars. _____

   _____

   _____

   _____

   _____

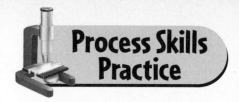

Use Models

You can use a model to study something that is too big to study in your classroom. For example, you may use a wall chart to study the solar system, or projections of stars on the ceiling to study the night sky.

Think About Using Models

When you want to see where you live in relation to the rest of the city, you can look at a map. A map is a model of your city. You can find the street you live on and, if the map is detailed enough, you can even figure out where your house is on the street. Astronomers have carefully measured the light from stars in our galaxy and have figured out how far away they are from the sun. They have used this information to draw maps of the galaxy as it would look from the side and from above.

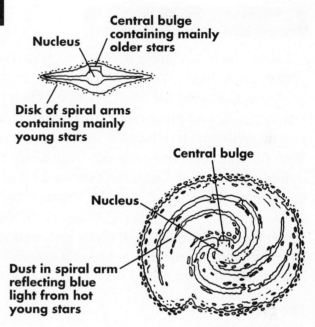

Nucleus

Central bulge containing mainly older stars

Disk of spiral arms containing mainly young stars

Central bulge

Nucleus

Dust in spiral arm reflecting blue light from hot young stars

1. Looking at the map, where in our galaxy do you think you would find most of the matter (that is, stars, gas, and dust)? _in the dense central bulge_

_____

2. Which of the two views shown do you think most resembles the Milky Way Galaxy as seen from Earth? Explain. _the side view, because we are located near the edge of the spiral in one of its curved arms_

_____

3. The entire galaxy is rotating. The inner stars are moving faster than the outer stars. How fast is the sun moving when compared to the rest of the galaxy? _It is moving slower than the center and than the stars that are closer to the center than itself, but faster than stars farther out._

_____

Identify Supporting Facts and Details

Read the selection. Then complete the outline below.

Discovering the Planets

Five of the nine planets in our solar system were discovered before 1700. Those planets are Mercury, Venus, Mars, Jupiter, and Saturn. These same five planets can be seen without the use of a telescope. When the telescope was invented, astronomy as a science grew dramatically. The next planet to be discovered was Uranus. William Herschel, a British astronomer, discovered this planet, seventh from the sun. After mapping out Uranus's orbit, Herschel discovered that it was indeed a planet, not a star. Neptune and Pluto were discovered by using mathematics. The director of the Urania Observatory in Berlin, Germany, and his assistant used John C. Adams's mathematical formula to locate Neptune on September 23, 1846. In 1930 Pluto appeared as a small dot on three photographs taken by Clyde Tombaugh at Lowell Observatory, which was built by Percival Lowell, who first predicted the existence of Pluto.

The Planets

A. Before 1700
   1. Five of the nine planets discovered
   2. Mercury, Venus, Mars, Jupiter, and Saturn
   3. All five planets can be seen with the unaided eye.

B. After Invention of the Telescope
   1. Uranus discovered next
   2. Discovered by William Herschel in 1781
   3. Named seventh planet in solar system

C. The Final Two Planets
   1. Neptune and Pluto discovered through mathematical predictions of their probable locations
   2. Neptune found in 1846 by scientists at Urania Observatory
   3. Pluto found in 1930 by Clyde Tombaugh

Name _____

Date _____

What Are Galaxies?

Lesson Concept

A galaxy is a group of stars, gas, and dust. The sun is in the Milky Way Galaxy, which is part of a galactic cluster called the Local Group.

Vocabulary

universe (D54) **galaxy** (D54) **light-year** (D55)

Answer each question with one or more complete sentences.

1. How are galaxies classified? _Galaxies are classified by shape._

2. You are looking through your telescope at the night sky, and you see a pinwheel-shaped object. What do you think it is? _It's probably a spiral galaxy._

3. What shape do irregular galaxies have? _Irregular galaxies have no obvious shape._

Mark the following statements with *True* or *False*. If the statement is false, write a correction next to it.

True **4.** Many galaxies rotate around a core. _____

True **5.** A nebula has no light of its own. _____

False **6.** A light-year is a unit of time. _A light-year is a unit of distance._

False **7.** Most galaxies are elliptical. _About half of all galaxies are elliptical._

False **8.** The Milky Way is an irregular galaxy. _The Milky Way is a spiral galaxy._

True **9.** Elliptical galaxies probably don't rotate. _____

Recognize Vocabulary

Listed below are the vocabulary terms from this chapter. Match the
terms in Column A with the definitions in Column B by writing in
the space next to the term the letter of the correct definition.

Column A

_D_ **1.** photosphere

_G_ **2.** corona

_B_ **3.** sunspot

_J_ **4.** solar flare

_A_ **5.** solar wind

_C_ **6.** magnitude

_I_ **7.** main sequence

_E_ **8.** universe

_F_ **9.** galaxy

_H_ **10.** light-year

Column B

A a fast-moving stream of particles released into
space from the surface of the sun

B dark places on the surface of the sun that are
cooler than the areas surrounding them

C the brightness of a star

D the part of the sun that we see

E everything that exists: planets, stars, dust, gases,
and energy

F a group of stars, gas, and dust

G the sun's atmosphere

H the distance light travels in one Earth year, about
9.5 trillion kilometers

I the most common combinations of color, size,
magnitude, and temperature of stars; plotted
on a special diagram, they appear in a band
stretching from the upper left of the diagram
to the lower right

J brief burst of energy from the sun's atmosphere

Write a Comic Strip About Sunscreen

Persuasive Writing–Promotion

Make up a comic strip for a children's magazine. Use your comic to convince children to wear sunscreen. Use what you know about the sun's radiation to support your message. Use the format below to plan your comic strip.

Panel 1: State your message.	**Panel 2: Give a reason to support your message.**
Panel 3: Give another reason to support your message.	**Panel 4: Restate your message in a memorable way.**

Chapter 1 • Graphic Organizer for Chapter Concepts

Matter and Its Properties

LESSON 1
PHYSICAL PROPERTIES THAT CAN BE MEASURED

1. mass _____
2. weight _____
3. volume _____

PHYSICAL PROPERTIES THAT HELP SCIENTISTS IDENTIFY DIFFERENT SUBSTANCES

4. density _____
5. solubility _____

LESSON 2
SIX PROCESSES THAT CAUSE MATTER TO CHANGE STATE

1. melting _____
2. freezing _____
3. boiling _____
4. condensation _____
5. sublimation _____
6. evaporation _____

LESSON 3
PHYSICAL OR CHEMICAL CHANGE?

1. Melting sugar _____ physical
2. Burning sugar _____ chemical
3. Mixing baking soda and vinegar _____ chemical
4. Burning steel wool _____ chemical
5. Steel rusting _____ chemical

Using Physical Properties to Identify Objects

Materials

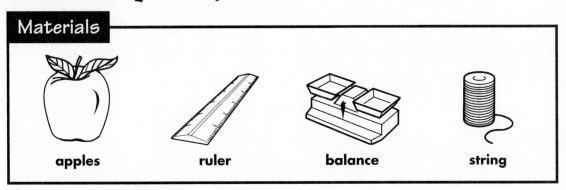

apples   **ruler**   **balance**   **string**

Activity Procedure

1 Carefully **observe** the apple your teacher gave you. What properties of your apple can you discover just by observing it? **Record** all the properties you observe.

2 Use the balance, ruler, and string to **measure** some characteristics of your apple. **Record** the properties you measure.

3 Put your apple in the pile of apples on your teacher's desk. Don't watch while your teacher mixes up the apples.

4 Using the properties that you recorded, try to identify your apple in the pile.

5 Using the balance, ruler, and string, **measure** this apple. **Compare** the measurements to those you recorded earlier. Then decide whether the apple you chose from the pile is yours. If someone else chose the same apple, comparing measurements should help you decide whose apple it really is.

Name _____

Investigate Log

Draw Conclusions

1. **Compare** your apple with a classmate's apple. How are the two apples alike? How are they different? Answers will vary. _____

_____

_____

2. Why was it helpful to **measure** some characteristics of your apple in addition to **observing** it? Measuring characteristics gives definite values. Observations can vary, even for the same object. _____

_____

3. How did you use the string to **measure** the apple? I wrapped the string around the apple and then measured the string to find the circumference of the apple. _____

4. **Scientists at Work** Scientists use both observations and measurements to identify substances. Which is faster, **observing** or **measuring**? Which provides more exact information? Observing is usually faster, but measuring provides more definite characteristics. _____

_____

Investigate Further Compare the list of your apple's properties with a classmate's list. Then, using your classmate's list, try to find his or her apple. Talk with your classmate about how he or she made the list. Did you and your classmate do things the same way? _____

_____

_____

_____

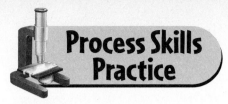
Process Skills Practice

Observe and Measure

Observing is learning facts about something by using your senses.
Measuring, a form of observation, is learning facts by using
instruments that can be used to extend your senses.

Think About Observing and Measuring

Tanya's science teacher told the class that chemical elements do not break down
during normal laboratory reactions. Then she said that the iron in fortified cereal
is not an iron compound, but pure iron! To demonstrate, she poured the contents
of a box of iron-fortified cereal into a large bowl and crushed the cereal into a
powder. She mixed water into the powder until it was very thin
and watery. Then she took a small bar magnet taped to a
glass rod and stirred the cereal and water mixture
for several minutes. When she pulled the bar
magnet out, tiny bits of iron were clinging to it.

1. Tanya observed the iron clinging to the magnet. How could her class measure
   the amount of iron in the box of cereal? Keep stirring the cereal and
   extracting the iron until no more can be observed clinging to the magnet.
   Then dry the iron and weigh it (on a milligram balance).

2. Tanya and her classmates read on the side panel of the cereal box that one
   serving of the cereal met the recommended daily allowance for iron and that
   one cup of cereal was one serving. What observation and measurement could
   they do to see if the cereal really provided the recommended daily allowance
   for iron? First they would need to look up the recommended daily allowance
   (RDA) for iron. Then they would need to use a fresh box of cereal to
   determine how many cups were in each box. Then they could divide the total
   amount of iron they measured in the first box by the number of cups of cereal
   and see if one serving would contain the RDA.

3. How did the iron become separated from the cereal? Did the matter in the
   cereal break down when Tanya's teacher mixed it with water? Explain.
   The iron was already pure iron and became physically separated when
   the cereal was crushed and mixed with water. Accept all reasonable answers.

Name _____

Date _____

Identify Supporting Facts and Details

Read the selection. Then complete the diagram to show supporting facts and details about mass and weight.

Mass Versus Weight

The terms *mass* and *weight* are often used to mean the same thing. However, in science these terms have very different meanings. Mass is a measure of the amount of matter an object contains. This measure is determined with a balance and is recorded in grams and kilograms. Weight is a measure of the pull of gravity on an object. The amount of weight is determined with a scale and is recorded in metric units called *newtons*.

Because gravity pulls on all objects on Earth with about the same force, the weight of an object remains fairly constant at all places on Earth. However, the weight of an object changes if the object is taken into space because the pull of gravity on the object changes. Despite this difference, the mass of the object remains the same in both locations because the object contains the same amount of matter.

Mass	Weight
a measure of the amount of matter an object contains	the measure of the pull of gravity on an object
determined with a balance	determined with a scale
recorded in grams and kilograms	recorded in newtons
mass remains the same in Earth's gravity or in space	weight differs from Earth's gravity to space

Name _____

Date _____

How Can Physical Properties Be Used to Identify Matter?

Lesson Concept

Matter has mass and takes up space. Physical properties can be used to identify different types of substances. Some physical properties, such as mass, volume, and density, can be measured.

Vocabulary

matter (E6)   **physical properties** (E6)   **mass** (E7)   **weight** (E7)

volume (E8)   **density** (E9)   **solubility** (E10)

Choose the answer that best completes the statement.

1. The effect of gravity on matter is the measure of _____.
   A mass   **B** weight   **C** density

2. An object has a mass of 120 g on Earth. On the moon it would have a mass of _____.
   A 20 g   **B** 60 g   **C** 120 g

3. The density of a steel hammer is 7.9 g/cm³ on Earth. On a spaceship it would have a density of _____.
   A 0 g/cm³   **B** 3.9 g/cm³   **C** 7.9 g/cm³.

4. Matter is anything that has mass and _____.
   A occupies space   **B** properties   **C** size

Decide whether the underlined term makes each statement true or false. If the statement is true, write the word *true* on the line. If the statement is false, write a word or phrase that makes the statement true.

___are not___   **5.** Materials <u>are</u> changed when physical properties are measured.

___true___   **6.** A milliliter is a unit of <u>volume</u>.

___solution___   **7.** In a <u>mixture</u>, the particles are evenly mixed.

Use with page E11.

Changing States of Matter

Materials

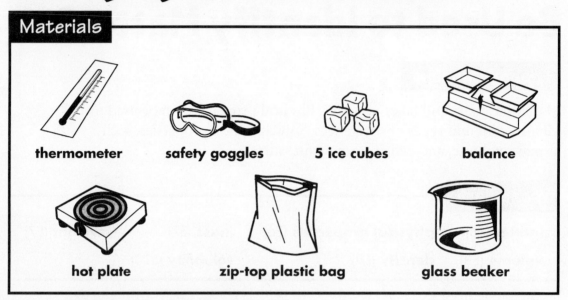

thermometer   safety goggles   5 ice cubes   balance

hot plate   zip-top plastic bag   glass beaker

Activity Procedure

1 Place five ice cubes in a zip-top plastic bag. Be sure to seal the bag. Use the balance to **measure** the mass of the ice cubes and the bag. **Observe** the shape of the ice cubes. **Record** your observations and measurements.

2 Set the bag of ice cubes in a warm place. **Observe** what happens to the shape of the ice cubes. Use the balance to **measure** the mass of the melted ice cubes and the bag. Unzip the bag slightly and insert the thermometer. Measure the temperature of the water. **Record** your observations and measurements. Use your observations to **infer** that a change of state is occurring.

3 After the ice has completely melted, pour the water into a glass beaker. Put the thermometer in the beaker. **Observe** what happens to the water's shape, and **record** the water's temperature.

4 **CAUTION** **Put on the safety goggles.** Your teacher will use a hot plate to heat the water in the beaker until it boils. **Observe** what happens to the water when it boils. **Record** the temperature of the boiling water. Use your observations to **infer** that another change of state has occurred.

Draw Conclusions

1. Identify the different states of water at different points in this investigation.
The ice cubes and the melted ice water are obvious. The water vapor cannot
be seen. Be sure students understand that the steam from the boiling water
is not water vapor, but condensed water vapor.

_____

2. Compare the mass of the ice to the mass of water after it melted. What does
this show about changes in state? The mass is the same. Changes in state do
not cause changes in mass.

_____

3. What temperatures did you **record** as the water changed states?
Accept answers within reasonable temperature range.

_____

4. Scientists at Work After scientists use their senses to **observe** the properties of
substances, they can **infer** whether a change in state has taken place. What did
you observe in this investigation? What did you infer about a change of state
from each observation? changes in the state and shape of water; that energy
in some form is present

_____

Investigate Further The physical change that happens to water when it is boiled
produces water vapor—an invisible gas. **Plan and conduct a simple experiment**
to test the following **hypothesis**: The mass of the water vapor is the same as the
mass of the liquid water. _____

_____

_____

_____

_____

Name _____

Date _____

Observe and Infer

Observation is collecting information about something by using your senses. Inferences are assumptions you make after considering your observations. Observations are facts, but inferences are guesses and may not always be correct.

Think About Observing and Inferring

Every night Dan could hear strange creaking noises in his bedroom and from the hallway outside his door. He finally asked his father about the noises and if the house was haunted. "That's just the house," explained his father. When Dan seemed doubtful, his father reached into the recycle bin and found a long-necked bottle. "After the sun goes down," he explained to Dan, "the house cools and contracts, that is, it actually gets smaller." To demonstrate, he partially inflated a balloon and put it over the bottle's neck as shown in the drawing. When he put the bottle into a bowl of ice water, the balloon shrank and fell over. When he put the bottle outside in the sun, the balloon slowly became inflated again.

1. What was Dan's first inference when he observed the noises in his house? Was his observation a fact? Was his inference correct? He inferred the house was haunted. His observation of noise was a fact. His inference was not correct.

2. What did he observe about the balloon and the bottle? When the bottle was cold, the balloon got smaller. When the bottle was warm, the balloon got bigger.

3. Why would Dan's house make noise expanding and contracting although the balloon did not? The balloon is elastic and expands and contracts evenly and easily. The house is rigid and made of many different materials that expand and contract at their own rates. Accept all reasonable answers.

Summarize and Paraphrase a Selection

Read the selection. Then summarize the concepts from each section.

Water and Other Matter

If you put a spoonful of solid sugar into a glass of liquid water and stir, what happens? The sugar seems to disappear!

Where did the sugar go? The answer is that the sugar and water formed a solution. In this case the sugar particles mixed with the water particles. You cannot see the sugar, but you can tell it's there because the water tastes sweet.

A solution is formed by one type of matter dissolving in another. After the sugar is stirred into the water, the sugar particles are mixed evenly with the water particles. If you mix too much sugar with the water, however, the extra sugar particles cannot mix evenly with the water. The extra sugar particles fall to the bottom of the glass.

Some solids dissolve in water. Other solids, such as sand, do not dissolve in water. The solubility of the water and sand mixture is zero because no amount of the sand dissolves in the water. When sugar dissolves in water, there is a high degree of solubility.

Concept: Solutions

Summary: A solution is a mixture in which the particles of different kinds of
             matter are mixed with each other.

Concept: Dissolving

Summary: One material forms a solution with another by dissolving. Sugar
             dissolving in water is one example.

Concept: Solubility

Summary: Solubility is a measure of the amount of a material that will
             dissolve in another material. Sugar has a high solubility in water,
             but sand has zero solubility.

Use with page E16.

Concept Review

How Does Matter Change from One State to Another?

Lesson Concept

Three states of matter are solid, liquid, and gas. Changes in state are physical changes. Particles of matter move faster as heat is added and slow down as heat is removed. Every substance has a melting point, the temperature at which it changes from a solid to a liquid. It also has a boiling point, the temperature at which it changes from a liquid to a gas.

Vocabulary

solid (E14)   **liquid** (E14)   **gas** (E14)

evaporation (E16)   **condensation** (E17)

Identify the following characteristics as belonging to solids (S), liquids (L), or gases (G). Some characteristics belong to more than one state of matter.

__S__ **1.** particles are held rigidly in place

__L, G__ **2.** takes the shape of the container

__S__ **3.** has a definite shape

__S, L__ **4.** particles are touching

__L__ **5.** particles slide over one another

__G__ **6.** particles are far apart

Choose the answer that best completes the statement.

7. The freezing point of a substance is the same as its __A__ point.

   A melting   **B** boiling   **C** condensation

8. Evaporation changes a __C__.

   A gas to a liquid   **B** liquid to a solid   **C** liquid to a gas

9. When a substance freezes, it __B__.

   A gains energy   **B** loses energy   **C** stays the same

10. Boiling involves the same change of state as __C__.

   A freezing   **B** condensation   **C** evaporation

Name _____

Date _____

Chemical Properties

Materials

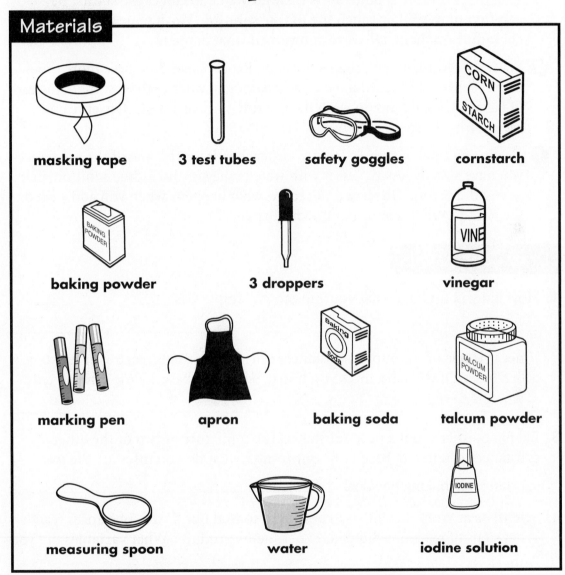

masking tape   3 test tubes   safety goggles   cornstarch

baking powder   3 droppers   vinegar

marking pen   apron   baking soda   talcum powder

measuring spoon   water   iodine solution

 ## Activity Procedure

1. Use the masking tape and marking pen to label your test tubes *water*, *vinegar*, and *iodine*.

2. **CAUTION** **Put on the apron and safety goggles. Leave them on for the entire activity.**

3. Put about $\frac{1}{3}$ spoonful of baking soda in each test tube. Add a dropper of water to the test tube labeled *water*. **Observe** and **record** what happens.

4 Add a dropper of vinegar to the test tube labeled *vinegar*. **Observe** and **record** what happens this time.

5 Add a dropper of iodine solution to the test tube labeled *iodine*.
CAUTION Iodine is poisonous if swallowed and can cause stains. Be careful not to spill or touch the iodine solution. Wash your hands if you get iodine on them. **Observe** and **record** what happens.

6 Wash the test tubes with soap and water. Repeat Steps 3–5 three more times using cornstarch, talcum powder, and baking powder in the test tubes instead of baking soda. Be sure to wash the test tubes between tests. **Observe** and **record** what happens each time.

7 Get an "unknown" sample from your teacher. It will be one of the substances you have already tested. Test it with water, vinegar, and iodine solution, just as you did before. **Observe** and **record** what happens when you add each of the liquids. What is your unknown substance?

Draw Conclusions

1. How did you find out what your unknown sample was? by comparing the way it reacted with the way the known samples react

2. Vinegar is one of a group of substances called *acids*. Acids react with substances called *bases*. Of the substances you tested, which are bases? How can you tell? baking soda and baking powder, because they reacted with the vinegar

3. Baking powder is not a pure substance. It is a mixture of two of the other substances you tested. Based on your results, what do you **infer** are the two substances in baking powder? baking soda and cornstarch

4. **Scientists at Work** Scientists **experiment** to find out if two substances react. What signs of reactions did your experiments produce? What **variables** did you **control**? A change in color and bubbling were evidence of a reaction; the quantity of substances and drops used.

Investigate Further Suppose you wanted to discover some of the chemical properties of chalk. **Hypothesize** whether chalk is an acid or a base. Then **plan and conduct a simple experiment** to test your hypothesis. _____

_____

_____

_____

_____

Experiment

One of the most basic of all activities in science is experimenting. Scientists state hypotheses and then design experiments to test them. Scientists change certain conditions in experiments and observe what happens. From these observations, they can see whether their hypotheses were correct.

Think About Experimenting

Sandra learned in science class that each substance has its own characteristic properties. One of those properties is density. Her teacher also said that the properties of a substance do not change even if the sample size changes. Sandra found that hard to believe. Sandra knew she could measure the density of a substance by putting it in water. If something floats, it is less dense than water. If it sinks, it is more dense than water. Sandra put some water in a clear jar and dropped in a piece of potato. The potato floated. Sandra hypothesized that a large enough piece of potato would sink. She put a large potato in the water and it also floated.

1. What was Sandra's hypothesis? A large potato is more dense than a small potato and would therefore sink.

2. What did Sandra observe? Was her hypothesis supported by her experiment? Why or why not? The large potato floated, too. No; because the density of a substance does not depend on its volume. A large piece has the same density as a small piece.

3. If the potato floats, then it is less dense than the water. Hypothesize what would happen if you could somehow make the potato more dense. If you get the potato dense enough, it would sink.

Draw Logical Conclusions

Read the selection. Then complete the chart by logically concluding the rate of corrosion for each common object, based on its metal makeup.

Corrosion

Corrosion is one of the most common chemical changes we observe in the environment around us. Corrosion occurs when a metal reacts with the oxygen in air, usually in the presence of water. It is a slow process. The first sign of corrosion is the metal losing its shiny appearance. As the corrosion spreads deeper into the metal, it begins to break down the metal's structure. Metals corrode at different rates. Some metals that corrode quickly and easily are potassium, sodium, magnesium, and aluminum. Metals that corrode more slowly and less easily are zinc, iron, copper, silver, and gold.

Object	Speed of Corrosion
A penny	slow
An aluminum baking sheet	fast
An iron stove	slow
A gold chain	slow
A silver teaspoon	slow

Name _____

Date _____

How Does Matter React Chemically?

Lesson Concept

Physical changes do not result in the formation of new substances. However, new substances are formed during chemical changes. Physical and chemical properties can be used to identify substances and to separate mixtures. Matter is neither produced nor destroyed during physical and chemical reactions.

Vocabulary

reactivity (E23)   **combustibility** (E24)

Answer each question with one or more complete sentences.

1. What is the difference between a physical change and a chemical change?

In a physical change, the original substance remains. In a chemical change, new substances are formed.

2. If you had a mixture of two substances and had your choice of using a physical change or a chemical change to separate them, which would you prefer? Explain. Probably a physical change because both substances could be recovered. In a chemical change, at least one substance would be changed into something else.

3. What is the relationship between the chemical properties of a substance and the chemical changes of a substance? The chemical properties of a substance, such as reactivity, determine what chemical changes it will undergo.

Identify each of the following as a physical or chemical change by writing *physical* or *chemical* on the line.

4. a snow bank shrinking on a cold day   physical

5. forming a bar of gold into wire   physical

6. bleaching a sheet and pillowcase   chemical

Recognize Vocabulary

Match the term on the left with its description on the right by writing the letter of the description in the blank next to the term.

____L____ **1.** matter

____J____ **2.** solid

____N____ **3.** liquid

____H____ **4.** physical properties

____A____ **5.** gas

____D____ **6.** mass

____F____ **7.** evaporation

____B____ **8.** weight

____C____ **9.** condensation

____M____ **10.** volume

____G____ **11.** reactivity

____I____ **12.** density

____K____ **13.** combustibility

____E____ **14.** solubility

A the state of matter that has no definite shape or volume

B the pull of gravity on matter

C changing from a gas to a liquid

D the amount of matter in an object

E the ability of a substance to dissolve

F the changing of a liquid to a gas

G the ability of a substance to react chemically

H the characteristics of a substance that can be measured without changing the substance

I mass per unit of volume

J the state of matter with a definite shape and volume

K the ability to burn

L anything that has mass and occupies space

M the amount of space anything occupies

N the state of matter with a definite volume but no definite shape

Use with pages E4–E27.

Name _____

Date _____

Write a Song About Matter

Expressive Writing—Song Lyrics

Write a song for a group of younger children, explaining how to tell the difference between the three states of matter. Give examples of each state in your song, and tell how matter changes states. Use the word web below to help you plan your lyrics.

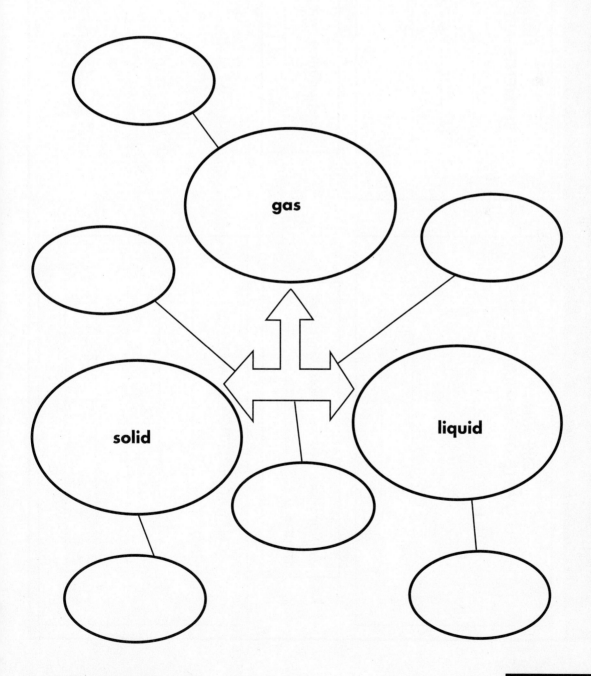

Chapter 2 • Graphic Organizer for Chapter Concepts

Atoms and Elements

LESSON 2
ELEMENTS ARE CLASSIFIED AS

1. metals _____
2. nonmetals _____
3. metalloids _____

Compounds can be written using
chemical formulas _____

LESSON 1
PARTS OF AN ATOM

1. nucleus _____
   protons _____
   neutrons _____
2. electrons _____

Two or more atoms linked together
form a   molecule _____

CHARACTERISTICS OF METALS

1. have luster _____
2. are malleable _____
3. are ductile _____
4. conduct electricity _____
5. conduct heat _____

Mystery Boxes

Materials

sealed box provided by your teacher

ruler

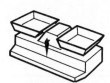

balance

magnet

Activity Procedure

1 With a partner, **observe** the sealed box your teacher gave you. **Record** any observations you think might help you learn about what's inside the box.

My observations: _____

2 Use the ruler to **measure** the outside of the box. Use the balance to find the mass of the box. **Record** your results.

My measurements: _____

3 Carefully tilt and shake the box. How many objects do you **infer** are in the box? How big do you infer the objects are? **Record** your inferences and the reasons for them.

My inferences: _____

4 Hold the magnet to the surface of the box. Then tilt the box. Are any of the objects in the box attracted to the magnet? Repeat this at several places on the surface of the box.

My observations: _____

5 What objects do you **infer** are inside the box? Base your inferences on your measurements and observations.

My inferences: _____

6 What do you **infer** about the inside of
the box? Draw a picture of what you think the inside of the box looks like.

7 Now open the box. **Compare** your inferences about the objects in the box
with the objects the box really contains. Also compare your inferences about
what the box looks like inside with what it really looks like.

My comparisons: _____

_____

_____

Draw Conclusions

1. How did what you **inferred** about the objects inside the box **compare** with
what was really inside? Students should point out both correct and incorrect
inferences.

_____

2. How did what you **inferred** about the inside of the box **compare** with the way
it really looked inside? Students should point out both correct and incorrect
inferences.

_____

3. Scientists at Work Different scientists may **infer** different things about objects
they can't **observe** directly. Compare your inferences about the contents and
the inside of the box with the inferences of other pairs. How were your

inferences similar? How were they different? Groups probably made many
different inferences about the contents and structure of the box.

_____

Investigate Further Construct your own mystery box, and place various objects
inside it. Give your box to a classmate. Your classmate will **observe** the box and
form a hypothesis about its contents and how it looks inside.

Name _____

Date _____

Observe and Infer

When you observe, you use one or more of your senses to perceive properties of objects and events. Observations can be made directly with the senses or indirectly through the use of instruments. When you infer, you use logical reasoning to draw conclusions based on observations. Inferences are explanations based on judgments and are not always correct.

Think About Observing and Inferring

During the investigation activity, you observed and inferred the characteristics of a mystery box. Below are some of the things you did during the investigation. After each action, write an *O* if you were observing or an *I* if you were inferring when you performed that step.

1. recorded things you noticed about the box	O
2. used a ruler to measure the outside of the box	O
3. listened to the sounds made and noticed the shifts in weight within the box when you tilted it and shook it	O
4. drew a picture of what you thought the inside of the box looked like before you opened the box	I

5. How did observing help you make an inference about the box?

Accept reasonable answers. Students may say that observations provided information to use to make logical judgments about what could or could not be in the box.

6. Suppose you receive a large envelope in the mail. Before opening it, you observe it and infer what is in it. What might you observe about the envelope?

Accept reasonable answers. Students may include size, weight, return address, handwriting, color, type of paper, stamps or type of postal service used, and so on.

7. What are some things you could infer about an unopened letter?

Accept reasonable answers. Students may include whom the letter is from, what's in the envelope, and so on.

Name ____________________

Date ____________________

Reading Skills Practice

Compare and Contrast

Compare and contrast the common elements by completing the chart below.

Common Elements

Name	Type of Matter	Possible Uses
oxygen	gas	breathing
sodium	solid	table salt
aluminum	solid	cooking pans and utensils, baseball bats, insulation
silicon	solid	electrical circuits
chlorine	gas	cleaning solution, disinfectant
iron	solid	manufacturing

Use with page E40.

Name _____

Date _____

What Are Atoms and Elements?

Lesson Concept

Atoms are tiny particles of matter. Elements are substances made up of only one kind of atom.

Vocabulary

nucleus (E39)   **proton** (E39)   **neutron** (E39)   **electron** (E39)

element (E40)   **atom** (E40)   **molecule** (E40)

Below is a list of terms and names from this lesson. Put each term or name into the correct category by writing it under one of the headings below.

heat conductor	ductile	sodium	electron
iron	oxygen	Dalton	neutron
silicon	proton	malleable	Bohr
electrical conductor			

Subatomic Particles	Common Elements	Properties of Metals	Scientists Who Studied Atoms
neutron	iron	ductile	Bohr
proton	silicon	malleable	Dalton
electron	oxygen	electrical conductor	
	sodium	heat conductor	

Draw a picture of Bohr's model of an atom, and label each part.

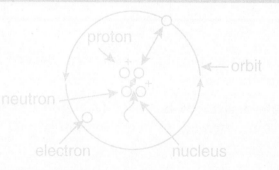

Name _____

Date _____

Grouping Elements

Materials

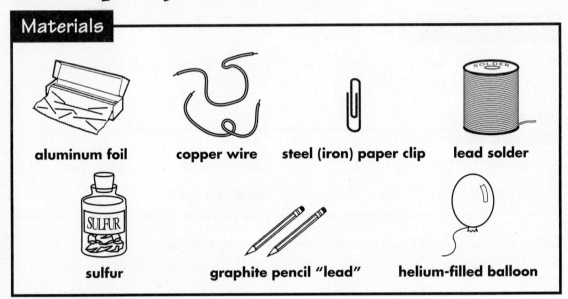

| aluminum foil | copper wire | steel (iron) paper clip | lead solder |

| sulfur | graphite pencil "lead" | helium-filled balloon |

CAUTION ## Activity Procedure

1 Use the chart below to **record** the properties of the elements you **observe**.

Object	Element	Phase	Color	Luster	Malleability
foil	aluminum	solid	silver	yes	yes
wire	copper	solid	copper	yes	yes
paper clip	iron	solid	silver	yes	yes
sulfur	sulfur	solid	yellow	no	no
graphite	carbon	solid	black	yes	no
solder	lead	solid	black	yes	yes
balloon	helium	gas	clear	no	no

2 What elements do the objects represent? **Record** your answers in the second column of the chart.

3 **Observe** each element. Is it a solid, a liquid, or a gas at room temperature? **Record** your observations in the column labeled "Phase" of the chart.

(page 1 of 2)

Use with pages E44–E45.

4 What is the color of each element?
(Carefully release some of the helium from the balloon.) **Record** what you **observe** in the chart.

5 Which elements have luster? (Which are shiny?) **Record** what you **observe** in the fifth column of the chart.

6 Which elements bend easily? **Record** what you **observe** in the column labeled "Malleability." **CAUTION** Wash your hands after handling the objects in this investigation.

Draw Conclusions

1. What similar properties did you **observe** in different elements?
Answers may include that aluminum, iron, and lead are silver-colored and shiny; that aluminum, copper, iron, and lead are bendable; and that sulfur and carbon are dull and don't bend.

2. Consider the properties you **observed** to form groups. Which elements could you group together? Explain. Aluminum, copper, iron, and lead; sulfur and carbon; reasons might include luster and bendability.

3. **Scientists at Work** Scientists have made a periodic table, in which elements are grouped by their properties. Using your observations, **predict** which elements from the activity are near each other in the periodic table. Students should suggest that the elements they grouped together should be near each other in the periodic table.

Investigate Further Think of other properties that could be used to group elements. Are there any you could test? **Plan and conduct a simple investigation** of one group of elements from this activity using these new tests.
Additional properties that students may test include magnetism, electrical and thermal conductivity, and melting point.

_____

_____

_____

_____

Observe and Predict

You can use observations to predict the outcomes of future events. Before making scientific predictions, you should think about previous observations you made of related events.

Think About Observing and Predicting

Observe the table below. Each element in the table is shown with its atomic number and atomic mass. The atomic mass is the mass of one mole (6.02×10^{23} atoms) of an element.

Element	Atomic Number	Atomic Mass in Grams
Helium	2	4
Carbon	6	12
Nitrogen	7	14
Oxygen	8	16
Sodium	11	
Iron		56

1. How many electrons circle around the nucleus of each atom of oxygen? _8_____

2. Describe the relationship between atomic number and atomic mass in the table. _The atomic mass seems to be twice the atomic number._____

3. The atomic mass of sodium is missing. What would you predict the atomic mass to be? _22 g_____

4. The atomic number of iron is missing. What would you predict the atomic number to be? _28_____

5. The atomic mass of sodium is actually 23 g. The atomic number of iron is actually 26. Compare these values to your predictions in Questions 3 and 4. What does this tell you about the relationship you saw between atomic number and atomic mass? _As the atomic number increases, the atomic mass increases. However, the atomic mass is not necessarily twice the atomic number._____

Name _____

Date _____

Use Context to Determine/Confirm Word Meaning

Complete the chart to determine or confirm the meanings of the terms listed in the chart.

Term	Sentence	Student Definition
elements	In nature most *elements* are joined with other elements to form compounds.	a substance made of only one kind of atom
alchemy	Changing other metals into gold could not be done after all. *Alchemy* was replaced by chemistry.	an ancient science based on the belief that gold could be made from other elements
chemistry	The students learned about chemical elements and compounds in *chemistry* class.	the study of chemical elements and compounds

Name _____

Date _____

Concept Review

What Are Compounds?

Compounds are molecules made of two or more elements.

Vocabulary

periodic table (E47)	**compound** (E48)

Chemists use shorthand to describe compounds. Use the table below to match each chemical symbol with the element it stands for.

C = carbon	Ca = calcium	Cl = chlorine	H = hydrogen
He = helium	O = oxygen	N = nitrogen	Na = sodium
Fe = iron			

1. Table salt (NaCl) has _____ atom(s) of _____ sodium _____
   and _____ atom(s) of _____ chlorine _____ .

2. One molecule of water (H_2O) has _____ atom(s) of _____ hydrogen _____
   and _____ atom(s) of _____ oxygen _____ .

3. One molecule of methane (CH_4) has _____ atom(s) of
   _____ carbon _____ and _____ atom(s) of _____ hydrogen _____ .

4. One molecule of ammonia (NH_3) has _____ atom(s) of
   _____ nitrogen _____ and _____ atom(s) of _____ hydrogen _____ .

Circle the choice that best completes each sentence below.

5. The order of elements in the periodic table is based on the
   ⟨*number of protons in one atom*⟩ / *atomic mass.*

6. Elements with properties of metals and nonmetals are called
   ⟨*metalloids*⟩ / *semi-metals.*

7. A Russian chemist named Dmitri Mendeleev organized elements by
   atomic number / ⟨*atomic mass.*⟩

Name _____

Date _____

Recognize Vocabulary

On the line, write the letter of the answer that best completes each sentence.

1. The ____ is the center of an atom.

  A nucleus   **B** proton   **C** compound   **D** molecule

2. A(n) ____ is made up of only one kind of atom.

  A compound   **B** element   **C** molecule   **D** atomic number

3. A(n) ____ is a subatomic particle with a negative charge.

  A electron   **B** nucleus   **C** neutron   **D** proton

4. The smallest unit of an element that has all the properties of that element is a(n) ____.

  A substance   **B** compound   **C** atom   **D** molecule

5. The elements are arranged in order of atomic number in the ____ table.

  A atomic   **B** Mendeleev   **C** periodic   **D** atomic mass

6. A(n) ____ is made of atoms of two or more elements.

  A neutron   **B** compound   **C** element   **D** molecule

7. A(n) ____ is a subatomic particle with a positive charge.

  A electron   **B** nucleus   **C** neutron   **D** proton

8. When two or more atoms are linked together, they form a(n) ____.

  A substance   **B** compound   **C** atom   **D** molecule

9. A(n) ____ is a subatomic particle with no charge.

  A electron   **B** nucleus   **C** neutron   **D** proton

Use with pages E36–E49.

Write a Science Lesson

Informative Writing–Explanation

Write a short science lesson explaining the periodic table of elements to another class. Think of ways to illustrate your lesson with charts or pictures. Use the topical outline below to help you plan your lesson.

The Periodic Table

   I. What does the periodic table look like?

      A. Words

      B. Illustrations

  II. What information does the periodic table provide?

      A. Words

      B. Illustrations

 III. How can you read the periodic table?

      A. Words

      B. Illustrations

 IV. Who invented the periodic table, and how has it changed over time?

      A. Words

      B. Illustrations

Chapter 1 • Graphic Organizer for Chapter Concepts

Forces

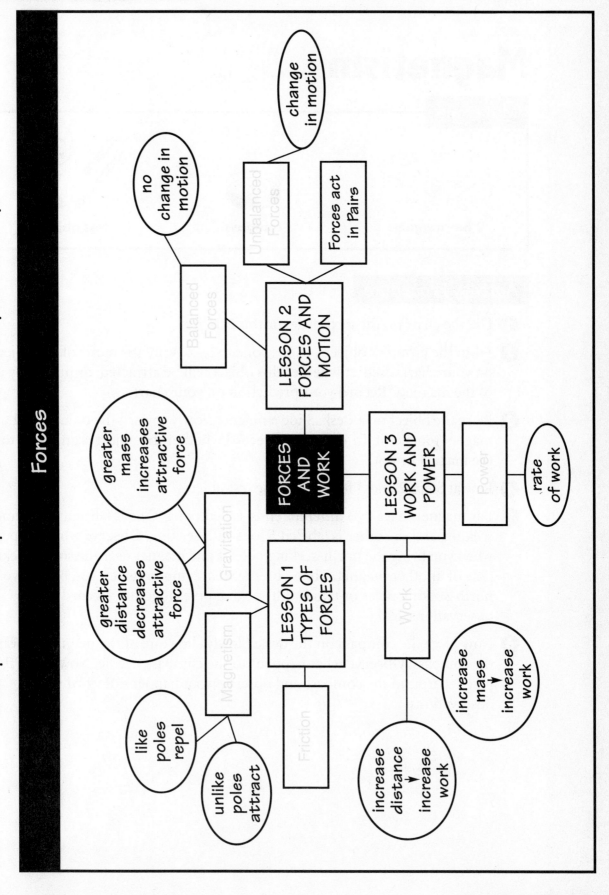

- change in motion
- no change in motion
- Unbalanced Forces
- Forces act in Pairs
- Balanced Forces
- LESSON 2 FORCES AND MOTION
- greater mass increases attractive force
- greater distance decreases attractive force
- Gravitation
- FORCES AND WORK
- LESSON 3 WORK AND POWER
- Power
- rate of work
- Magnetism
- LESSON 1 TYPES OF FORCES
- Work
- like poles repel
- unlike poles attract
- Friction
- increase distance → increase work
- increase mass → increase work

Name _____

Date _____

Magnetism

Materials

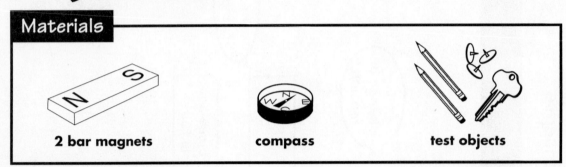

2 bar magnets   **compass**   **test objects**

Activity Procedure

1. Use the chart on the next page for this activity.

2. From the group of objects, choose one to test. Write the name of the object on your chart. **Predict** whether this object will be attracted, or pulled, by one of the magnets. **Record** your prediction on your chart.

3. Place the object on a desk. Slide a magnet slowly toward the object until the magnet touches it. In your chart, **record** whether the object is attracted to the magnet or not.

4. Repeat Steps 2 and 3 for each of the test objects.

5. Bar magnets have two different ends, called poles. One is labeled *N* for north seeking, and the other is labeled *S* for south seeking. **Observe** what happens when you bring the north-seeking pole of one magnet near the south-seeking pole of another magnet. Then observe what happens when you bring two north-seeking poles or two south-seeking poles together. **Record** your observations.

6. Now place the compass on the desk. Slowly slide one of the magnets toward the compass. **Observe** what happens to the compass needle. Now move the magnet around the compass and observe what happens. **Record** your observations.

Investigate Log

Object	Prediction	Test Result

Draw Conclusions

1. What characteristic of an object determines whether or not it is attracted by a magnet? Some metallic objects are attracted by magnets; or iron objects are attracted by magnets.

2. Infer what characteristic of a compass needle accounts for your observations of the compass and the magnet. Students may infer that a compass needle is also a magnet.

3. Scientists at Work Scientists often **hypothesize** about why things happen. Then they **plan and conduct investigations** to test their hypotheses. Form a hypothesis about why unlike magnetic poles attract each other while like magnetic poles repel, or push away, each other. Then plan and conduct an investigation to test your hypothesis. Students' hypotheses should relate to the magnetic fields around the magnets. Their investigations should use magnets and iron filings to show the shapes of these fields around like and unlike poles.

Investigate Further Experiment to find out if this **hypothesis** is correct: A compass needle always points to the north.

Students may bring in various compasses to prove the validity of this statement.

Name _____

Date _____

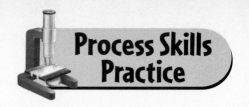

Hypothesize

When you hypothesize, you make an educated guess about the relationship between variables. A hypothesis must be something that can be tested. A hypothesis is often changed because of the outcome of experiments that test it.

Think About Hypothesizing

Leona's mother bought a small car because lightweight cars can go farther than heavy cars on the same amount of gasoline. Because weight is important to fuel efficiency, Leona wondered how the weight of the gasoline itself affects gas mileage. She hypothesized that a car probably gets better gas mileage when it has less gas in it. Therefore, to save both gas and money, it is better to fill the gas tank half-full than to fill it full. Her mother suggested they experiment to test the hypothesis.

1. How could Leona test her hypothesis? Record the fuel gauge reading. Fill the tank half-full. Record the number of gallons put in. Use the trip odometer to see how many miles the car goes before the fuel gauge reading is the same as before filling. Then divide the number of miles by the number of gallons to get miles per gallon. Repeat the experiment with a full tank of gas, and compare the results.

2. What are some variables in this experiment? the type of driving (for example, city or highway), the type of gas, the driver (driving styles differ), the weight of passengers and cargo, and the amount of gas

3. Which of the variables should be held constant in this experiment? all but the amount of gas

4 What results would support Leona's hypothesis? better gas mileage on half a tank of gas

5. Suppose Leona and her mother discovered that their gas mileage increased by 0.5 mile per gallon of gas by driving with the tank half-full. How much more often would they have to stop at the gas station to get this extra mileage? Do you think it would be worth the extra stops at the gas station? They would have to stop twice as often. It would probably not be worth it.

Reading Skills Practice

Identify Supporting Facts and Details

Read the selection. Then complete the outline with facts about the location and the direction of Earth's magnetic poles.

North and South Magnetic Poles

Earth has two other poles aside from the geographical North and South Poles. These poles are the north and south magnetic poles. Earth's north magnetic pole is located in northern Canada, about 800 miles from the North Pole. Earth's south magnetic pole is located in Antarctica, about 1,600 miles from the South Pole.

At Earth's magnetic poles, the magnetic field is vertical. The force of Earth's magnetic field at the north magnetic pole is pulled downward, into the ground. At the south magnetic pole, the magnetic force is pulled upward, away from the ground. At all other points on Earth, the magnetic field points toward the ground or angles away from it. Earth's magnetic poles can be found by using a compass. Follow the north-pointing end of the compass to find the north magnetic pole and the south-pointing end to locate the south magnetic pole.

Earth's Magnetic Poles
I. Location of north and south magnetic poles
  A. located far from Earth's geographical poles

  B. north magnetic pole located in northern Canada

  C. south magnetic pole located in Antarctica
II. Direction of Earth's magnetic force
  A. at north magnetic pole, magnetic force pulled into the ground

  B. at south magnetic pole, magnetic force pulled upward, away

    from the ground

  C. at all other areas on Earth, magnetic force pulled toward

    the ground or angled toward the ground

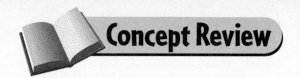

What Forces Affect Objects on Earth Every Day?

Lesson Concept

A force is a push or a pull that can move an object, stop it, or change its direction. Some forces are direct; others work at a distance. Where two surfaces rub against each other, the force of friction opposes motion. Magnetism pulls the poles of magnets together or pushes them apart. Gravity, which pulls objects toward each other, depends on the masses of the objects and how far apart they are.

Vocabulary

force (F6)   **friction** (F6)   **magnetism** (F7)   **gravitation** (F8)

Complete each sentence below by writing the word *friction*, *magnetism*, or *gravitation* in the blank.

1. The moving parts of an automobile engine are coated in oil or grease to reduce the _____friction_____ between the metal parts.

2. Some toys let you draw hair, eyebrows, and other features with a special wand that moves iron filings around by _____magnetism_____.

3. A balance scale works by using _____gravitation_____ to compare the weights of two objects.

4. A parachute uses the force of air pushing up on a large area of silk to resist the force of _____gravitation_____.

5. When you apply the brakes on your bike, you are clamping down on the bike's wheel to increase the force of _____friction_____.

6. Hikers can use a compass to guide them along a trail because the compass needle is pulled to the north by _____magnetism_____.

7. You can tape lightweight objects to a wall, but if you try to tape something heavy to a wall and it falls off, you'll know the tape isn't strong enough to overcome the force of _____gravitation_____.

Name _____

Date _____

Forces That Interact

Materials

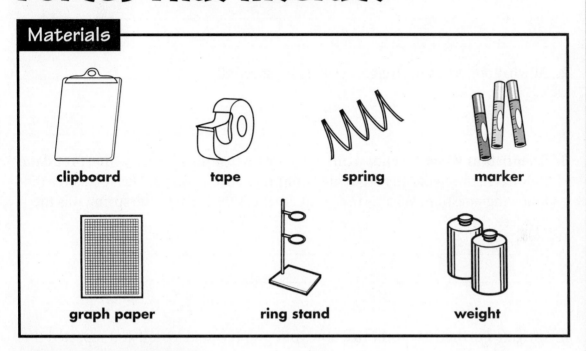

clipboard   tape   spring   marker

graph paper   ring stand   weight

Activity Procedure

1 Tape the graph paper to the clipboard. Across the bottom of the graph paper, draw a line and label it *Seconds*. Starting at one end of the line, make a mark every 2.5 cm.

2 Tape the spring to the ring stand. Then tape the weight to the free end of the spring. Tape the marker to the bottom of the weight so that its tip points toward the back of the setup.

3 Have a partner hold the clipboard with the graph paper taped to it behind the weight. The marker point should just touch the graph paper. Pull the weight until the spring is fully stretched.

4 Have your partner slide the clipboard across a table at a steady rate of about 2.5 cm per second. As soon as the clipboard starts to move, drop the weight. As it bounces, it traces its movements on the graph paper.

5 **Interpret the data** on your graph. Identify and mark the points where the weight was not moving up or down for an instant. Identify and mark the direction (up or down) the weight was moving along each sloping line. Identify and mark the places where the weight was moving most rapidly.

Name _____

Investigate Log

Draw Conclusions

1. At what points was the weight not moving? at the top and bottom of each
cycle
_____

2. At what point was the weight moving most rapidly? at the midpoint of each
cycle
_____

3. Scientists at Work Scientists often **draw conclusions** after they **interpret data** they have collected. After studying your graph, draw conclusions to answer the following question: What is the point at which the force of the spring was the greatest?

at the bottom of each cycle
_____
_____

Investigate Further Hypothesize how your graph would look if you repeated the activity with a heavier weight. **Plan and conduct a simple experiment** to test your hypothesis. Encourage students to formulate testable hypotheses and select and use appropriate equipment. Ask students to analyze and critique the strengths and weaknesses of their hypotheses based on their results.
_____
_____

Name _____

Date _____

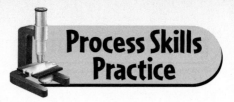

Interpret Data and Draw Conclusions

When you interpret data, you look for patterns or meaning in information that is given to you or information you have gathered from your own observations.

Think About Interpreting Data and Drawing Conclusions

The table below shows the force required to lift various objects on Earth as well as on two other planets, Planet X and Planet Y. The force is expressed in newtons (N). Study the data table, and then answer the questions that follow.

Force Needed to Lift Objects				
Object	On Earth (N)	On Planet X (N)	On Planet Y (N)	Mass (g)
1	20.0	8	4	2040.8
2	7.5	3	1.5	765.3
3	12.5	5	2.5	1275.5
4	5.0	2	1	510.2
5	25.0	10	5	2551.0

1. Which of the three planets has the strongest gravitational pull? Explain.
   Earth; the largest force is required to lift the objects on Earth.

2. Which of the three planets has the weakest gravitational pull? Explain.
   Planet Y; the least amount of force is required to lift the objects on Planet Y.

3. List the objects in order, starting with the one having the greatest mass and ending with the one having the least mass. Objects 5, 1, 3, 2, and 4

4. How did you use your knowledge of interpreting data to help you decide what the information in the data table means? Answers will vary, but students should recognize that having the data arranged in a table allowed them to make comparisons and draw conclusions about the gravitational forces of the planets, and the effect of mass on gravitational force.

Use with page F11.

Identify Cause and Effect

Read each statement. Identify the effect of each cause by underlining it. Then circle "Balanced" or "Unbalanced" to describe the forces used.

A strong wind moves the <u>sailboat across the water at a constant velocity</u>.

(Balanced)   Unbalanced

A person using a wheelchair applies the brakes and <u>slows down</u>.

Balanced   (Unbalanced)

A soccer ball rolls across a field and <u>is stopped by a tree</u>.

Balanced   (Unbalanced)

A skateboarder <u>slows down</u> while skating up a ramp.

Balanced   (Unbalanced)

Name _____

Date _____

What Are Balanced and Unbalanced Forces?

Lesson Concept

Balanced forces occur when two forces acting on an object are equal in size and opposite in direction. Unbalanced forces occur when forces acting on the same object are not opposite and equal. When forces are unbalanced, a net force occurs, causing acceleration. When you calculate the net force on an object, you must account for both the size and the direction of the forces.

Vocabulary

balanced forces (F12)   **unbalanced forces** (F13)

net force (F14)

Decide whether the underlined term or phrase makes each statement true or false. If the statement is true, write the word *true* on the line. If the statement is false, write a word or phrase that makes the statement true.

true _____ **1.** <u>Balanced</u> forces are equal in size and opposite in direction and therefore cancel each other out.

true _____ **2.** The change in motion of an object is always caused by <u>a force or forces</u>.

no force _____ **3.** If balanced forces are acting on an object, it will seem as if <u>a net force</u> is acting on the object.

in pairs _____ **4.** Forces always act <u>alone</u>.

adding or subtracting _____ **5.** <u>Balancing</u> the forces acting on an object gives you the net force.

unbalanced _____ **6.** When <u>balanced</u> forces act on an object, the object speeds up, starts to move, slows down, stops, or changes direction.

true _____ **7.** If <u>two equal forces</u> act on an object in opposite directions, the net force will be balanced.

true _____ **8.** <u>Unbalanced forces</u> can stop a moving object.

Measuring Work

Materials

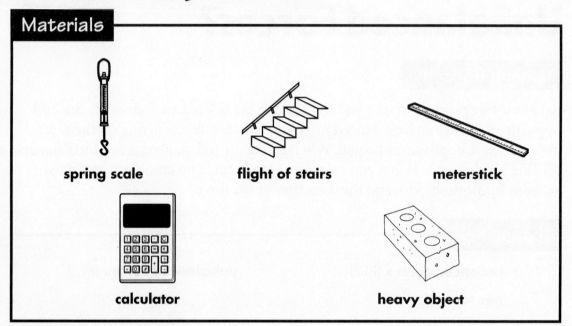

spring scale   flight of stairs   meterstick

calculator   heavy object

Activity Procedure

1 Use the table below for this activity.

2 Weigh the object using the spring scale and **record** its weight in the table, next to *Trial 1*.

3 **Measure** the total height of the flight of stairs in meters. **Record** the measurement in your table, also next to *Trial 1*.

4 Work can be **measured** as the product of force (in newtons) and distance (in meters). **Calculate** to find the number of newton-meters, or *joules*, of work you would do if you carried the object up the flight of stairs. **Record** the product in the table.

Work			
Trial	Weight (newtons)	Height (meters)	Work (joules)
1			
2			
3			
4			

5 Suppose you carried the object up two flights of stairs. Beside *Trial 2* on the table, **record** the new height and **calculate** the work done.

6 For *Trial 3*, **calculate** how much work you would do if you carried the object up three flights every day for a week.

7 For *Trial 4*, suppose your weight is 300 newtons. **Record** this new data and **calculate** the work you do climbing the stairs without carrying the object.

Draw Conclusions

1. **Compare** the amount of work a person weighing 300 newtons does climbing one flight of stairs to the total amount of work the same person does climbing three flights of stairs every day for a week. Twenty-one times as much work is done in a week.

2. **Interpret** your **data** and **draw conclusions** about how work is related to force and distance. As force or distance increases, the amount of work done also increases.

3. **Scientists at Work** When scientists **interpret data**, they often **draw conclusions** based on the data they collected. What can you conclude about the amount of work done by people who weigh more than 300 newtons? they do more work

Investigate Further *Power* is the measure of how quickly work is done. You can measure power in *joules per second*. **Hypothesize** about how much power you use walking up a flight of stairs compared to running up a flight of stairs. Then **plan and conduct an experiment** to test your hypothesis.

_____

_____

_____

_____

_____

Name _____

Date _____

Interpret Data

When you interpret data, you look for patterns or meaning in information that has been given to you or information that you have gathered.

Think About Interpreting Data

The table below provides data about five students who participated in a fitness test. Look at the data, and then answer the questions that follow.

Name	Student Weight	Vertical Distance	Time
Darcy	369 N	100 m	120 seconds
Carla	392 N	100 m	116 seconds
Tyler	400 N	100 m	122 seconds
Tasha	382 N	100 m	126 seconds
Daniel	419 N	100 m	130 seconds

1. Which of the five students exerts the most force to move his or her body? Explain. Daniel weighs the most and therefore requires the most force to move his body.

2. Which of the five students did the most work? Explain. Daniel; because all the students moved the same vertical distance, the student who moved the most weight did the most work.

3. Write a mathematical sentence that describes the amount of work done by Daniel. 419 N × 100 m = 41,900 J

4. Which student is the most powerful? Explain. Carla; Carla did the greatest amount of work in the shortest amount of time and was therefore the most powerful.

5. How did having the data in a table help you interpret it to answer the questions? Answers will vary, but students should recognize that having the data arranged in a table made it easier to make comparisons and draw conclusions.

Use with page F17.

Use Context Clues

Read the selection. Then complete the chart, using context clues from the selection.

Archimedes

Archimedes was one of the world's first known scientists. He lived and worked in Greece around 250 B.C. His many scientific inventions include the Archimedes' screw, which is still used today. An Archimedes' screw is a simple machine used to lift water from rivers and move it into canals for irrigation. An Archimedes' screw turns inside a tight cylinder. One end of the cylinder is placed under water. When the screw is turned, water moves up the threads and flows out the top of the cylinder. A similar screw is used today in meat grinders to move meat to the cutting blades and in sewage treatment plants as a pumping device.

Term	Ancient Use	Modern Use
Archimedes' screw	to lift water from rivers and move it into irrigation canals	in meat grinders to move meat to the cutting blades and in sewage treatment plants as a pumping device

Concept Review

What Is Work and How Is It Measured?

Lesson Concept

Work is the force applied to an object times the distance the object is moved. Work is measured in joules. Power is a measure of the speed at which work is done. Power is measured in watts. Machines are devices that make work seem easier by changing the size or direction of a force. Pulleys, levers, wheels and axles, inclined planes, wedges, and screws are simple machines.

Vocabulary

work (F18)　　　　　**power** (F19)　　　　　**machine** (F20)

Rewrite the descriptions in Questions 1–4 as mathematical sentences. Express values in newtons (N), meters (m), joules (J), and watts (W). Do any calculations necessary to find these values.

1. Vanessa and her father have built a sandbox for a neighborhood playground. They need to fill the sandbox with 20 bags of sand. Each bag weighs 50 pounds.

   How many newtons of force will be needed to lift the sand? 50 lb × 20 bags
   = 1000 lb; 1000 lb × 4.5 = 4500 N

2. The closest Vanessa and her father can get the back of their truck to the sandbox is 5 meters. How much work will Vanessa and her father have to

   do to move all the sand to the sandbox? 4500 N × 5 m = 22,500 J

3. Figure out how much work Vanessa's father must do to move one bag of sand.
   50 lb × 4.5 = 225 N × 5 m = 1125 J

4. It takes Vanessa's father three minutes to lift one bag of sand from the truck and carry it to the sandbox. How much power does Vanessa's father use to move one bag of sand?
   3 min × 60 sec/min = 180 sec; 1125 J ÷ 180 sec = 6.25 J per

   second = 6.25 W

Name _____

Date _____

Recognize Vocabulary

Choose from the following terms to solve each riddle. Use each term only once.

balanced forces	**work**	**power**	**forces**
net force	**magnetism**	**acceleration**	**gravitation**
friction	**machines**	**unbalanced forces**	

___magnetism___   **1.** I am a repulsing force, and my partner is an attracting force. Together we are forces between the poles of a magnet. What are we?

___balanced forces___   **2.** I am a force pushing on an object, and you are a force pushing back on the object, but neither of us is moving the object. What are we?

___work___   **3.** When you catch a football and run with it, I am what you are doing when you move the ball and yourself over the distance you run. What am I?

___machines___   **4.** We can change force into distance and distance into force. What are we?

___forces___   **5.** We are pushes or pulls. What are we?

___power___   **6.** The faster you work, the more you have of me. What am I?

___friction___   **7.** I am a force, I oppose motion, and you find me where the surfaces of two objects meet. What am I?

___unbalanced forces___   **8.** We are both pulling the same object in opposite directions. At first the object doesn't move. Then it does. What are we when the object moves?

___gravitation___   **9.** I am the force that keeps your feet on the ground. What am I?

___net force___   **10.** I am a way of measuring the effect of two forces on an object.

___acceleration___   **11.** I am a change in movement, caused by unbalanced forces. What am I?

Name _____

Date _____

Describe an Everyday Machine

Informative Writing–Description

Think of a machine you use every day. Imagine you are writing a page in a technical manual that describes this machine. Your page should describe the function of the machine, the simple machines it is made up of, and the forces it uses. In the box below, draw the machine you have chosen and label its parts. Then use the organizer to make notes on the machine for your page.

Everyday Machine _____

Drawing of Machine with Parts Labeled	Description of Machine for Technical Manual
	Function:
	Simple machines:
	Forces:

Chapter 2 • Graphic Organizer for Chapter Concepts

Motion

LESSON 1
WAYS TO DESCRIBE MOTION

1. Speed _____

2. Velocity _____

3. Acceleration _____

LESSON 2
THE THREE LAWS OF MOTION

First Law: An object at rest will

remain at rest, and an object in

motion will continue to move in a

straight line at a constant speed

until an outside force acts on it.

Second Law: An object's

acceleration depends on the size

and direction of the force acting on it

and the mass of the object.

Third Law: For every action force,

there is an equal and opposite

reaction force.

LESSON 3
WHY PLANETS STAY IN ORBIT

Law of Universal Gravitation:

All objects in the universe are

attracted to all other objects.

Investigate Log

Changes in Motion

Materials

clear plastic bottle
with cap

water

small piece
of soap

Activity Procedure

1 Fill the bottle nearly to the top with water. Leave only enough space for a small air bubble. Add a small piece of soap to the water. This will keep the air bubble from sticking to the side of the bottle. Put the cap tightly on the bottle.

2 Lay the bottle on its side on a flat surface. You should see one small bubble in the bottle. Hold the bottle steady until the bubble moves to the center of the bottle and stays there.

3 **Predict** what will happen to the air bubble if you turn the bottle to the left or right. Turn the bottle and **observe** what happens. **Record** your observations.

4 Now **predict** what will happen to the air bubble if you move the bottle straight ahead at a steady speed. Move the bottle and **observe** what happens. **Record** your observations.

5 Repeat Step 4, but this time slowly increase the bottle's speed. **Observe** what happens to the air bubble. **Record** your observations.

Investigate Log

Draw Conclusions

1. Compare your predictions and your observations. What happened when you turned the bottle to the left or right, or moved it forward? The bubble moved in the same direction as the bottle.

_____

2. From what you **observed**, how did a change in speed affect the bubble?
A change in speed caused the bubble to move in the direction of the change.

_____

3. Scientists at Work Were you surprised by the way the air bubble moved? When scientists get surprising results, they often **hypothesize** about the cause of those results. Form a hypothesis about why the bubble moves the way it does. Students' hypotheses should include the idea that the bubble moves in reaction to the water. As the bottle moves, the water tends to stay where it is at first, pushing the bubble in the direction of the movement.

_____

Investigate Further Hypothesize about what will happen to the air bubble if the bottle is moving at a steady speed and its direction changes. **Plan and conduct an experiment** to test your hypothesis. _____

_____

_____

_____

_____

Hypothesize

When you hypothesize, you make an educated guess about the relationships between variables. A hypothesis must be something you can test in an experiment, and it may be proven wrong in an experiment. A hypothesis is based upon observation, prior knowledge, and prior experimental outcomes.

Think About Hypothesizing

Suppose you want to find out the effect of an inclined surface on an object's speed. In addition to a stopwatch, you have the following materials to work with:

   a smooth board, 15 centimeters wide by 30 centimeters long

   a cylindrical glass jar weighing 75 grams

   a cylindrical glass jar weighing 150 grams

   2 blocks of wood, 2 centimeters thick

   2 blocks of wood, 4 centimeters thick

1. State a hypothesis about how the slope of an inclined surface might affect an object's speed. Possible answers: The steeper the slope of an inclined surface, the faster an object will travel.

2. Describe an experiment, using the materials listed above, that would test this hypothesis. Possible answers include timing how long it takes one of the jars to roll down the board, when one end of the board is propped up by various combinations of the 2-centimeter and 4-centimeter blocks.

3. State a hypothesis about how the weight of a jar might affect its speed down the inclined board. Possible answers: The heavier jar will roll faster; both jars will roll at the same speed.

4. Describe an experiment that would test your hypothesis. Answers may include holding the slope of the inclined board constant while timing the speed of both jars.

Use Context Clues

Read the selection. Then complete the chart, using context clues.

Speed, Velocity, and Acceleration

What are the differences among speed, velocity and acceleration? These terms are *fundamental* to studying *motion*. You have heard people talk about speed. You speed up or slow down on a bicycle or in a car or when you are walking. **Speed** is a measure of the distance an object moves in a given amount of time. If you are riding in a car that goes 45 mi/h in a straight line, that is its speed. However, if your car is going 45 mi/h in a circle, you are describing its velocity. **Velocity** is an object's speed in a particular direction. Any change in the velocity of an object is called **acceleration**. Any time an object stops, starts, speeds up, slows down, or changes direction, it is called acceleration. Can you infer what *deceleration* is?

Term	What You Think It Means	Definition
fundamental		basic, original
motion		movement of objects
deceleration		another name for slowing down

How Are Motion and Speed Related?

Lesson Concept

Motion is a change in an object's position. Speed is a measure of the distance an object moves in a given amount of time. Velocity is speed in a particular direction. Acceleration is a change in velocity, either in direction or in speed. Momentum, the product of an object's velocity and its mass, is a measure of how hard it is to slow down or stop an object.

Vocabulary

position (F34)   **speed** (F35)   **velocity** (F35)

acceleration (F35)   **momentum** (F36)

Fill in each blank with a vocabulary term. Each term may be used more than once.

1. When track runners finish a race, they don't just suddenly stop at the finish line. The runners' _____ momentum _____ carries them well past the finish line, before they can slow down and then stop.

2. You can usually tell when an object is in motion because you can see its _____ position _____ changing.

3. Some people think that _____ acceleration _____ just means speeding up, but it can also mean slowing down.

4. _____ Velocity _____ isn't just an object's _____ speed _____, it's also the object's direction of travel.

5. Earth is moving through space. One way we can tell Earth is moving is by observing how our _____ position _____ changes in relation to the stars.

6. If an object is traveling at a constant speed and then changes direction, we say its _____ velocity _____ has changed. We call this change _____ acceleration _____.

How Mass and Velocity Affect Momentum

Materials

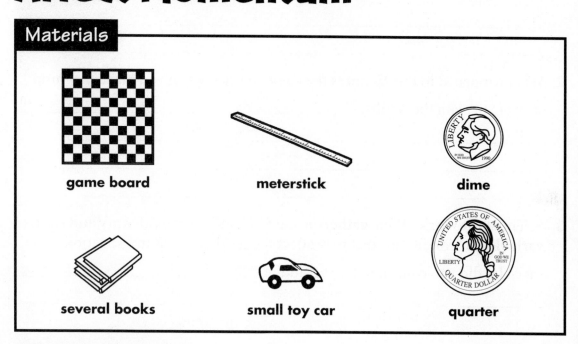

game board

meterstick

dime

several books

small toy car

quarter

Activity Procedure

1 Make a ramp by setting one end of the game board on a stack of books about 15 cm high. Place another book as a barrier about 10–15 cm from the bottom of the ramp.

2 Position the car at the top of the ramp. Put the dime on one end of the car. Let the car roll down the ramp and strike the barrier. **Observe** what happens to the dime. **Measure** and **record** its distance from the barrier.

3 Repeat Step 2, this time placing the quarter on the car instead of the dime. **Observe** what happens to the quarter. **Measure** and **record** its distance from the barrier.

4 Repeat Steps 2 and 3 several times. **Measure** and **record** the distance for each trial.

5 **Predict** how the results would differ if the ramp were steeper. Add another book to the stack under the ramp, and repeat Steps 2 and 3 several times. **Measure** and **record** the distances for each trial.

Investigate Log

Draw Conclusions

1. Make a table to organize your data. **Compare** the results for the dime with the results for the quarter. **Infer** how the mass of the coin is related to the distance it travels. The quarter travels farther than the dime. Students should infer that the greater the coin's mass, the farther it travels.

_____

2. What happened to the distances the coins traveled when you made the ramp steeper? Explain the results. Both coins traveled farther. Making the ramp steeper increases the velocity of the cart, which increases the momentum of the coins.

_____

3. Scientists at Work While **gathering data**, scientists try to **identify and control variables**, or conditions, that may affect the results. In this investigation, what variables did you control in Steps 2 and 3? the height of the ramp (velocity of the car) and the distance the car traveled

_____

What variable did you test? the size (mass) of the coin

_____

Investigate Further Plan and conduct a simple investigation to test various methods of keeping the coin on the car when it strikes the barrier. Carefully select the equipment you will need, and conduct several trials for each method you test. Students must devise a "seat belt" for the coin. Challenge them to use their results to encourage people to wear seatbelts in automobiles.

_____

Identify and Control Variables

When you identify and control variables, you find out which conditions in an experiment make a difference in the outcome. Controlling variables means changing one condition while keeping all the other conditions the same.

Think About Identifying and Controlling Variables

Ann and Barbara decide to ride their bicycles from their houses to the park. Ann claims that her bicycle is faster than Barbara's, and that therefore, she will get to the park first. They both live the same distance from the park. The road from Ann's house is paved. The road from Barbara's house is dirt and gravel. Ann takes off her coat before she rides. Barbara likes the sound of her coat flapping in the wind, so she leaves her coat on. The two of them race from their separate houses, and Ann wins. Did she win because her bicycle is faster?

1. Was the race a fair test of which bicycle is faster? Explain. No; two different people rode the bikes, road surfaces produced different amounts of friction, and a coat produced air resistance.

2. What were some variables in the race? bicycles, riders, road surfaces, and air resistance

3. Which condition was the same? In other words, which variable was controlled? distance

4. Which variables were not controlled? bicycle, rider, road surface, and air resistance

5. What would be a good way of testing the hypothesis that Ann's bicycle is faster than Barbara's? Accept all reasonable answers. Possible answer: One friend should not wear a coat and should ride one bike over one road while the other friend times the ride. This ride should be repeated, and the average time should be taken. Then the same rider should take the same ride on the other bike. The average times should be compared.

Make Generalizations

Read the selection. Then write a generalization based on the information.

For Every Action . . .

Sir Isaac Newton identified three laws of motion and changed forever the way we look at the world. These laws have become a part of our everyday lives, but we're not always aware of them acting on us. Many people have a hard time understanding Newton's third law of motion: *For every action, there is an equal and opposite reaction.* Yet this law is demonstrated in several sports you may be familiar with. Perhaps you have watched sprinters begin a race. Do you remember how they started? By pushing off a starting block, the sprinters demonstrated Newton's third law of motion. As the sprinters push off the block, they are launched forward. At the same time, the starting block and Earth are pushing back. It's easy to see the motion, or action, of the sprinter, but it's not possible to see the reaction of the starting block and Earth because these forces do not cause a measurable change in the motion of the Earth or the starting block. Now think about roller-skating. Roller-skating demonstrates all three laws of motion. The third law is demonstrated when gravel is thrown backward as skates go forward. The action is the skater moving forward. The reaction is the gravel being thrown backward. Can you think of any other sports that demonstrate the third law of motion?

Generalization:

Newton's third law of motion is demonstrated in natural, everyday activities.

_____

_____

_____

Name _____

Date _____

What Are the Three Laws of Motion?

Lesson Concept

The first law of motion is that an object at rest tends to remain at rest and an object in motion tends to move in a straight line at a constant speed, unless an outside force acts on it. The second law is that an object's acceleration depends on the mass of the object and on the size and direction of the force acting on it. The third law is that for every action, there is an equal and opposite reaction.

Vocabulary

inertia (F41)	action force (F43)	reaction force (F43)

Write *true* in front of the true statements and *false* in front of the false statements. If the statement is false, write a correction in the space provided.

_____true_____ **1.** The same force that causes a pencil to fall to the floor also causes the moon to orbit Earth. _____

_____true_____ **2.** A moving object tends to continue moving in a straight line unless something pushes or pulls it out of its path. _____

_____

_____false_____ **3.** The inertia of an object depends directly on its motion.

The inertia of an object depends directly on its mass.

_____true_____ **4.** Newton's first law of motion explains why when you are riding in a car, you feel forced outward, away from the direction of turns.

_____

_____false_____ **5.** An action force makes a rocket move. A reaction force makes

a rocket move.

_____true_____ **6.** Newton's second law of motion explains how an unbalanced force on an object causes it to accelerate. _____

_____

Name _____

Date _____

Orbits and Inertia

Materials

2-m string   **safety goggles**   **metal washers**

CAUTION Activity Procedure

1. Tie three or four metal washers securely to one end of the string.

2. **CAUTION** **Take the string with the washers outside to an open area. Be sure that you are far from any buildings or objects and that no one is standing close to you. Put on the safety goggles.** Hold the loose end of the string. Slowly swing the string and washers in a circle above your head. **Observe** the motion of the washers.

3. **Predict** what will happen if you let go of the string while swinging it in a circle.

4. **CAUTION** **Again, make sure that there are no people, buildings, or other objects near you.** Swing the string and washers in a circle again. Let the string slip through your fingers. **Observe** the motion of the washers. How does it **compare** with your prediction?

5. Using a drawing, **record** the motion of the washers in Steps 2 and 4. Be sure to show the forces acting in each situation. Now make a drawing of the moon orbiting Earth. **Compare** the two drawings.

Name _____

Draw Conclusions

1. **Compare** the path of the washers while you were swinging them with their path once you let go of the string. While the student swings the string, the washers move in a circular path because of the force exerted by the string. When the string is let go, the washers fly off in a straight-line because of inertia.

2. The string and washers can be used to **model** the moon orbiting Earth. **Compare** the motion of the washers circling your head with the motion of the moon orbiting Earth. Inertia keeps the washers and the moon moving. The force exerted by the string keeps the motion of the washers circular, while gravitation keeps the moon orbiting Earth.

3. **Scientists at Work** When scientists **experiment**, they must **communicate** their results to others. One way of doing this is with diagrams. Look at the drawing you made of the washers. What motions and forces does it show? Student diagrams should show the circular and straight-line motions of the washers. They should also show the force exerted by the string on the washers and the force exerted by the washers on the string.

Investigate Further Hypothesize about the effect the length of the string has on the time the washers take to complete one revolution. Then **plan and conduct an experiment** to test your hypothesis. _____

_____

_____

_____

_____

Communicate

When you communicate in science, you are showing the results of an activity, such as an experiment, in an organized fashion so that the results can be interpreted later. If you communicate well, you or someone else can repeat the experiment to demonstrate it to others, or you can build on the work to make further discoveries.

Think About Communicating

In the 1600s a mathematician named Johannes Kepler was given an assignment to analyze records of the motions of the planets to figure out the nature of their orbits. This was before telescopes, before Newton's laws of motion, and at a time when people knew very little about the planets. The records he studied had been kept very carefully by an astronomer named Tycho Brahe (TEE•koh BRAH•hee) and were considered very accurate. After studying the data, Kepler was able to describe the orbits of Mars and Earth as ellipses. He used this new information to figure out three laws of planetary motion, and he published his findings in two books. A few years afterward, a young scientist named Isaac Newton used the information communicated by Johannes Kepler to figure out the law of universal gravitation.

1. What kind of communication enabled Kepler to reach his conclusions?
   the accurate records kept by Tycho Brahe

2. How did Kepler communicate his own discoveries? He wrote books.

3. Kepler's books described the orbits of planets. If you were helping him write his books, how would you suggest he communicate his findings?
   Possible answers include using drawings of the orbits or making a chart of
   how the distances of the planets from the sun changed during their orbits,
   forming ellipses.

4. Part of effective scientific communication is making sure others will understand the information you are sharing. Do you think Brahe's scientific communication was effective? Was Kepler's? Explain. Yes. Kepler was able to
   use Brahe's communication to deduce his laws of planetary motion. Isaac
   Newton was able to use Kepler's communication to figure out the law of
   universal gravitation.

Use Graphic Sources for Information

Look carefully at the illustration and read the paragraph. Then answer the questions below.

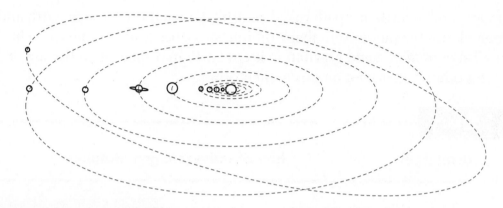

Pluto and Neptune

Most of the time, Pluto is the planet farthest away from the sun. It takes Pluto 247 Earth years to orbit the sun. Yet during some periods, such as between 1979 and 1999, Pluto's orbit brings it inside the orbit of Neptune, making Neptune for those years the farthest planet from the sun. Neptune is about four times the size of Earth. It has eight satellites and lies 2.8 billion miles from the sun. Neptune's atmosphere is made up of poisonous gases. Pluto is only one-fifth the size of Earth. It is so cold and its atmosphere is so extremely thin that life is not thought to exist there. Like Earth, Pluto has one moon.

When is Pluto *not* the farthest planet from the sun? It is closer to the sun than Neptune is during some periods while it orbits the sun.

In relation to Earth, what is the size of Neptune? Neptune is about four times larger than Earth.

Which planet has more satellites, Neptune or Pluto? Neptune has eight satellites; Pluto has one.

Why are Neptune and Pluto planets that would not support human life? Students should mention that these planets are too far from the sun to provide much light or heat. The planets' atmospheres are poisonous and thin.

Name _____

Date _____

Why Do the Planets Stay in Orbit?

Lesson Concept

The moon circles Earth in a path called an orbit. Gravitation between Earth and the moon keeps the moon from flying off into space because of its inertia. The balance between inertia and gravitation keeps Earth in orbit around the sun. It also keeps other planets and moons in their orbits.

Vocabulary

orbit (F48)   **law of universal gravitation** (F49)

Answer each question with one or more complete sentences.

1. If Earth suddenly disappeared, the moon would no longer be under its gravitational influence. Would the moon then fly off in a straight line? Explain. No; because it would still be under the influence of the sun's gravitation, the moon would continue to orbit the sun.

2. Newton's law of universal gravitation says that all objects in the universe are attracted to all other objects. You already know this means that the moon is attracted toward Earth. Does the law of universal gravitation also mean that Earth is attracted toward the moon? Explain. Yes; the moon is also an object with a huge mass and therefore pulls Earth toward it.

3. Gravitational force decreases with distance. What does this mean for a space traveler who leaves Earth in a spaceship? As you travel away from Earth in a spaceship, the farther away you get, the less you feel the pull of Earth's gravitation.

4. As you travel through space away from Earth, what does the universal law of gravitation say about objects you may encounter that have huge masses? You will be attracted to them as you were attracted to Earth when you were closer to it.

Recognize Vocabulary

Use the following terms to solve the crossword puzzle.

position	speed	velocity
acceleration	momentum	inertia
action force	reaction force	orbit
law of universal gravitation		

Across

2. a measure of the distance an object travels in a certain length of time
6. the force that pushes or pulls back in response to another force
7. an object's speed in a particular direction
8. any change in velocity
9. a force that acts on an object
10. the property that resists any change in an object's motion

Down

1. an object's place or location
3. a measure of how hard it is to slow down or stop an object
4. If you say that everything is attracted to everything else, you are stating the law of universal ____.
5. the path an object in space takes as it revolves around another object

Crossword grid answers:

1-Down: POSITION
2-Across: SPEED
3-Down: MOMENTUM
4-Down: GRAVITATION
5-Down: ORBIT
6-Across: REACTION FORCE
7-Across: VELOCITY
8-Across: ACCELERATION
9-Across: ACTION FORCE
10-Across: INERTIA

Writing Practice

Write a Public Service Announcement

Persuasive Writing–Promotion

You have been asked to develop a one-minute public service announcement for television, promoting the use of automobile safety belts by children. Write a script for the public service announcement. Support your position by including details about the effects of mass, velocity, and momentum. Use the storyboard outline below to plan your script.

Elapsed Time (in seconds)	Visual	Narration
00:00–00:12		**Main argument:**
00:12–00:24		**Supporting point 1:**
00:24–00:36		**Supporting point 2:**
00:36–00:48		**Supporting point 3:**
00:48–00:60		**Restate argument:**

Chapter 3 • Graphic Organizer for Chapter Concepts

Forms of Energy

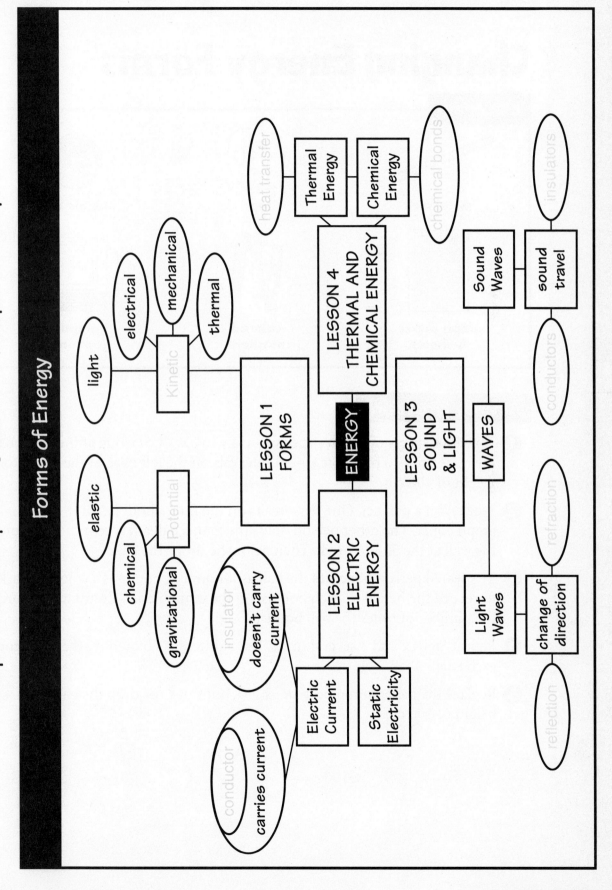

Changing Energy Forms

Materials

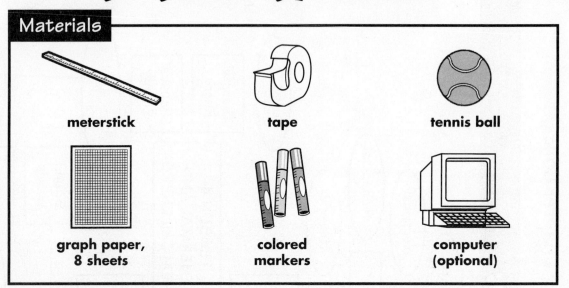

meterstick	tape	tennis ball
graph paper, 8 sheets	colored markers	computer (optional)

Activity Procedure

1 Tape four sheets of graph paper vertically to a wall. Starting at the floor, use the meterstick to mark off 10-cm intervals on the left edge of the paper to a height of 100 cm.

2 Work with a partner. One person sits on the floor about 0.5 m from the graph paper. The other person holds the tennis ball a few centimeters from the wall at the 50-cm mark. Then he or she drops the ball.

3 The seated person **observes** the ball as it bounces, and uses a colored marker to **record** the height of each bounce on the graph paper. **Count** and record the number of times the ball bounces.

4 Repeat Steps 2 and 3 several times. Use a different-colored marker to **record** each trial.

5 Replace the paper and repeat Steps 1–4, but this time drop the ball from a height of 100 cm.

Name _____

Draw Conclusions

1. Compare the drop height to the bounce height for each trial in the experiment. How are the heights related? _The higher the drop height, the higher the bounce height._

2. When you hold the ball in the air before dropping it, it has *potential energy* because of its position and because of gravitation. When you let go of the ball, it has *kinetic energy* because of its movement. **Infer** the point at which the ball has the most kinetic energy. _at its point of greatest speed—just before it hits the floor for the first time._

3. Draw a conclusion about how potential energy and kinetic energy are related in the bouncing ball. _They are inversely related, as kinetic energy increases, potential energy decreases._

4. Scientists at Work Scientists often use computers to help them **interpret data** and **communicate** the results of an experiment. Use a computer graphing program, such as *Graph Links*, to **compare** the height of each bounce and the number of bounces from one trial of the 50-cm drops and one trial of the 100-cm drops. Make a different-colored line graph for each trial.

_____

_____

_____

Investigate Further Analyze the data you graphed in Step 4 and **hypothesize** how high and how many times a ball dropped from a height of 200 cm will bounce. Then **experiment** and **compare** your results to your hpothesis.

_____

_____

_____

_____

Communicate

When you communicate, you transmit data or information to others. You can use spoken or written words, graphs, drawings, diagrams, maps, and charts to communicate. Communicating in science means showing the results of an activity in an organized fashion so that the data can be interpreted or the activity repeated.

Think About Communicating

Here is some data from an experiment to observe the potential and kinetic energy of a basketball.

Dropped from 1 meter. Trial 1: Bounced 60 cm. Trial 2: Bounced 70 cm. Trial 3: Bounced 80 cm.

Dropped from 2 meters. Trial 1: Bounced 1 m 40 cm. Trial 2: Bounced 1 m 25 cm. Trial 3: Bounced 1 m 40 cm.

Communicate these results on the graphs.

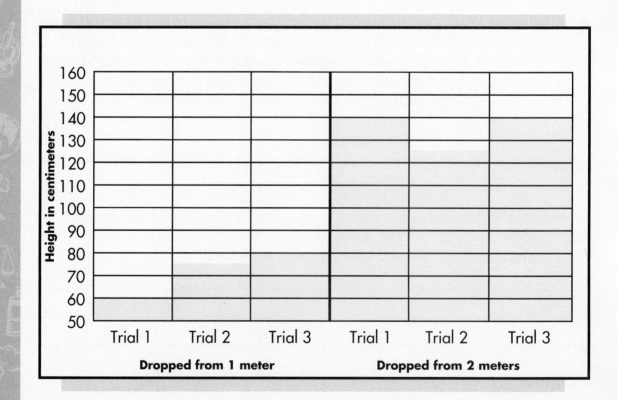

Predict Probable Future Actions and Outcomes

Read the selection. Then predict probable future outcomes of the use of solar energy by answering the questions.

Solar Energy

The sun produces a form of energy called *solar energy*. The sun's radiation is Earth's largest energy source. Solar energy first became popular as a source of energy during the twentieth century. The fact that it is both abundant and clean makes it very attractive to many people. Its nonpolluting quality adds to its attractiveness since coal, oil, and natural gas have been destructive to Earth's environment.

Earth receives radiation from the sun and converts it to either electrical energy or thermal energy. Concentration collectors and flat-plate collectors capture solar energy. The collectors must be very large—about 430 square feet—to produce enough energy for one person for one day. Most solar energy has been used to operate boilers for power plants, to provide power for communications and weather satellites, and even to power watches and calculators.

Solar energy also has been used to produce salt from sea water and to power solar ovens for cooking. Despite its wide use, this type of energy has been limited because of its high cost for collection, conversion, and storage.

Predict the Outcome

The search for cheaper, cleaner energy has increased during the last century. What problems might the sun have as an energy source? These uses of solar energy could be limited by the cost of converting solar energy to electricity.

_____

_____

Predict the Outcome

Currently, the sun's energy powers many devices. What might be some future uses of solar energy for homes, businesses, and transportation? Solar energy could be used to power cars and buses. It could provide electricity to power appliances in homes and businesses. It could even be used to produce clean drinking water from sea water.

Name _____

Date _____

What Are Kinetic and Potential Energy?

Lesson Concept

Energy is the ability to cause changes in matter. There are two basic types of energy—kinetic energy and potential energy. Kinetic and potential energy can be found in many forms. Electric energy, thermal energy, mechanical energy, light, and sound are all forms of kinetic energy. Chemical potential energy, gravitational potential energy, and elastic potential energy are forms of potential energy. The law of conservation of energy says energy can change form but cannot be created or destroyed.

Vocabulary

energy (F62)   **kinetic energy** (F62)   **potential energy** (F62)

Decide whether the underlined term or phrase makes each statement true or false. If the statement is true, write the word *true* on the line. If the statement is false, write a word or phrase that makes the statement true.

___true___ **1.** Energy is the ability to do work.

___true___ **2.** The energy of motion is called kinetic energy.

___true___ **3.** The energy an object has because of where it is or because of its condition is called potential energy.

___kinetic___ **4.** A boulder rolling down a hill has potential energy.

___kinetic___ **5.** Mechanical energy is a form of potential energy.

___can change___ **6.** Energy never changes from one form to another during any one activity.

___kinetic___ **7.** Thermal energy and light energy are two forms of potential energy.

___true___ **8.** An apple that is ready to drop from the tree to the ground has gravitational potential energy.

___potential___ **9.** The energy stored in a compressed spring is called elastic kinetic energy.

Electric Circuits

Materials

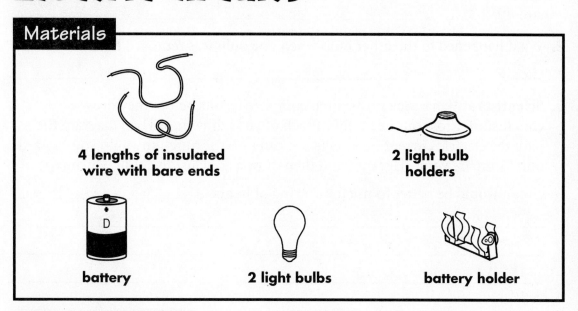

4 lengths of insulated wire with bare ends

2 light bulb holders

battery

2 light bulbs

battery holder

Activity Procedure

1 To make electricity flow between the terminals, or charged ends, of a dry cell or battery, you need to connect the terminals in some way, such as with a wire. Electricity will then flow through any device you put along this path. Connect the wires, bulb holders, and battery holder as shown in Picture A on page F67.

2 Insert the light bulbs and batteries. **Observe** what happens and **record** your observations.

3 Remove one of the bulbs from its holder. **Observe** and **record** what happens to the other bulb.

4 Now reconnect the wires, bulb holders, and battery holder as shown in Picture B on page F67. **Observe** what happens and **record** your observations.

5 Again remove one of the bulbs from its holder. **Observe** and **record** what happens to the other bulb.

6 Draw diagrams of both of the circuits you built. Use arrows to **compare** the path of the electric current in each circuit.

Name _____

Draw Conclusions

1. What happened to the other bulb when one bulb was removed from the first circuit? It went out. _____

2. What happened to the other bulb when one bulb was removed from the second circuit? It stayed on. _____

3. **Scientists at Work** Scientists often **compare** results before they **draw a conclusion**. Cross out one bulb in each of your drawings. Then diagram the path the electric current must take if it can't pass through the bulb you crossed out. Compare your diagrams, and then draw a conclusion about which type of circuit would be better to use for a string of lights. The second circuit would _____ be better because one burned-out bulb wouldn't stop the electricity from _____ reaching the other bulbs. _____

   _____

   _____

Investigate Further In the investigation you demonstrated that electricity flowing through a circuit produces light and heat (the glowing bulbs were warm). Now **plan and conduct a simple investigation** to demonstrate that electricity flowing through a circuit can also produce sound and magnetism. Decide what equipment you will need to use in your investigation. _____

_____

_____

_____

_____

Name _____

Date _____

Compare and Draw Conclusions

When you compare, you identify common and distinguishing characteristics of objects or events. When you draw a conclusion, you pull together all that you have discovered in observing, researching, and investigating.

Think About Comparing and Drawing Conclusions

Comparing the characteristics of different things is a good way to learn those characteristics and draw conclusions about them. Look at the data in the chart below and then answer the questions that follow.

	Materials That Allow Electricity to Flow	**Materials That Do Not Allow Electricity to Flow**
Porous	watery substances, salt solutions, acid solutions	Leather, cotton, wool, parchment, ashes, chalk, hair, feathers, wood
Nonporous	iron, copper, silver, graphite, charcoal	rubber, porcelain, vinyl, plastics, precious stones, ceramic, glass, resin, amber

1. When you plug something into an electrical outlet, you don't want electricity to flow from the wires into your hand. The plug must therefore be made of material that does not allow electricity to flow. Compare the properties of the materials listed in the chart. Draw a conclusion about which materials would be good for making plugs. Possible answers include rubber, porcelain, vinyl, plastics, precious stones, ceramic, glass, resin, and amber.

2. Explain why you chose those materials. Students should choose materials that do not allow electricity to flow and that are nonporous so perspiration on a person's hands (a salt solution, which is a material that allows electricity to flow) could not seep through the plug covering and allow electricity to flow.

3. List two materials that would be good to use for wires to carry electricity in a circuit and explain why. silver and copper; Both allow electricity to flow and can be shaped into wire.

Name _____

Date _____

Use Prefixes and Suffixes to Determine Word Meanings

Read the words in the chart. Then write your own definition of the words, based on the meanings of the prefix and the root. Check your definitions with a dictionary.

Prefix + Root	Your Definition	Dictionary Meaning
electro- (electric) + *magnetism* (power to attract)	Student definitions will vary but should closely match the dictionary definition.	magnetism produced by an electric current
electro- (electric) + *mechanical* (operated by machinery)	Student definitions will vary but should closely match the dictionary definition.	a mechanical device or operation that is controlled by electricity
re- (back, returning to previous state) + *action* (state of being in motion)	Student definitions will vary but should closely match the dictionary definition.	a returning or opposing action or force
com- (with) + press (push steadily against)	Student definitions will vary but should closely match the dictionary definition.	make more compact by or as by pressure

Use with page F70.

What Is Electric Energy?

Lesson Concept

Electric energy is the movement of electrons between areas that have opposite charges. When objects with opposite charges are close enough together or when the charges are very large, electrons move between the objects. Electric current moves through an electric circuit. When electric current flows through a conductor, it produces a magnetic field, turning the conductor into an electromagnet.

Vocabulary

electric charge (F68)   **electric force** (F69)   **electric current** (F69)

conductor (F70)   **electric circuit** (F71)   **insulator** (F71)

resistor (F71)   **electromagnet** (F72)

Match the term in the left column with its description in the right column.

___D___ **1.** positive charge

___F___ **2.** static electricity

___I___ **3.** series circuit

___G___ **4.** proton

___A___ **5.** electric energy

___H___ **6.** electric current

___J___ **7.** conductor

___K___ **8.** generator

___B___ **9.** electron

___L___ **10.** resistor

___E___ **11.** electric force

___C___ **12.** negative charge

A the energy produced by the movement of electrons

B an atomic particle with a negative charge

C the charge an object has when it has gained electrons

D the charge an object has when it has lost electrons

E the attraction or repulsion that unlike or like charges have

F the potential electric energy of a charged object

G an atomic particle with a positive charge

H the flow of electrons

I a circuit with only one path for the electrons

J a material that carries electrons easily

K a source of electrons

L a material that resists electric current

Name _____

Date _____

The Path of Reflected Light

Materials

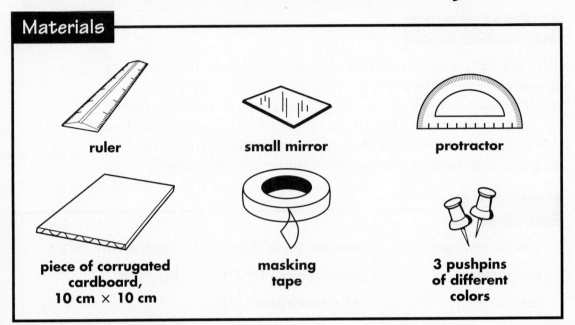

ruler

small mirror

protractor

piece of corrugated cardboard, 10 cm × 10 cm

masking tape

3 pushpins of different colors

Activity Procedure

1. Lay the cardboard flat. Use the tape to attach the mirror vertically to one end of the cardboard. Push two of the pins into the cardboard, about 5 cm from the mirror.

2. Position yourself at eye level with the mirror. Align yourself so that your view of one pin lines up with the reflection of the other pin. Push a third pin into the cardboard at the edge of the mirror, right in front of where you see the reflection of the second pin. The first pin, the third pin, and the reflection of the second pin should appear to be in a straight line.

3. Draw lines on the cardboard to connect the three pins. These lines show how the reflected light from the first pin traveled to your eye.

4. Using the protractor, **measure** the angle between each line and the edge of the mirror. You will probably have to trace the edge of the mirror and then move it out of your way to make this measurement. **Record** your results.

5. Now remove the original pins and place two of them 10 cm from the mirror. Repeat Steps 2–4 with this new arrangement of pins. **Measure** the angles of the new lines, and **record** your results.

6 Now draw diagrams to **communicate**
the results of the two experiments. Each diagram should show the locations
of the pins and the mirror and the path of the reflected light.

Draw Conclusions

1. **Compare** the two angles you **measured** in each experiment.

The two angles should be congruent in each case.

_____

2. The angle at which light strikes a mirror is the *angle of incidence*. The angle at
which it reflects from the mirror is the *angle of reflection*. **Draw a conclusion**
about the angle of incidence and the angle of reflection from a flat surface.

The angle of incidence and the angle of reflection have the same

measurement.

_____

3. **Scientists at Work** When scientists **observe** a pattern that seems to always be
true, they try to come up with a clear, simple rule. This helps them **predict**
what will happen in the future. Predict what the angle of incidence and the
angle of reflection would be if the pins were 20 cm from the mirror.

Students should predict that the angles will still be congruent.

_____

Investigate Further **Hypothesize** how light would be reflected from a mirror that
was not flat. Then **plan and conduct a simple experiment** to test your hypothesis.

_____

_____

_____

_____

Name _____

Date _____

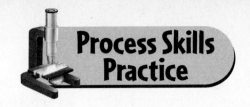

Predict

When you predict, you anticipate outcomes of future events, basing your ideas on your prior experience, observations, or knowledge.

Think About Predicting

Louise was given a toy guitar for her birthday. She noticed that plucking on the thicker strings made a sound lower in pitch than the sound made by plucking on the thinner strings. She also noticed that if she tightened a string, the sound it produced would become higher in pitch. She also noticed that all the strings on her mother's guitar produced sounds lower in pitch than the strings on her toy guitar. She observed that all the strings on her mother's guitar were longer than the strings on her toy guitar.

Louise inferred from her observations that the thinner, the shorter, or the tighter the string, the higher the pitch of its sound. She thought she could use this inference to predict the sounds that other stringed instruments would make.

1. What is Louise trying to predict? how the length, thickness, and tension of a musical instrument's strings will affect the pitch of the sound it makes

2. What information does she have that will help her predict? Shorter, tighter, or thinner strings make higher-pitched sounds.

3. A cello is a stringed instrument that looks like a very large violin. What could Louise predict about the sounds that a cello might make? Explain.
The cello would probably sound like a violin except much lower in pitch because its strings are thicker and longer.

4. Louise knew that a piano is a stringed instrument. What could she predict about the strings that would be hammered when she played the keys that produce low-pitched sounds? They would probably be thicker and longer than the other strings.

5. If you used Louise's observations, what could you predict about the sounds different-sized drums might make? Explain your answer by using Louise's inference. Larger drums would probably produce sounds lower in pitch than sounds produced by smaller drums. Students may also predict that drawing the skin tighter over the drum will change the sound to a higher pitch.

Use with page F75.

Name _____

Date _____

Arrange Events in Sequence

The Human Ear

Read the selection on page F79, and look at the diagram of the ear. Then number the steps below according to the order in which they occur.

___3___ The vibrating eardrum starts the hammer, anvil, and stirrup moving.

___6___ When hair cells move in the cochlea, they change their mechanical energy to electrical energy. Nerve impulses are sent along the cochlear nerve to the brain.

___1___ Sound waves enter the ear canal as air pressure changes.

___2___ The change in air pressure causes the eardrum to vibrate in and out.

___7___ The brain interprets the impulses.

___4___ The stirrup transfers vibrations to the fluid in the cochlea.

___5___ The vibrating fluid moves the hair cells that line the cochlea.

Name _____

Date _____

What Are Light and Sound Energy?

Lesson Concept

Light energy is electromagnetic energy that travels through space and through certain materials. When light waves strike an obstacle, they are absorbed, reflected, or refracted. Lenses are curved pieces of transparent matter that refract light rays. Sound energy is vibrations that travel through matter. Solids and liquids conduct sound better than gases.

Vocabulary

reflection (F76)	**refraction** (F76)	**lens** (F77)
pitch (F79)	**volume** (F79)	

Choose the answer that best completes each statement.

1. A _____ lens is thicker in the middle than at the edges.

   A concave   **B** convex   **C** reflection

2. The bending of light rays is called _____

   A reflection   **B** absorption   **C** refraction

3. When light rays bounce off an object, the bouncing is called _____

   A absorption   **B** refraction   **C** reflection

4. The colors of light that objects _____ are the colors we see.

   A absorb   **B** reflect   **C** refract

5. Sound waves have two parts, compression and _____

   A rarefaction   **B** refraction   **C** reflection

6. Light energy moves as waves called _____

   A magnetic waves   **B** vibrating waves **C** electromagnetic waves

7. The _____ is the colored part of the eye that narrows and widens to control the amount of light entering the eye.

   A pupil   **B** iris   **C** cornea

Use with page F81.

Heat

Materials

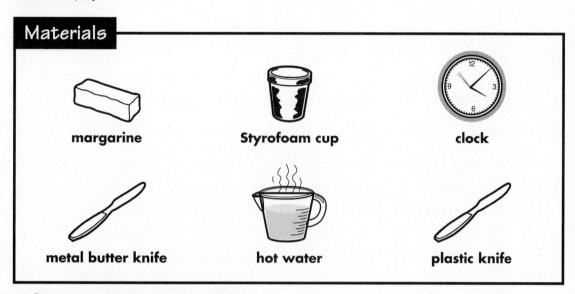

margarine

Styrofoam cup

clock

metal butter knife

hot water

plastic knife

CAUTION

Activity Procedure

1. Place a dab of cold margarine near the middle of the metal knife. Place another dab of margarine the same size near the tip of the knife's blade.

2. **CAUTION** Be careful when pouring the hot water. Half-fill the cup with hot water. Put the metal knife's handle into the water. The dabs of margarine should be above the level of the water.

3. **Predict** which dab of margarine will melt first—the one near the middle of the knife or the one near the end of the knife.

4. **Observe** the metal knife for ten minutes and **record** your observations.

5. Repeat Steps 1–4 using the plastic knife.

6. **Experiment** to find out which material transfers heat faster—metal or plastic. Be sure to **identify and control variables** that might affect the results.

Investigate Log

Draw Conclusions

1. Draw conclusions about how heat moves through the metal knife.

Heat moves from one end of the knife to the other, since the margarine near

the middle of the knife melted first.

_____

2. Draw conclusions about which material transfers heat faster.

Metal transfers heat faster.

_____

3. Scientists at Work Scientists must **identify and control variables** in an experiment to see how changing one variable affects the results. What variables did you control in your experiment? What variable did you test?

Controlled variables should include the lengths of the knives and

temperatures and amounts of both the margarine and the water.

The only variable that should change is the material through which the

heat is transferred.

_____

Investigate Further Hypothesize about which knife will lose heat more quickly. Then **experiment** to find out which knife cools faster. _____

_____

_____

_____

Name _____

Date _____

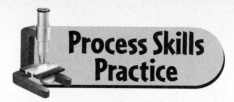

Identify and Control Variables

When you identify and control variables that affect the outcome of an experiment, you state which factors could affect the outcome of the experiment and you make sure that only one of those factors, or variables, is changed in any given test.

Think About Identifying and Controlling Variables

Suppose you are an architect trying to design an energy-efficient house. You want to know which wall and ceiling insulating materials work best so the house can be cooled and heated as inexpensively as possible. You also want lots of windows in the house so you can take advantage of natural light during the day. Windows, however, are where a house loses most of its warmed or cooled interior air. So you want windows that are good insulators but still allow light to pass through freely. You have a choice of three wall and ceiling insulating materials, and you have a choice of two window materials. You decide to build several small buildings the size and shape of doghouses for your test.

1. What are you testing? _the insulating efficiency of three wall and ceiling_
   insulators and two window materials

2. What are some variables in your tests? _the size of the house, the heating or_
   cooling source, the starting temperature inside the houses, the materials
   the houses are made of, the amount of insulating material in each house,
   the type of insulating material, the type of window material, the amount of
   time you measure the interior temperature of each house, temperatures
   outside the houses, the number of windows, and possibly others suggested
   by the students

3. Which of the variables will you control? _all but the one you are testing for;_
   that is, all but the type of insulating material or all but the type of
   window material

4. Will using doghouse-sized models give you accurate results? Explain.
   Yes; although an actual-size house will give you different results, as long as
   you keep all the houses the same size, that is, keep house size a controlled
   variable, you will still know which insulating materials work best. You are
   testing the material, not the house. Accept all reasonable answers.

Name _____

Date _____

Summarize and Paraphrase a Selection

Read the selection. Then, list three facts you learned about electromagnetism.
Finally, write a summary of the selection.

Electromagnetism

In the 1700s scientists thought that electricity and magnetism might be related.
They began experimenting to see whether this was true. Alessandro Volta
discovered that he could make electricity with pieces of two different metals. What
he invented was the first battery. The battery moved electricity steadily through a
conductor, such as a salt solution, instead of giving off the electricity all at once,
like a lightning bolt or a spark.

The key to understanding the connection between electricity and magnetism
came about when Hans Oersted, a Danish scientist and teacher, observed
something while teaching a class. Oersted noticed that when he put a compass
over a wire carrying electricity, the compass needle moved. He proved later that an
electric current always produces a magnetic field. Scientists continue to build on
Oersted's discovery of the connection between electricity and magnetism.

Facts: 1.

In the 1700s scientists thought that electricity and magnetism might be related.

Facts: 2.

Alessandro Volta invented the first battery.

Facts: 3.

Hans Oersted proved that electric current always produces a magnetic field.

Summary:

Scientists tried to find a connection between electricity and magnetism in the
1700s. Two scientists, Alessandro Volta and Hans Oersted, made major
contributions to the field of electromagnetism. Volta invented the battery and
Oersted proved that electric current produces a magnetic field. The discoveries
of these two scientists continue to help present-day scientists who work in the
field of electromagnetism.

What Are Thermal and Chemical Energy?

Lesson Concept

Thermal energy is the kinetic energy of molecules. The average kinetic energy of the molecules in an object is the object's temperature. Heat is the transfer of thermal energy from one object to another. Conduction is the direct transfer of thermal energy between objects that touch. Convection is the transfer of thermal energy through currents in a gas or a liquid. Radiation is the transfer of thermal energy by electromagnetic waves. When atoms join to form molecules, thermal energy can be stored as chemical energy. Chemical energy can be released as kinetic energy.

Vocabulary

temperature (F84)   **heat** (F84)   **conduction** (F85)

convection (F85)   **radiation** (F85)

Fill in each blank with a vocabulary term. You may use each term more than once.

1. When you add _____ heat _____ to an object, you increase the kinetic

   energy of the object's molecules, which increases its _____ temperature _____.

2. If you leave a metal stirring spoon in a pot of soup while the soup is heating,

   the spoon will quickly get hot because of _____ conduction _____.

3. When you sit near a campfire, the heat of the fire is transferred to you mostly

   by _____ radiation _____.

4. If your house is heated by a furnace that blows hot air into the rooms, you are

   depending on the process of _____ convection _____ to stay warm.

5. A lizard sometimes stretches out on a rock to warm itself. The rock is warm

   because the sun has transferred thermal energy to it by _____ radiation _____.

   The rock then transfers thermal energy to the lizard by

   The rock also transfers thermal energy to air above it and the lizard through a

   process called _____ convection _____.

Name _____

Date _____

Recognize Vocabulary

Write the letter of the definition in the right column next to the
term that it matches in the left column.

_____ **1.** conductor

_____ **2.** temperature

_____ **3.** electric circuit

_____ **4.** lens

_____ **5.** electric current

_____ **6.** convection

_____ **7.** potential energy

_____ **8.** heat

_____ **9.** insulator

_____ **10.** electric charge

_____ **11.** pitch

_____ **12.** electromagnet

_____ **13.** refraction

_____ **14.** energy

_____ **15.** electric force

_____ **16.** radiation

_____ **17.** conduction

_____ **18.** resistor

_____ **19.** volume

_____ **20.** reflection

_____ **21.** Kinetic energy

A a magnet formed by the flow of electric current

B energy of motion

C a material that doesn't carry electrons

D what an object gets when it gains or loses electrons

E the loudness of a sound

F the average kinetic energy of all the molecules in an object

G the transfer of thermal energy by electromagnetic waves

H energy an object has because of its condition

I a quality determined by the speed of vibration of sound waves

J a material that conducts electrons easily

K light that bounces off an object

L the attraction or repulsion between objects with a positive or negative charge

M the direct transfer of thermal energy between objects that touch

N the bending of light rays

O the ability to cause changes in matter

P the flow of electrons

Q the transfer of thermal energy from one substance to another

R a piece of clear material that bends light rays passing through it

S the transfer of thermal energy through currents in a liquid or a gas

T a material that resists the flow of electrons

U any path along which electrons can flow

Use with pages F60–F87.

Name _____

Date _____

Writing Practice

Write a Letter About Sound Waves

Expressive Writing—Business Letter

Write a letter to a sound engineer at a radio or TV station. Tell the engineer one thing you have learned about sound waves. Ask the engineer to answer some questions about sound waves. Use the format below to plan your letter.

Heading: _____
_____

Inside address: _____
_____
_____
_____

Greeting: _____
_____
_____
_____

Body of letter: _____
_____
_____
_____
_____
_____
_____
_____

Closing: _____
_____
_____

Signature: _____

Hint   Remember to thank the recipient for his or her time.

Chapter 4 • Graphic Organizer for Chapter Concepts

How People Use Energy

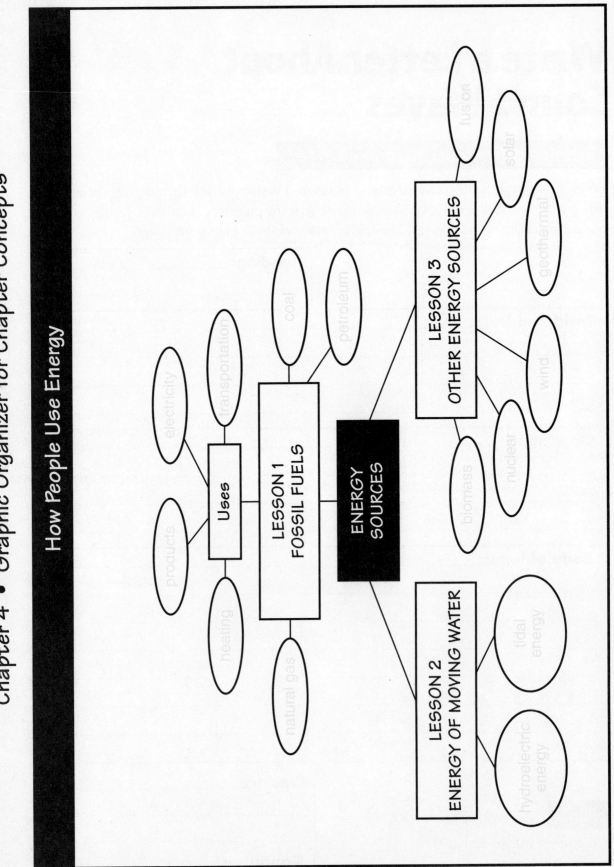

- electricity
- transportation
- products
- heating
- **Uses**
- **LESSON 1 FOSSIL FUELS**
- coal
- petroleum
- natural gas
- **ENERGY SOURCES**
- **LESSON 3 OTHER ENERGY SOURCES**
- fusion
- solar
- geothermal
- wind
- nuclear
- biomass
- **LESSON 2 ENERGY OF MOVING WATER**
- tidal energy
- hydroelectric energy

How Stored Energy Is Released

Materials

water	measuring cup	Styrofoam cup	thermometer
clock with second hand	safety goggles	calcium chloride	spoon

Activity Procedure

1 Use the table on the next page for this activity. Measure 50 mL of water in the measuring cup, and pour it into the Styrofoam cup. Put the thermometer in the water. After 30 seconds, **measure** the temperature of the water and **record** it in the table.

2 **CAUTION** **Put on the safety goggles.** Add 2 spoonfuls of calcium chloride to the cup of water. Stir the water with the spoon until the calcium chloride dissolves. Wait 30 seconds. Then **measure** and **record** the temperature.

3 **Measure** and **record** the temperature of the water two more times, after 60 seconds and after 120 seconds. Then **compare** the temperature of the water before and after you added calcium chloride.

Substance	Temperature
Water without chemical	
Water with chemical after 30 seconds	
Water with chemical after 60 seconds	
Water with chemical after 120 seconds	

Draw Conclusions

1. How did the temperature of the water change when you added calcium chloride? The temperature increased.

2. **Infer** whether the calcium chloride gives off heat or absorbs heat as it dissolves in water. It gives off heat as it dissolves.

3. What do you **infer** might have caused the water temperature to change?
Possible answer: As the calcium chloride reacted with the water, chemical bonds were broken and heat was given off.

4. **Scientists at Work** Scientists **observe** and **measure** to gather as much data as they can from an experiment. What did you learn from this experiment about how the chemical energy in some compounds can be released?
The chemical energy in some compounds can be released by dissolving the compounds in water. The energy is released as heat.

Investigate Further Hypothesize what will happen when a different chemical, such as magnesium sulfate (Epsom salts), is placed in water. Then **plan and conduct a simple experiment** to test your hypothesis. _____

_____

_____

_____

Name _____

Date _____

Observe and Measure

When you observe, you use one or more of your senses to perceive properties of objects and events. One type of observing is measuring. When you measure, you are making observations with the aid of instruments, such as stopwatches or thermometers.

Think About Observing and Measuring

Before you can effectively measure anything, you have to know what you will be measuring. Then you choose the appropriate instrument for the type of measuring you will be doing. In the following questions, you will be asked to make those decisions.

1. You are working for a veterinarian. It is your job to feed the dogs. Your instructions are to feed each dog twice a day, one-half cup at each feeding for every 15 pounds that the dog weighs. What observations will you be making, and what measuring instruments will you be using? observations: the weight of the dog, the time of day, and the volume of food; measuring instruments: volume by a measuring cup, and weight by a scale

2. You are part of a mapping expedition that is going into unexplored territory. The expedition plans to take a boat up the river until it reaches the river's source. Your job is to map the course of the river for later expeditions. What observations will you make? What instruments and what units of measure will you use? observations: landmarks, directions the river turns, distance traveled each day. instruments: compass; possible devices, such as surveying instruments for measuring distance, GPS, and other devices students may suggest. units: kilometers or miles, and degrees.

3. A local television station has asked you to be part of a weather watch. They expect you to call the station every day at 4:00 P.M. and tell them the temperature, sky conditions, the wind speed, and any other observation you think might be important. What will you be observing and what instruments will you use? observations: the weather, general sky conditions, and the times of day so you can report in at 4:00 P.M. instruments: wind vane, anemometer, thermometer, clock or watch, and possibly others the students may suggest.

Name _____

Date _____

Identify Supporting Facts and Details

Read the selection. Then use facts from the selection to complete the outline.

Finding Oil at Sea

Not all oil is produced from oil wells on land. Oil also is found miles below the ocean's floor through offshore drilling.

In order to find oil under the sea, two ships conduct a *seismic survey*. The first ship, called the firing ship, sets off charges in the sea. The second ship, called the recording ship, picks up the signals from the charges, which reveal where the oil reserves are most likely to be found. Next, an exploration rig is set up at sea. When oil is discovered, the exploration rig is towed away and replaced by a production platform. This platform is fixed to the sea bed and contains the derrick, the living quarters for the workers, and all the equipment needed to drill for oil.

Offshore drilling supplies many countries with much-needed petroleum. However, environmental groups have objected to offshore drilling because of the destruction of natural habitats and ocean life. Ways to tap into the sea's petroleum beds while not harming the environment are being researched today.

How Oil Is Drilled Offshore

A. Seismic Surveys

- charges set off by one ship send information to another _____

- probable sites are found _____

B. Exploration Rigs

- set up temporarily to discover whether there is oil at that site _____

C. Production Platforms

- set up for drilling purposes _____

- contain a derrick, sleeping quarters, and equipment _____

D. Benefits and Harmful Effects

- supplies many countries with much-needed petroleum _____

- destruction of natural habitats and ocean life _____

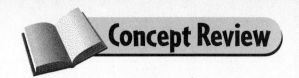

How Do People Use Fossil Fuels?

Lesson Concept

Coal, natural gas, and petroleum are fossil fuels, formed from once-living matter that has been buried for millions of years. Fossil fuels are used to heat homes, move cars, and generate electricity. Because fossil fuels take millions of years to form, they are nonrenewable.

Vocabulary

chemical bonds (F98)

Answer each question with one or more complete sentences.

1. How did energy from sunlight become stored in fossil fuels?

Fossil fuels are the remains of once-living things. The living things stored

energy from the sun in the chemical bonds of their molecules.

2. How does burning fuel of any kind turn solar energy into thermal energy?

Solar energy is stored as chemical energy in living things. The fuel is made

of material that used to be one or many living things. Burning the fuel turns

the chemical energy into thermal energy by breaking chemical bonds.

3. Why are fossil fuels the main source of energy for so many people?

They release more energy when they are burned than other fuels.

4. Where is most of the chemical energy in living organisms stored?

It is stored mostly in chemical bonds that join carbon atoms to each other

and to atoms of hydrogen and other elements.

5. What type of fossil fuel is the main source of energy for transportation?

Petroleum is the main source of energy for transportation.

6. Give at least two reasons other sources of energy besides fossil fuels should be

used. Fossil fuels are nonrenewable resources; they are needed to make

new materials such as plastics; burning fossil fuels releases large amounts of

carbon dioxide into the air.

Water Power

Materials

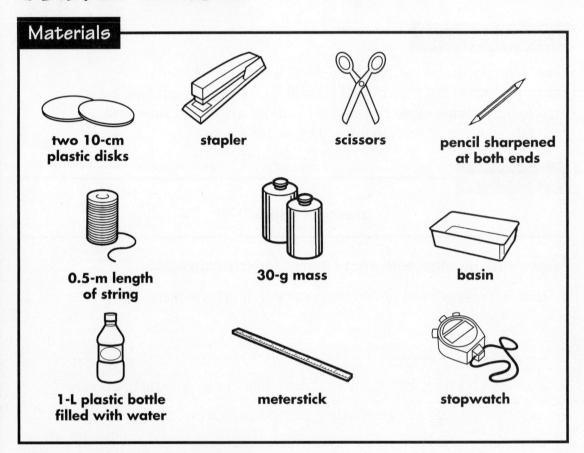

two 10-cm plastic disks

stapler

scissors

pencil sharpened at both ends

0.5-m length of string

30-g mass

basin

1-L plastic bottle filled with water

meterstick

stopwatch

Activity Procedure

1 **CAUTION** **Be careful when using the scissors.** Staple the plastic disks together near their centers. Using the scissors, cut four 3-cm slits into the disks as shown on page F103. At each slit, fold the disks in opposite directions to form a vane.

2 Again using the scissors, punch a 0.5-cm hole at the center of the disks. Insert the pencil. It will serve as the axle on which the water wheel rotates.

3 Use the scissors to make a smaller hole next to the pencil hole. Insert one end of the string into the hole, and tie a knot in the string to keep it in place. Tie the mass to the other end of the string.

4 Place the basin near the edge of the desk. Hold your water wheel over the basin. Your fingertips should hold the pencil points so the pencil can turn. The mass on the string should hang over the edge of the desk.

5 Have a partner slowly pour water over the wheel from a height of about 10 cm. Using the stopwatch, **measure** and **record** the time it takes for the mass to reach the level of the desk. Repeat this step several times.

6 Now repeat Steps 4 and 5, but have your partner pour the water from a height of about 20 cm. Again, **measure** and **record** the time it takes for the mass to reach the level of the desk.

Draw Conclusions

1. What **variables** did you **control** in your investigation? the amount of water in the bottle and the rate at which the water was poured

What variable did you change? the height from which the water fell

2. Recall that the greater the power, the more quickly work is done. Which of your trials produced more power? Why? the trial in which the water fell from the greater height, because work was done more quickly during this trial

3. **Scientists at Work** Scientists often look beyond the results of an investigation. For example, how does the height from which the water is poured affect the speed at which the water wheel turns? **Plan and conduct a simple experiment** to find out. Be sure to **identify and control variables**, changing only the height from which the water falls. Students should hypothesize that increasing the height from which the water falls produces more force, which turns the wheel faster. Investigations should confirm this hypothesis.

Investigate Further Hypothesize about the rate of flow and the speed at which the water wheel turns. Then **plan and conduct a simple experiment** to test your hypothesis. Be sure to **identify and control variables**, changing only the rate of flow of the water. _____

_____

_____

_____

_____

Name _____

Date _____

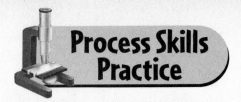
Identify and Control Variables

Identifying and controlling variables involves stating or controlling factors that affect the outcome of an experiment. It is important that only one variable be altered in any given test.

Think About Identifying and Controlling Variables

Read the descriptions of the experiments below. Then identify the variables that affect the outcome of each experiment.

1. People noticed that the number of a certain type of fish that live in a river seemed to have decreased since a dam was built on the river. Scientists who were concerned about the situation captured some of the fish and put them in giant tanks to study them. Both tanks were filled with river water. Plants, rocks, and insects from the river were also introduced into each tank. In one tank the water was 8 meters deep, the average depth of the undammed river. The water in the other tank was 30 meters deep, the depth of the river behind the dam. What is the variable in this experiment, and what could scientists learn by controlling it?

   The variable is the depth of the river. By controlling it, scientists might learn if

   the increased depth of the water on the dammed river is harming fish.

2. Many fish died in both tanks in the investigation in Question 1. Trying to determine the cause of the fish deaths, the scientists set up two tanks each with 8 meters of water in them. New fish were introduced, along with stones, insects, and plants from the river. One tank was lit by light that simulated sunshine. The other was kept dark. What is the variable in this experiment, and

   what could scientists learn by controlling it? The variable was sunlight. The

   scientists could find out whether fish were dying because they weren't getting

   enough sunshine in the deep reservoir.

3. Patricia built two water wheels by placing a dozen plastic slats between two plastic coffee-can lids. On one water wheel, she placed the slats so they pointed straight to the center from the edge of the lids. On the other wheel, she placed the slats so they were tilted at a sharp angle from the edge of the coffee-can lids. Using a pencil as the axle, she suspended each wheel over a basin and asked an assistant to pour water over them at a steady rate from 10 centimeters above the wheel. What is the variable in Patricia's experiment, and

   what could she learn by controlling it? The variable is the angle of the slats.

   She could learn which design allows the wheel to turn more quickly.

Name _____

Date _____

Arrange Events in Sequence

Read the selection. Then fill in the graphic organizer to show how a tidal energy station operates.

A Unique Hydroelectric Power Station

Most hydroelectric stations get their power from the energy released by falling water. Another kind of hydroelectric power comes from the energy released by the rising and falling of tides.

Tidal energy stations are built in tidal areas that experience the greatest difference between high and low tides. Tidal energy plants produce electricity by holding back water at high tide and letting it fall through turbines at low tide. The turbines are usually reversible so they can operate on both incoming and outgoing tides.

When the tide comes in, water levels rise on one side of the station. Once the difference in water level is about 10 feet or more, the force of the water is great enough to spin the turbines, which are connected to electric generators. When water is at the same level at both sides of the plant, the gates are closed. The tide goes out, leaving higher water behind the station. Then the gates are opened and water again flows through the turbines, this time spinning them in the opposite direction.

1. When the tide comes in, water levels rise on one side of the station.

⬇

2. Once the difference in water level is about 10 feet or more, the force of the water is great enough to spin the turbines, which are connected to electric generators.

⬇

3. When water is at the same level at both sides of the plant, the gates are closed.

⬇

4. The tide goes out, leaving higher water behind the station.

⬇

5. The gates are opened and water again flows through the turbines, this time spinning them in the opposite direction.

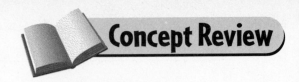
How Can Moving Water Generate Electricity?

Lesson Concept

An electric generator changes mechanical energy to electric energy. One source of this mechanical energy is moving water. Hydroelectric energy stations use the energy of falling water to spin turbines that generate electricity. The mechanical energy present in ocean tides can also generate electric energy.

Vocabulary

hydroelectric energy (F104)   **tidal energy** (F106)

Write a phrase from the chart to complete each sentence .

hydroelectric energy can be traced back to the sun
the potential energy of water under pressure
by holding back water at high tide and letting it fall through turbines at low tide
of falling water to spin turbines that generate electricity
to electric energy
the turbine spins the shaft of an electric generator
can also generate electric energy

1. An electric generator changes mechanical energy _to electric energy_ .

2. The energy that spins a hydroelectric turbine comes from _the potential energy of water under pressure_ .

3. Hydroelectric energy stations use the energy _of falling water to spin turbines that generate electricity_ .

4. The mechanical energy present in ocean tides _can also generate electric energy_ .

A Steam-Powered Turbine

Materials

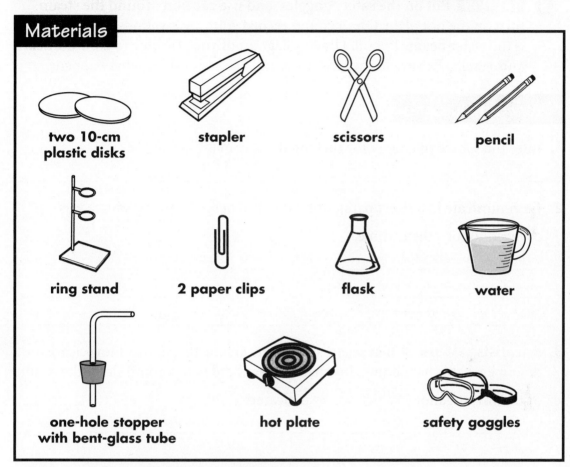

two 10-cm
plastic disks

stapler

scissors

pencil

ring stand

2 paper clips

flask

water

one-hole stopper
with bent-glass tube

hot plate

safety goggles

 CAUTION CAUTION

Activity Procedure

1 You can modify the water wheel you made in the last investigation by adding 12 more vanes to the wheel and enlarging the hole. Or you can follow Steps 2 and 3 to make your turbine.

2 **CAUTION** **Be careful when using the scissors.** Staple the plastic disks together near their centers. Using the scissors, cut sixteen 3-cm slits into the disks as shown on page F109. At each slit, fold the disks in opposite directions to form a vane.

3 Again using the scissors, cut a 0.5-cm round hole in the center of the disks. Make the hole as round as possible. Insert the pencil. It will serve as the axle on which the turbine rotates. The turbine should spin freely on its axle. Now suspend the axle and turbine from the ring stand arm with two bent paper clips.

4 Fill the flask with water. Put the stopper with the bent glass tube in the flask. Set the flask on the hot plate. Point the open end of the glass tube toward the vanes on the bottom of the turbine.

5 **CAUTION** **Put on the safety goggles, and use caution around the steam.** Turn on the hot plate. **Observe** and **record** your observations of the turbine as the water begins to boil. Draw a diagram of your turbine to **communicate** your results. Be sure to include labels and arrows to show what happens.

Draw Conclusions

1. **Infer** the source of energy for turning the turbine. the hot plate _____

_____

2. **Communicate** in a short paragraph how the energy from the source was changed to turn the turbine. The water is heated by the hot plate until it boils. The water turns to steam. The steam expands and is forced out of the flask through the glass tube. As the steam rushes out of the glass tube, it pushes against the vanes of the turbine, causing it to spin.

3. **Scientists at Work** When scientists **communicate**, they try to show clearly or describe what is happening. In what two ways did you communicate the results of this investigation? Which way was clearer? By writing a paragraph and by drawing a diagram; the diagram may have communicated the results of the investigation more clearly.

Investigate Further **Plan and conduct a simple experiment** to determine how much work your turbine can do. Decide what hypothesis you will need to test and what equipment you will need to use. Students could attach a weight on a string to the turbine. By increasing the weight, they could measure about how much work the turbine can do.

_____

_____

Name _____

Date _____

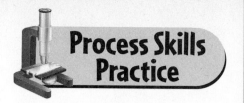

Communicate

Communicating involves the passing on of data. This may be done through spoken or written words, graphs, drawings, diagrams, maps, and charts. Communicating in science means showing the results of an activity in an organized fashion so the results can later be interpreted or the activity can be repeated.

Think About Communicating

In the questions below, you will find four types of information that a scientist might want to communicate. In the space provided, describe what you think would be the best way to communicate the information.

1. A laboratory was studying the nutritional requirements of a new breed of mouse they had developed for cancer research. They discovered that the healthiest mice were those fed a diet consisting of 15 percent protein, 75 percent carbohydrates, and 10 percent fats. What sort of graph, drawing, or chart would best communicate these results? Answers may vary. The best graphic would probably be a pie chart.

2. A group of scientists was surveying a large open area for the placement of windmills. They wanted to be sure each windmill would receive the greatest amount of wind possible, so they placed wind vanes in the area and kept track of the wind speed and direction over a period of six months. Then they took the average for each position. What would be the best way for them to communicate their results? Possible answers include showing average wind speed and direction on a map. Accept all reasonable answers.

3. A fisher was keeping track of the height of the tides in a certain area as part of a study being done at a local university. He drove a long measuring stick into the ground at the water's edge at low tide. Then, every hour, he checked the water's depth on the measuring stick. What kind of graphic would best communicate what he discovered? Possible answers include a line graph plotting water depth on the *y* axis and time on the *x* axis. Accept all reasonable answers.

4. Scientists were studying the relative top running speeds of animals in East Africa. They clocked a cheetah at 100 kilometers per hour (km/hr), a gazelle at 72 km/hr, a wildebeest at 36 km/hr, a leopard at 65 km/hr, and a jackal at 40 km/hr. What would be the best way to communicate this information? Possible answers include using a bar chart. Accept all reasonable answers.

Compare and Contrast

Use information from the selection to fill in the chart below.

Nuclear Energy: Fission and Fusion

Just as molecular bonds contain energy, so do the bonds holding together the protons and neutrons of an atom's nucleus. This energy is called *nuclear energy*. Nuclear energy can be released two ways—by nuclear *fission* and nuclear *fusion*.

Fission occurs when a nucleus breaks into two parts, forming the nuclei of two smaller atoms. Fission can take place only in very large atoms, such as those of uranium, that can be broken apart easily. The reaction also releases two or three other neutrons and a large amount of energy. The neutrons released may hit other uranium nuclei, causing a chain reaction. In a chain reaction, a huge amount of energy is released. Fission reactions can be controlled to generate electricity.

Unlike fission, fusion occurs when two nuclei join together to form the nucleus of a single larger atom. Fusion takes place easily between nuclei of very small atoms. Even more energy is produced from fusion than from fission. However, today it is not yet possible to control fusion reactions to generate electricity.

Fission and Fusion	Compare	Contrast
How the Reaction Occurs	Both reactions involve one or more nuclei.	In fission, a nucleus breaks into two parts, forming the nuclei of two smaller atoms. In fusion, two nuclei join together to form the nucleus of a single larger atom.
Energy Released	Both release a large amount of energy.	In fission, there is potential for a chain reaction, and the energy can be controlled to generate electricity. More energy is released from fusion, but the energy cannot be controlled to generate electricity.

What Other Sources of Energy Do People Use?

Lesson Concept

In addition to fossil fuels and hydroelectric energy, the United States uses small amounts of energy from other sources. These sources include biomass, nuclear energy, wind, geothermal energy, and solar energy. Researchers continue to work on new sources of energy, such as fusion.

Vocabulary

nuclear energy (F110)   **biomass** (F110)   **solar energy** (F111)

fusion energy (F112)   **geothermal energy** (F111)

List the advantages and disadvantages of each type of energy.

Type of Energy	Advantages	Disadvantages
Biomass	virtually free; can be made into liquid fuel	not very efficient
Nuclear	produces large amount of energy from small amount of fuel	fuel and waste products very dangerous to living organisms
Solar	free, nonpolluting, inexhaustible	not always available; collectors and cells can be expensive
Wind	free, nonpolluting, inexhaustible	expensive equipment; inconstant
Geothermal	free, nonpolluting, inexhaustible	technology could be expensive; not available everywhere
Ocean Thermal	free, nonpolluting, inexhaustible	technology could be expensive; not available everywhere
Hydrogen	potential low cost, low risk	requires expensive energy to start process; still experimental

Recognize Vocabulary

Choose one of the words from the box to answer each riddle.

biomass	**nuclear energy**
hydroelectric energy	**solar energy**
geothermal energy	**chemical bonds**
fusion energy	**tidal energy**

1. I'm alive now, or I was fairly recently. Burning me doesn't release a lot of energy, but I'm free or very inexpensive, so a lot of people use me. What am I?
biomass
_____

2. I'm not a wallet, and I'm not a purse or a backpack. I'm not a bank account, but I'm the thing that all living things keep their "saved-up" energy in. What am I?
chemical bonds
_____

3. Look for me at Niagara Falls or Glen Canyon Dam! I'm on the Missouri River and the Tennessee River, too. What am I? hydroelectric energy _____

4. Atoms are very tiny, but if you split them apart, you'll get me, the most powerful source of thermal energy on Earth. What am I? nuclear energy _____

5. If you want to get your energy directly from the source, you'll come to me. Too many cloudy days, however, could make it hard for you to get enough of me. What am I? solar energy _____

6. Dig deep to find me, preferably near a volcano or an earthquake zone. What am I? geothermal energy _____

7. I result from something that happens twice a day. See you at the beach! What am I? tidal energy _____

8. I'm in the experimental stages. Scientists know how I work, but the heat needed to get me started is so high that it burns all known materials. What am I? fusion energy _____

Name _____

Date _____

Write a Speech About Energy and the Environment

Persuasive Writing—Opinion

Some scientists believe that the use of fossil fuels is causing Earth's temperature to rise. Find out more about global warming. Then write a short speech expressing your opinion about global warming. Use the organizer below to plan your speech.

State your opinion.
State reasons.   **Reason 1:**
Reason 2:
Reason 3:
Restate your opinion or call for action.

Unit Experiments
Grade 5

Name _____

Date _____

Experiment Log

Use these pages to plan and conduct a science experiment to answer a question you may have.

1 Observe and Ask Questions

Make a list of questions you have about a topic. Then circle a question you want to investigate. _____

_____

2 Form a Hypothesis

Write a hypothesis. A hypothesis is a suggested answer to the question you are investigating. You must be able to test the hypothesis.

_____

_____

3 Plan an Experiment

Identify and Control Variables

To plan your experiment, you must first identify the important variables. Complete the statements below.

The variable I will change is _____

_____

The variable I will observe or measure is _____

_____

The variables I will keep the same, or control, are _____

_____

_____

Name _____

 **Experiment Log**

Develop a Procedure and Gather Materials

Write the steps you will follow to set up an experiment and collect data.

_____

_____

_____

_____

_____

_____

_____

_____

_____

_____

Materials List Look carefully at all the steps of your procedure and list all the materials you will use. Be sure that your teacher approves your plan and your materials list before you begin. _____

_____

_____

_____

_____

_____

_____

_____

_____

_____

_____

_____

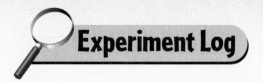

Experiment Log

4 Conduct the Experiment

Gather and Record Data Follow your plan and collect data. Make a table or chart to record your data. Observe carefully. Record your observations and be sure to note anything unusual or unexpected. Use the space below and additional paper, if necessary.

Interpret Data

Make a graph of the data you have collected. Plot the data on a sheet of graph paper or use a software program.

5 Draw Conclusions and Communicate Results

Compare the hypothesis with the data and the graph. Then answer these questions.

Do the results of the experiment make you think that the hypothesis is true?

Explain. _____

_____

How would you revise the hypothesis? Explain. _____

_____

What else did you observe during the experiment? _____

_____

Prepare a presentation for your classmates to communicate what you have learned. Display your data table and graph.

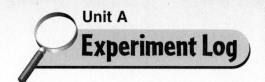
Plants and Light

1 Observe and Ask Questions

How do plants respond to light? For example, does a plant grow toward a light
source? Make a list of questions you have about plants and light. Then circle a
question you want to investigate. _____Do plants respond to light?_____

_____Do different colors of light make plants grow differently?_____

_____How does the amount of light affect plant growth?_____

2 Form a Hypothesis

Write a hypothesis. A hypothesis is a suggested answer to the question you are
investigating. You must be able to test the hypothesis.

_____A plant will grow toward a light source._____

_____

3 Plan an Experiment

To plan your experiment, you must first identify the important variables.
Complete the statements below.

Identify and Control Variables

The variable I will change is _____the position of the light source._____

The variable I will observe or measure is _____the plants' movement or growth.____

The variables I will keep the same, or *control*, are _____the type of plant, the amount____
_____of water the plants receive, and the temperature._____

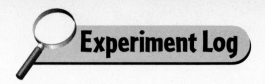
Experiment Log

Develop a Procedure and Gather Materials

Write the steps you will follow to set up an experiment and collect data.

a. Cut a hole about 2 inches wide in the middle of one end of a shoe box.

b. Divide the box into thirds by taping two cardboard squares inside the box. One square will extend from the left side of the box to the middle of the box. The other square will extend from the right side of the box to the middle of the box.

c. Put one plant in the box at the end opposite the hole.

d. Place the lid on the box. Put the box in a sunny location so that the hole is facing the light source.

e. Place the second plant next to the box.

f. Observe the growth of the plants daily, and record all observations.

Use extra sheets of blank paper if you need to write down more steps.

Materials List
Look carefully at all the steps of your procedure, and list all the materials you will use. Be sure that your teacher approves your plan and your materials list before you begin. two potted lima bean seedlings, light source or sunny location, shoe box with lid, cardboard, tape, scissors

Name _____

4 Conduct the Experiment

| Gather and Record Data | Follow your plan and collect data. Use the chart below or a chart you design to record your data. **Observe** carefully. **Record** your observations and be sure to note anything unusual or unexpected.

Observation Log

	Plant Observations						
Plant	**Day 1**	**Day 2**	**Day 3**	**Day 4**	**Day 5**	**Day 6**	**Day 7**
In Box							
Control							

	Plant Observations						
Plant	**Day 8**	**Day 9**	**Day 10**	**Day 11**	**Day 12**	**Day 13**	**Day 14**
In Box							
Control							

Interpret Data

Make sketches that illustrate the appearance of both plants on Day 14. Use the sketches to compare and contrast the growth of the plants.

5 Draw Conclusions and Communicate Results

Compare the **hypothesis** with the data and chart, then answer these questions.

1. Given the results of the experiment, do you think the hypothesis is true?

Explain. _____

_____

2. How would you revise the hypothesis? Explain. _____

_____

3. What else did you **observe** during the experiment? _____

_____

Prepare a presentation for your classmates in which you **communicate** what you have learned. Display your data table and diagram.

Investigate Further Write another hypothesis that you might investigate.

_____

_____

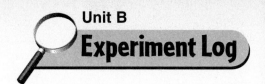
Cleaning Up Pollution

1 Observe and Ask Questions

Does the type of material used in a water filter affect how clean filtered water becomes? For example, will layers of pebbles, fine sand, and paper towel clean water better than layers of gravel, coarse sand, and cotton? Make a list of questions you have about water pollution and how to remove pollutants. Then circle a question you want to investigate. _Will layers of pebbles, fine sand, and paper towel clean water better than layers of gravel, coarse sand, and cotton?_

_____

2 Form a Hypothesis

Write a hypothesis. A hypothesis is a suggested answer to the question you are investigating. You must be able to test the hypothesis.

Water that seeps through layers of pebbles, fine sand, and paper towel will be cleaner than water that seeps through layers of gravel, coarse sand, and cotton.

3 Plan an Experiment

To plan your experiment, you must first identify the important variables. Complete the statements below.

Identify and Control Variables

The variable I will change is _the materials used to make a water filter._

The variable I will observe or measure is _how clean the water becomes._

The variables I will keep the same, or *control*, are _the mixture of polluted water, the amount of water poured into each filter, and the number and thickness of layers._

Name _____

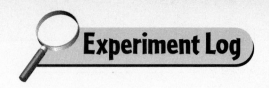
Experiment Log

| Develop a Procedure and Gather Materials |

Write the steps you will follow to set up an experiment and collect data.

1. Construct a filter from one of the bottles with the bottom cut off as follows: a. Punch a hole into the cap of the bottle and screw the cap in place; b. Turn the bottle upside down and place it in a large beaker; c. Place a folded paper towel into the neck of the bottle; d. Pour a layer of fine sand on top of the paper towel; e. Pour a layer of pebbles on top of the fine sand.

2. Using the second 2-liter bottle, repeat the procedure above, using cotton, coarse sand, and gravel as the filter layers.

3. Pour water into the last 2-liter bottle until it is about 2/3 full. Add the soil and debris to the water. Put the cap on the bottle and shake it until the contents are thoroughly mixed.

4. Alternate pouring the water mixture into each of the filters, ensuring that a near-equal amount is poured each time, until the bottle is empty. Shake the mixture between pourings as needed to keep the water, soil, and debris thoroughly mixed.

5. Allow the water to seep through the filter layers and collect in the beakers.

6. Observe how clean each collected water sample is.

Use extra sheets of blank paper if you need to write down more steps.

| Materials List | Look carefully at all the steps of your procedure and list all the materials you will use. Be sure that your teacher approves your plan and your materials list before you begin. 3 two-liter bottles (2 with bottoms cut off), gravel, pebbles, coarse sand, fine sand, cotton, paper towel, scissors, 2 large beakers, water, soil, bits of debris

Name _____

4   Conduct the Experiment

Gather and Record Data   Follow your plan and collect data. Use the chart below or a chart you design to record your data. **Observe** carefully. **Record** your observations and be sure to note anything unusual or unexpected.

Water Filter Observations

Water Filter Layers	Description of Filtered Water
Pebbles, fine sand, and paper towel	
Gravel, coarse sand, and cotton	

Name _____

| Interpret Data | Compare the two samples of water collected from the two water filters.

5   Draw Conclusions and Communicate Results

Compare the **hypothesis** with your **observations.** Then answer these questions.

1. Based on the results of the experiment, do you think the hypothesis is true? Explain. _Students should justify their responses with observations._

_____

_____

2. How would you revise the hypothesis? Explain. _Students may revise their hypotheses to match the results of the experiment more closely._

_____

3. What else did you **observe** during the experiment? _Encourage students to use their notes and to be as specific as possible._

_____

_____

Prepare a presentation for your classmates to **communicate** what you have learned. Display your collected water samples.

| Investigate Further | Write another hypothesis that you might investigate.

Water that seeps through double layers of pebbles, fine sand, and paper towel will be cleaner than water that seeps through one layer of pebbles, fine sand, and paper towel.

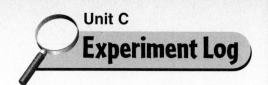
Wave Action

1 Observe and Ask Questions

Do artificial structures built along beaches change the shoreline? Do large artificial structures have the same effect on a beach as small structures do? Make a list of questions you have about how artificial structures might affect a beach.

Then circle a question you want to investigate. Will large artificial structures affect erosion and deposition along a shoreline in the same way as small structures will?

_____

_____

2 Form a Hypothesis

Write a hypothesis. A hypothesis is a suggested answer to the question you are investigating. You must be able to test the hypothesis.

Jetties and groins will cause a beach to become larger.

_____

_____

3 Plan an Experiment

To plan your experiment, you must first identify the important variables. Complete the statements below.

Identify and Control Variables

The variable I will change is _the size of the artificial structure._

The variable I will observe or measure is _how much sand is deposited and eroded around the barrier._

_____

The variables I will keep the same, or *control*, are _the size of the beach and of the waves._

_____

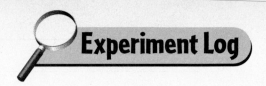
Experiment Log

Develop a Procedure and Gather Materials

Write the steps you will follow to set up an experiment and collect data.

a. Use the sand and water to make a model beach in the stream table.

b. Place the long plastic block at right angles to the shoreline.

c. When the water is calm and the sand has settled, use the ruler to generate waves that strike the beach at approximately a 45° angle. Continue this motion until a "longshore current" develops.

d. Carefully observe and sketch how the amount of sand changes when it is upcurrent, as well as downcurrent from the structure.

e. Make another model beach that is the same as the first.

f. Place the small plastic block at right angles to the shoreline.

g. Repeat steps c and d.

Use extra sheets of blank paper if you need to write down more steps.

Materials List
Look carefully at all the steps of your procedure and list all the materials you will use. Be sure that your teacher approves your plan and your materials list before you begin. stream table; water; sand; ruler; large interlocking plastic blocks; small interlocking plastic blocks

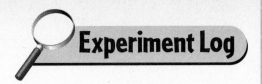

4   Conduct the Experiment

| Gather and Record Data | Follow your plan and make careful observations. Use the space below to draw and label changes in the beach that result from placing the large artificial structure at right angles to the beach. Draw and label the changes in the beach that result from placing the small structure at right angles to the beach. Below each drawing, **summarize** your **observations.**

Changes to Beach As a Result of the Large Structure

Changes to Beach As a Result of the Small Structure

Observations _____

_____

Name _____

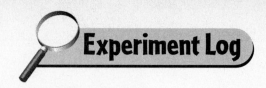
Experiment Log

5 Draw Conclusions and Communicate Results

Compare your **hypothesis** with your drawings, and then answer these questions.

1. Given the results of the experiment, do your observations support your

   hypothesis? Explain. _____

   _____

   _____

2. How would you revise the hypothesis? Explain. _____

   _____

   _____

3. What else did you **observe** during the experiment? _____

   _____

   _____

Prepare a presentation for your classmates to **communicate** what you have learned. Display your data table and graph.

| Investigate Further | Write another hypothesis that you might investigate.

_____

_____

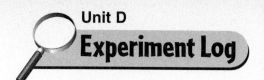
Designing Rockets

1 Observe and Ask Questions

Does the arrangement of the parts of a rocket affect how far the rocket will travel? For example, will a rocket with stages arranged on top of each other travel farther than one with the rockets clustered side by side? Make a list of questions you have about the arrangement of rocket parts. Then circle a question you want to investigate. _Will a rocket with parts that are side by side travel_

farther on the same amount of fuel than a rocket with parts arranged

on top of each other?

_____

2 Form a Hypothesis

Write a hypothesis. A hypothesis is a suggested answer to the question you are investigating. You must be able to test the hypothesis.

A rocket with parts that are side by side will travel farther on the same

amount of fuel than a rocket with parts arranged on top of each other.

_____

3 Plan an Experiment

To plan your experiment, you must first identify the important variables. Complete the statements below.

Identify and Control Variables

The variable I will change is _the arrangement of parts in a model rocket._

The variable I will observe or measure is _how far each rocket travels on the_

same amount of fuel (the volume of air in the balloons).

The variables I will keep the same, or *control*, are _the total volume of air in_

each fuel cell (balloon), and the slope of the fishing line and how tightly

it is drawn.

Name _____

Develop a Procedure and Gather Materials

Write the steps you will follow to set up an experiment to test two model rockets.

1. For the first model, use the pump to inflate two balloons with the same volume of air, for example, 20 pumps each. Tightly close the balloons with twist-ties or clothespins.

2. Carefully tape the balloons to each other (or side by side) and to the straw so they are all parallel to each other, with the straw sandwiched in the middle.

3. Thread the straw onto the piece of fishing line. Line up the side-by-side balloons at the starting line. Remove the twist-ties or clothespins at the same time.

4. Observe the rocket. Use the meterstick to measure the distance it traveled.

5. For the second model, use the pump to inflate the other two long balloons with a total volume of 40 pumps: one balloon with 25 pumps and the other balloon with 15 pumps. Tightly close the balloons with twist-ties or clothespins.

6. Remove the twist-tie from the smaller balloon without letting any air out of it and tuck the balloon neck under a rubber band that is placed about in the middle of the larger balloon. Keep the neck of the larger balloon twisted as you place the rubber band and put the smaller balloon neck under the rubber band. The pressure from the larger balloon against the rubber band will hold the smaller balloon in place and closed. The smaller balloon should be mounted behind the larger balloon, with the twisted neck held in place by the rubber band. Tape both balloons to a straw.

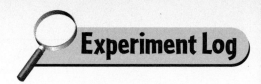

7. Thread this model rocket onto the piece of fishing line. Line up the balloons at the starting line.

8. Remove the twist-tie from the larger balloon. Observe the rocket. Measure the distance this rocket traveled.

Use extra sheets of blank paper if you need to write down more steps.

Materials List Look carefully at all the steps of your procedure and list all the materials you will use. Be sure that your teacher approves your plan and your materials list before you begin. 4 balloons, bicycle pump, twist-ties or spring-type clothespins, straws, scissors, thick rubber band, fishing line, tape, meterstick

4 Conduct the Experiment

Make Observations Follow your plan and make careful **observations**. Use the space below to draw and label your two model rockets. Below the drawings, **summarize** your **observations**.

Rocket with Two Parts Side by Side

Rocket with Two Parts One Behind the Other

Experiment Log

Observations

Students will observe that the model rocket whose parts are mounted one
on top of the other travels farther with the same volume of fuel (air) than the
model rocket whose parts are in a side-by-side arrangement.

5 Draw Conclusions and Communicate Results

Compare your **hypothesis** with your **observations,** and then answer these
questions.

1. Based on your results, do your observations support your hypothesis?
Explain. Students should use their observations to support or revise their
hypotheses.

2. How would you revise the hypothesis? Explain. Students may revise their
hypotheses so that they match the observations made in this experiment.

3. What else did you **observe** during the experiment? Encourage students to
be as specific as possible. One observation might be that the model
rockets traveled forward because of the air escaping from the necks of the
balloons.

Prepare a presentation for your classmates to **communicate** what you have
learned. Demonstrate your two model rockets.

| Investigate Further | Write another hypothesis that you might investigate.

Answers will vary but might include investigating how far one large rocket will
travel when compared with several smaller rockets with the same arrangement
of parts.

Name _____

Date _____

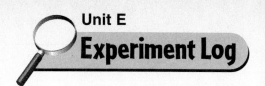
Solubility

1 Observe and Ask Questions

What substances dissolve in water? For example, do all white powders or granules, such as salt, sugar, baking soda, flour, chalk dust, talc, baking powder, and cornstarch, dissolve in water? Make a list of questions you have about what kinds of things dissolve in water. Then circle a question you want to investigate.

Do all white powders dissolve in water?

Do rocks, dirt, or sand dissolve in water?

Do all solids dissolve in water?

2 Form a Hypothesis

Write a hypothesis. A hypothesis is a suggested answer to the question you are investigating. You must be able to test the hypothesis.

All white powders will dissolve in water.

3 Plan an Experiment

To plan your experiment, you must first identify the important variables. Complete the statements below.

Identify and Control Variables

The variable I will change is the type of white powder or granules I will try to dissolve.

The variable I will observe or measure is how well each substance dissolves.

The variables I will keep the same, or *control*, are the amount of powder substance; amount of water (to dissolve each substance); temperature of water; and time spent stirring, settling, and observing (before, during, and after stirring).

Name _____

Experiment Log

Develop a Procedure and Gather Materials

Write the steps you will follow to set up an experiment and collect data.

a. Label a clear plastic cup with the type of powder to be dissolved.

b. Put 125 mL (about 1/2 cup) water into the cup.

c. Put 1 teaspoon of powder into the water. Wait 30 seconds before stirring. Observe and record what happens.

d. Stir the substance in the water for 60 seconds. Observe and record results.

e. Wait 5 minutes for the water and substance to settle. Observe and record the results.

f. Observe the solution again after another 10 minutes. Record the results.

g. Repeat the experiment, using a different powder.

NOTE: Use a clean, dry measuring spoon, stirring spoon, and plastic cup for each new test. Make sure that powders and solutions do not get mixed.

Use extra sheets of blank paper if you need to write down more steps.

Materials List
Look carefully at all the steps of your procedure, and list all the materials you will use. Be sure that your teacher approves your plan and your materials list before you begin. plastic cups, measuring cup, measuring spoon, stirring spoons or rods, timer or clock, water, 5–10 white powders (salt, sugar, cornstarch, baking powder, baking soda, chalk dust, talc or baby powder, flour, artificial sweetener, dishwasher or laundry powder)

Name _____

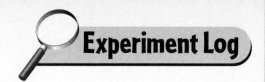
Experiment Log

4 Conduct the Experiment

| Gather and Record Data | Follow your plan and collect data. Use the chart below or a chart you design to record your data. If needed, make up a new chart for each substance you test. **Measure** and **observe** carefully. **Record** your observations, and be sure to note anything unusual or unexpected.

Observations of Substances in Water

Substance	Unstirred (30 seconds)	After stirring (60 seconds continuous stirring)	After settling (5 minutes)	After settling (15 minutes)	Dissolved? How well?

Other Observations _____

_____

_____

_____

_____

Name _____

5 Draw Conclusions and Communicate Results

Compare your **hypothesis** with the data and graph and then answer these questions.

1. Given the results of the experiment, do you think the hypothesis is true?

Why or why not? _____

_____

_____

2. How would you revise the hypothesis? Be specific. _____

_____

_____

3. What else did you **observe** during the experiment? _____

_____

_____

Prepare a presentation for your classmates to **communicate** what you have learned. Display your data table.

Investigate Further | Write another hypothesis you might investigate about how substances dissolve. _____

_____

_____

_____

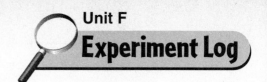
Changing Pitch

1 Observe and Ask Questions

What are some ways to change the pitch of a sound? For example, on stringed instruments, does shortening the length of a vibrating string cause the string to make a higher sound or a lower one? Make a list of questions you have about pitch and how it can be changed. Then circle a question you want to investigate.

How can I change the pitch of a note played on a guitar or other stringed instrument? Will shortening the vibrating length of a guitar string produce a higher-pitched note? How can I produce sounds of higher and lower pitches when blowing across the mouth of a bottle? Can I change the pitch by adding different amounts of water to the bottle?

2 Form a Hypothesis

Write a hypothesis. A hypothesis is a suggested answer to the question you are investigating. You must be able to test the hypothesis.

Shortening the length of a vibrating guitar string is one way to raise the pitch of the sound the string produces.

3 Plan an Experiment

To plan your experiment, you must first identify the important variables. Complete the statements below.

Identify and Control Variables

The variable I will change is the length of the vibrating portion of a guitar string.

The variable I will observe or measure is the pitch of the sound produced.

The variables I will keep the same, or *control*, are the guitar used, the string used, how hard I pluck the string.

Experiment Log

Develop a Procedure and Gather Materials

Write the steps you will follow to set up an experiment and collect data.

_____

_____

_____

_____

_____

_____

_____

_____

_____

_____

_____

_____

_____

Use extra sheets of blank paper if you need to write down more steps.

Materials List Look carefully at all the steps of your procedure, and list all the materials you will use. Be sure that your teacher approves your plan and your materials list before you begin. _____

_____

Name _____

4 Conduct the Experiment

Gather and Record Data Follow your plan and collect data. Use the chart below or a chart you design to record your data. (Make additional copies of the chart as needed for testing additional strings or other instruments.) **Observe** carefully. **Record** your observations, and be sure to note anything unusual or unexpected.

Pitch Observations

String Tested (name or description):	
String Length (vibrating section only)	**Pitch**

Other Observations _____

_____

_____

_____

Name _____

Experiment Log

Make a bar graph of the data you have collected. Plot the graph on a sheet of graph paper, or use a software program.

5 Draw Conclusions and Communicate Results

Compare the **hypothesis** with the data and graph, and then answer these questions.

1. Given the results of the experiment, do you think the hypothesis is true?

   Why or why not?_____

   _____

2. How would you revise the hypothesis? Explain. _____

   _____

   _____

3. What else did you **observe** during the experiment?_____

   _____

   _____

Prepare a presentation for your classmates to **communicate** what you have learned. Display your data table and graph.

Investigate Further Write another hypothesis that you might investigate about sound and pitch. _____

_____

_____